BEHIND THE TEAK CURTAIN

This work seeks to challenge conventional studies on Burma, which focus on the behavior and actions of the military elite in Rangoon and treat the military regime as a unitary actor. It will be shown how and why the same autocratic and repressive military leaders who are perceived by a particular sector of the population as "illegitimate" may, at the same time, be favorably seen and accepted by another group of citizens. Finally, this study draws out the implications of these findings for other authoritarian governments in developing societies. It will demonstrate a more comprehensive foundation of legitimacy in authoritarian countries by highlighting the varying perceptions and attitudes in society toward central government authorities, toward local officials, and the different bases of legitimacy enjoyed by these two different levels of authority.

Ardeth Maung Thawnghmung, a native of Burma, is an assistant professor in the Department of Political Science, University of Massachusetts, Lowell. She came to the United States in 1990 to pursue her education after the Burmese military government closed down all universities and colleges for fear of students' call for democracy. She earned her bachelor's degree in political science from Indiana University-Fort-Wayne, and master's degree in International Relations from Yale University. Her Ph.D in political science is from the University of Wisconsin-Madison. *Behind the Teak Curtain* is the product of her one-year field research project in Burma in 1999, and two week- interviews in 2002.

BEHIND THE TEAK CURTAIN

Authoritarianism, Agricultural Policies and
Political Legitimacy in Rural Burma/Myanmar

ARDETH MAUNG THAWNGHMUNG

Routledge
Taylor & Francis Group

LONDON AND NEW YORK

First published 2003 by Kegan Paul.

2 Park Square, Milton Park, Abingdon, Oxon OX14 4RN
711 Third Avenue, New York, NY 10017, USA

Routledge is an imprint of the Taylor & Francis Group, an informa business

First issued in paperback 2016

Copyright © 2003 Taylor & Francis.

British Library Cataloguing in Publication Data
A catalogue record for this book is available from the British Library

ISBN 978-0-7103-0935-8 (hbk)
ISBN 978-1-138-96453-2 (pbk)

Publisher's Note
The publisher has gone to great lengths to ensure the quality of this reprint
but points out that some imperfections in the original copies may be
apparent. The publisher has made every effort to contact original copyright
holders and would welcome correspondence from those they have been
unable to trace.

To Neil and Diana Sowards
who have touched upon many lives in Burma

Contents

Acknowledgements

When I was about to conduct my field work in Burma's countryside, I had absolutely no idea the kind of environment I would be encountering. The pathetic-looking research proposal I submitted barely covered ten pages, in which I struggled with unconnected theories and irrelevant case studies. There had been only a few studies on Burma's agrarian relationships to guide my research, and most of them were out-of-date. I decided to study the economic and political impacts of various agricultural policies implemented by the military regime, but I did not know what to expect.

Taw or rural areas have never been strange places to me. As a child, I occasionally accompanied my grandfather on his visits to Burma's rice villages. He deliberately took us with him because he did not want us to sever our ties with rural people. I also went to taw to attend a number of summer bible camps. My siblings and I enjoyed our stays in paddy villages particularly because we could jump up and down on a big yellow haystack, and catch fish and swim in the river. To me, villages or ywa were my temporary vacation places. Nothing else.

By the time I went back to Burma in 1999, I was full of curiosity about people I have long known. My research, drawn heavily on one-year's fieldwork in Burma's countryside in 1999, was mainly based on conversations and observations of Burmese farmers. For about five months I focused on one rice farming village in Upper Burma and another in Lower Burma. Both villages had been early experimental sites for various agricultural programs. I stayed with rice farm families, observed their social and economic activities, and had lengthy conversations with them and with local officials. I accompanied agricultural extension agents to their field extension camps, and to government offices. I witnessed interactions between rice farmers and agricultural extension agents, local officials, and soldiers. The rest of my year long research in Burma was spent visiting several other villages in Pegu, Rangoon, Magwe, and Irrawaddy divisions. I stayed a minimum of several days to observe, talk with farmers and government officials, and investigate experiences in agriculture. To get a more comprehensive view of the nature of Burma's agricultural policies, I also interviewed researchers in the Agriculture

Institutes, retired and active agricultural officials at the provincial level, and agricultural officials in embassies and other foreign agencies.

During my stay in these villages, I eschewed using rigidly structured interview questions. Rather I listened closely to what farmers had to say. My conversations with Burmese rice farmers covered broad and seemingly endless and random issues, ranging from past and present agricultural policies, farmers' daily economic activities, religious and cultural practices, living conditions, rumors, gossip and popular movie stars and singers. All the while, I began to notice a framework of analysis emerging out of our conversations. It gradually transformed into a firmer pattern, 'the 'atek lu (those from above) and auk lu (those from below) scenario.' It is the study of Burmese farmers' different dispositions towards local and central authorities. After that, I started focusing on the issues relevant to atek lu (central authorities) and auk lu (local authorities).

Some changes have taken place since I left Burma in 1999. The year 2002 was one of the worst years for the agricultural sector, with farmers' experiencing drought in the early season and severe flood in the pre-harvest and harvesting periods. The military government eliminated the rice procurement policy in April 2003 to cope with sky rocketing prices on rice. I returned to Burma very briefly toward the end of 2002, and interviewed seven farmers from Rangoon, Pegu, and Irrawaddy divisions to re-assess their perceptions of authorities and political system, which were not fully developed from my previous analysis.

This book is a revised version of my dissertation submitted to the political science department at University of Wisconsin-Madison. I am indebted to my dissertation committee members, Don Emmerson, Paul Hutchcroft, and Ed Friedman for their insightful comments and constructive criticism. Without their suggestions and encouragement, I would never have thought of publishing this project.

I would like to express my profound gratitude to the Henry Luce foundation and the Australian National University fellowship for Southeast Asian Studies which provided generous funding and the opportunity to revise my manuscript. I have received valuable critiques and suggestions through the presentation of my work at an International Workshop for Political Science Ph.D. Students Working on Southeast Asia, San Diego, Cornell Southeast Asian Studies brownbag seminar, University of Wisconsin-Madison Southeast Asian Studies brownbag seminar, and a Burma Studies conference at the Northern Illinois University.

Thanks are also extended to the following scholars, who read parts of the original or/and revised manuscript and gave me the benefit of their critical comments: Robert Taylor, James Scott, John Badgley, David Steinberg, Gerald Houseman, David Mathieson, Yoshinori Nishizaki, Joseph Silverstein, Kikue Hamayotsu, and Philip Taylor. I am particularly grateful to Professor Ben Kerkvliet who made detailed suggestions for revising the original draft of the manuscript, read all draft chapters, and offered invaluable comments. I am also greatly indebted to Mark Selden, who taught me how to write a great prospectus and gave me valuable advice on my thesis. I would also like to thank Allison Ley for her thorough suggestions on my writing style and manner of presentation.

I owe a special debt to my colleague and a very tolerant office-mate, David Mathieson. The moment I arrived at my office in Political and Social Change Department at the Australian National University, David greeted me with a big smile, a shelf full of books on Burma, a formidable knowledge on Burmese history and politics, and a willing heart to teach and to comment on my work. It must have been very painful for David to share an office with a colleague who is computer illiterate and who lacks attention to detail. A specialist on Burma, David has condoned all my annoying behavior and gracefully commented on and provided relevant information on my work. He also formatted, edited, and drew graphs for my project. The months I shared the office with David will always be the most cherished memories of my stay in Canberra. Thanks so much Davie!!

Every lucky person has a few friends and mentors to count on in time of trouble and desperation. In this respect, I would like to thank four wonderful people, my borrowed parents, Neil and Diana Sowards, and my two former professors, Gerald Houseman and Paul Hutchcroft, who never fail to lend me their helping hands. I shall always be grateful for their generosity and unflagging support. I dedicate this book to Neil and Diana Sowards, who gave me and many other Burmese students a second opportunity to pursue education in the United States, and who have touched upon many lives in Burma.

Research in Burma would not have been possible without the help of my rice farmer friends in Burma whose love, hospitality, generosity were bigger than their life-time earnings. I very much appreciate their willingness to offer me a place to live and to share with me their life experiences. I would also like to express my profound gratitude for those who assisted me in various ways with my research in Burma.

My family in Burma welcomed me back home with a hearty meal during my short stay in Rangoon in 1999. My mother traveled from

Burma to help take care of our new born baby and help me finish my dissertation in 2001. She came back to the United States again in 2002 to look after the same little girl whom she had previously cared for eight months. This time, mom was by herself with the strong-headed, hyper-active girl for four and a half months, wrestling her on a daily basis, while I revised my manuscript at the Australian National University. Without mom, this project would have taken much longer to complete. I also appreciate the help and support of our relatives who have given their love and care to Dai, our little girl, while I was overseas. For this, I thank Puu Puu Edward, Pee Pee Annie, Aunt Mary, Uncle Will, Uncle John, Aunt Ruth, Aunt Martha, Daww Cookie, Daww Zippo, and Tee Pupeh.

In Canberra and Sydney, Australia, Ester Kyaw, Ohmar Khin Zaw, Aung Kyaw Htut and Ma Judy, David Mathieson, and Kikue Hamayotsu created a separate social space for me to enjoy life like other normal people. These fun-loving and food-loving friends kept my life sane and made my intellectual pursuits even more stimulating and productive.

While I was revising this book I was constantly torn between my moral responsibility as a former Burmese student who witnessed the atrocities of the regime and my intellectual obligation as an "emotionally detached" scholar who must "objectively" analyze identifiable patterns and practices. This dilemma reflects the broader trend that has long dominated Burma studies or any studies that examine authoritarian countries (e.g. Marco's Philippines and Soeharto's Indonesia). The debates over the negative and positive depictions of the military regime in Burma have created animosities among scholars on Burma, and between "detached" scholars who study the country from the ivory tower, and activists who experienced at first hands the regime's brutality and ruthlessness. It becomes almost impossible or politically unacceptable to portray any positive aspects of the military regime.

This book is not about how popular the Burmese military regime is. Rather, this book analyzes the very rare and specific situations under which the authoritarian military enjoys popularity in Burma's rural areas. My project aims to engage pro- and anti-regime scholars, and journalists and activists in intellectual cooperation and in a more fruitful and productive debate by reflecting on my findings on Burmese farmers' political behavior and practices. This field-based analysis, though not claiming to be completely free from contamination due to the restrictive nature of the environments under which the research was conducted, is supported by factual evidence, anecdotes, and stories of actual rural conditions. Whether I have succeeded in engaging those for and against Burma's military regime is up to readers to decide. To demonstrate my commitment toward the methodological procedures underpinning the social science discipline, I submit this work to rigorous judgment and scrutiny by any thorough reader.

My greatest appreciation is to my most wonderful and loving husband, Mawi Mawi, who has sacrificed everything to help achieve my dream, and who has been by my side for more than ten years. I would not have made it to where I am without the love, support, patience, and understanding of my husband.

Ardeth Maung Thawnghmung
Madison

Introduction

Behind the Teak Curtain

Scandals and crop failures in the countryside

On a dry, hot evening in the summer of 1998, a group of angry farmers in a small village in upper Burma silently walked toward their paddy fields located outside their village. They were accompanied by a camera crew from town. The cameraman began to videotape the dying paddy fields. A few minutes later, a woman appeared in front of the camera. She cried out loud, beat her chest, and pointed towards the dying crops. Once the farmers believed they had made a satisfactory record of the damaged crops, they returned home. Nervously, they waited for the next morning when they would meet with local military officials.

These paddy cultivators had been forced by the local ruling authorities to provide a small percentage of their crops to them. They resisted, arguing that most of their crops failed because the local irrigation officers did not provide enough water. The farmers also accused these officers of illegally channeling water to their relatives and friends who were not included in the summer paddy project. In addition, they pointed out that both the local irrigation officials and military officials accepted bribes from some of the area's better- off farmers in return for more water. This led to a shortage of water in the area and crop failure.

The next day, the cultivators met with the township Peace and Development Council chairman, a military officer. They threatened to take the videotape to the highest authorities in the capital city and reveal the corrupt activities if the local officials insisted on exacting a portion of their produce. Immediately, the township chairman withdrew his initial demand and agreed that the farmers could keep whatever remained after their harvest.

Although this kind of incident usually goes unpublicized, Burmese farmers have often been able to play one level of governmental authority against another. This calls into question the widely held image of the military regime in Burma as a unitary actor, and sheds light on the crucial, yet neglected, role of the local authorities, who exert significant control and influence over local affairs. The Burmese farmers' tendency to rely on the highest authorities as the small farmers' ultimate source of remedy against local abuses also indicates that local residents' attitudes toward local officials and central authorities are not necessarily the same. Sometimes the central authorities enjoy popularity in the countryside because of their perceived role as the protector from rural abuses and exploitation. This situation is not unique to Burma. Similar practices can also be found elsewhere in Third World authoritarian countries, including contemporary China, Vietnam, Marcos' martial law regime, Suharto's Indonesia, Trujillo's Dominican Republic, Mexico, and the Russian Federation.

This generally missing analysis of local authority structure contributes to a misunderstanding about the political reality of poor countries, whose local activities and political arrangement are not readily accessible to casual observers. Many authoritarian regimes, including Burma's, have been portrayed by foreign media and academia as single entities, operating as hierarchic and unitary regimes. This typical portrayal of dictatorial governments, however, can hardly reflect a comprehensive image. Such a view rarely incorporates the perceptions of diverse elements of society, which may not always converge with the stereotypical depiction of despotic practices. It is only beneath the surface, and behind the teak or iron curtains that one discovers the multiple images of autocratic regimes. It is only through the analysis of the struggle and/or accommodation between various parts of the state and society that incomprehensible phenomena become comprehensible. And it is only through a sharp and critical focus on local authorities' interactions with residents that one can understand why "socially-baseless tyranny and despotic or autocratic rule" has, on closer examination, pockets of acceptance and societal support.[1]

The case study of Burma will provide a new perspective on the study of political legitimacy in authoritarian countries. I will demonstrate how and why the Burmese military regime, often considered one of the least legitimate governments in the international community by human rights activists, can in fact be favorably looked upon and accepted by a particular group of citizens; and in this case, by poor rice farmers.

In this first in-depth look at authorities' interactions with the local population in Burma, I shall analyze four different agricultural policies that have been implemented by the Burmese military regime. I will evaluate farmers' perceptions of local and central authorities

[1] Richard Turits, "The Foundation of Despotism: Peasants: Property, and the Trujillo Regime (1930-1961)", (Ph.D. Dissertation, History Department, University of Chicago, August 1997).

through the implementation of these policies, and highlight various circumstances under which rural residents see the military leaders in the capital both favorably and, sometimes, unfavorably. My intention is to move away from the Rangoon-centered and elitist-oriented analysis into a more localized approach to the authority structure in Burma, and to explore the relationship between local government authorities and paddy farmers. Theoretically, this study seeks to make a contribution by shedding light on a more comprehensive foundation of legitimacy in authoritarian countries because it analyzes rural societies' varying perceptions of central and local authorities, and the different bases of legitimacy for these two levels of government.

Understanding Burmese Politics: Theory and Practice
The current military government in Burma, in power since 1962, has incarcerated approximately one thousand political prisoners, invalidated the results of the 1990 election (which the National League for Democracy easily won), and committed violence, torture and rape in ethnic regions. It has extensively relied on conscripted labor to build roads, bridges, irrigation, and other infrastructures, and forcibly relocated between 500,000-1,000,000 of its own citizens in major cities (such as Rangoon and Mandalay) as well as in border areas. For these and other reasons, analysts have argued that the Burmese government lacks popular legitimacy. Is this, however, really the case?

This book, the first fieldwork-based study of Burmese rural politics and development, shows that other factors, long ignored in the literature, may be central to regime legitimacy. Especially in the countryside, Burma's government hinges less on the high profile issues singled out by the international press and more on the agrarian agenda. Consequently, the issues that have mesmerized Western scholars and journalists, the high profile battles between the junta and the NLD and the riveting clashes with Aung San Suu Kyi appear to have different resonance throughout the villages where the majority of Burmese live and work.

This study makes four main assertions. First, it attempts to expand on the concept of "legitimacy by economic performance" by proposing two issues that have equal impact on the legitimacy of the state. I argue that whether the legitimacy of the state can be enhanced or undermined depends on the types of development policies it sets out, as well as the ways in which these are implemented at the local level. The indicators of macro-performance at the national level are too broad to inform us of the society's specific views towards the state. We must thus incorporate more detailed and comprehensive features of state-societal relationships to understand the complicated nature of legitimacy in authoritarian countries.

Second, this work seeks to challenge conventional studies on Burma, which focus on the behavior and actions of the military elite in Rangoon, and treat the military regime as a unitary actor. The present approach aims to disaggregate the state into different levels of analysis, and to focus on the importance of the interaction between the implementors of the policies and the local population.

Third, it will be shown how and why the same autocratic and repressive military leaders who are perceived by a particular sector of the population as "illegitimate" may, at the same time, be favorably seen and accepted by another group of citizens.

The last theme of this book concerns the broader implications for Third World authoritarian countries. It will demonstrate a more comprehensive foundation of legitimacy in authoritarian countries by highlighting the varying perceptions and attitudes in society toward central government authorities, toward local officials, and the different bases of legitimacy enjoyed by these two different levels of authority.

Performance, political legitimacy, and authoritarianism
The first theme to be taken deals with the relationships between economic performance and political legitimacy in authoritarian regimes. Everyday the front pages of official newspapers in Burma reveal a score of military leaders making offerings to the monastery, giving *alu* (feeding or presenting gifts) to monks, worshiping at pagodas, putting umbrellas on top of pagodas, and thereby symbolically portraying themselves as "legitimate" leaders in Burma. Public speeches by military commanders repeatedly emphasize the regime's effort to promote the welfare of farmers through various development schemes. Why does a repressive government need to perform symbolic gestures and rely on rhetorical statements to justify its domination, despite its apparent ability to eliminate and neutralize societal forces that challenge its authority? Alagappa answers that

> If acceptance of commands issued by authorities is based solely or even largely on naked force, then the right to rule will be challenged and political change will be sought through resistance, rebellion, and revolution. The government's survival will consume the bulk of its resources, and its effectiveness will be considerably reduced. If the government is perceived as legitimate, however, the social, political, and economic cost of governance will be low and the government's capacity to promote its political and socioeconomic goals will be enhanced.[2]

---

[2] Muthiah Alagappa, "Introduction", in Political Legitimacy in Southeast Asia: The Quest for Moral Authority, ed. Muthiah Alagappa (California: Stanford University Press, 1995), 4.

4

In addition to its potential impact on the reduced social, political, and economic costs of governance, the symbolic acts of legitimization also bring psychological satisfaction to the rulers. Alagappa thus notes that "(f)rom the rulers' viewpoint, legitimacy is not just a stratagem to secure more effective control or perpetuate themselves in office. Self-justification in moral terms is crucial for most rulers. They need to believe they are serving the national interest or a moral cause even if it necessitates a noble lie. By enhancing self-esteem, such a belief justifies domination and enjoyment of the privileges of power."[3]

For these reasons, authoritarian governments have used a variety of rationales to legitimize their rule. Among them "performance" (the ability to promote the collective interests of the community, such as the provision of law and order and the cultural and material welfare of citizens) poses as the most appealing and viable strategy (Huntington 1991, Liddle 1992, Schwarz 1994, Alagappa 1995). David Beetham, for instance, writes that a military regime lacks enduring bases of political legitimacy by failing to adhere to the rules regarding the ascension to power and the entertaining of popular consent. Thus "performance" becomes everything, and "the achievements and capacities of the regime have to be disproportionately magnified."[4]

Although many authors agree that "performance" can alleviate, if not eliminate, the legitimacy problems of authoritarian governments, the extent to which positive economic performance enhances the citizens perception of the government's right to rule remains an issue of scholarly debate. Alagappa, for instance, contends that economic performance is not a sufficient or durable basis for political legitimacy. He writes that "while good performance has contributed to the legitimacy of the Soeharto government, the New Order's legitimacy has been challenged on the grounds of equity and corruption...and the growth of more independent middle and working classes is likely to accentuate this contestation."[5]

Alagappa's argument has two important implications. First, it questions the feasibility of relying on aggregate economic performance at the national level or even at the local level as the basis of legitimacy. In other words, the aggregate data of agricultural growth and development inadequately captures the type and level of popularity enjoyed by the government. Second, there are many

---

[3] Ibid.,
[4] David Beetham, The Legitimation of Power, 234-235.
[5] Alagappa, "Seeking a more durable basis of authority", in Political Legitimacy in Southeast Asia: the Quest for Moral Authority, 309-310.

different kinds of policies that can be implemented to promote "growth" or "equity," or both, and the contributions they make with regard to enhancing, or undermining a government's legitimacy are varied. Simply put, the types of policies and the ways in which they are implemented can have varying impacts on the societal perception of the state. Thus an analysis of how different types of agricultural policies and their implementation affect the government's popularity in Burma will provide us with improved understanding of the relationship between economic policies and political legitimacy.

Different local authorities will of course implement the same agricultural policy in slightly different ways, and their treatments of particular policies have a wide range of consequences for farmers' perception of the local and central authorities. Since agriculture is the paddy producers' main concern, a change in agricultural policies clearly and dramatically affects their lives. Because both the policies themselves and the implementation determine rural support for the government, it is not sufficient to look at improved economic conditions of citizens as the basis of governmental popularity. This book will look at how the "processes" of implementing agricultural policies (in addition to the "end results," which are measured in terms of improved or worsened living conditions) affect the image of central government authorities.

The disaggregated state
The Burmese military government is not a single entity. It has established a hierarchical chain of command, and has generally transmitted national policies through local state agencies and departments. Thus it is important to look at diverse activities that occur within Burma's villages to understand the institutional, organizational, personality and socio-economic factors that influence hostile and friendly interactions between various components of state and society and farmers' attitudes toward local and central authorities.

Generally speaking, Burmese cultivators have to deal with two different types of authorities on a regular basis. They are the local leaders (native authority) and the centrally appointed officials (non-native authority). Their relationships with these authorities vary depending on a variety of circumstances. These include the objectives and organizational resources of the local agencies, socioeconomic status, and the occupational and educational backgrounds of local authorities. The second thesis of this book centers upon rice farmers' interactions with local agencies and government authorities.

There are several local agencies that deal directly with paddy farmers in Burma, but only four agencies have significant interaction with farmers. They are the Myanma Agriculture Services (MAS), the Irrigation Department, the Settlement and Land Records Department, and the township and village Peace and Development Councils. Although these agencies have their headquarters in the capital, farmers only deal with local branches. The central headquarters of agriculture-related ministries and departments usually formulate policies, which are then passed down to their respective subordinate departments at the district level. The district authorities then divide up responsibilities and guide their organizations at the next lower tier, the township and village tract level. These township and village tract departments and agencies must implement policies that are assigned to them from the top down, and they deal directly with the farmers.

The actions of local officials provide a basis upon which farmers develop different attitudes toward the highest authorities in Rangoon. It is, however, very difficult to discern farmers' overall attitudes toward the highest authorities in Rangoon because of their varying relationships with different local departments and native leaders. Ultimately, farmers' attitudes toward the central government are determined by their relationship with agencies that have the most direct and most significant impact on their lives. Nonetheless, the dynamic nature of these interactions at the local level not only challenges the misconception of a singular governmental structure in Burma but also sheds light on rice farmers' predominant concerns with good local leadership and governance structure.

Burmese rice farmers particularly value village chairmen and local authorities who are impartial, honest, responsive to their needs, sympathetic to their plight, protective of their interests, and who are not too corrupt and abusive of their power and authority. The rice farmers are complacent as long as these qualities are present in local leaders, be they military or civilian officials. Most officials are expected to engage in illicit deals among themselves and with farmers, but they do not necessarily create negative repercussions in rural areas unless these activities take place at the expense of farmers' tremendous loss. Farmers also prefer local officials who share similar interests with them, who dispense resources with a minimum level of corruption, who do not rigidly enforce central policies that are inimical to the interests of farmers, and to whom farmers can openly and frankly express their problems.

Multiple images of authoritarianism
The third theme of this book examines the varying circumstances under which the top echelon of military officials enjoy high or low regard in the countryside. I argue that despite the international

communities and human rights activists' overwhelming perception of the military regime as "illegitimate," the military government has continued to enjoy pockets of support and societal acceptance in rural areas. The level of support for military officials in the capital, however, has varied over time.

Specifically, rural residents held high regard for the military elite in the capital when a specific development program demonstrably improved their lives. Moreover, when convinced that the central authorities were unaware of local officials' abuses and exploitation in the implementation of these programs, farmers looked to the central government to solve their problems and sought channels to make their grievances known to the highest executive authority in Rangoon.

Rural support for the central government, however, was weak when it instituted policies that adversely impinged on farmers' economic position. This low regard for the central government, however, rarely translates into similar regard for the local government. Rural attitudes toward the local authorities have largely been based on their execution of programs; specifically, local authorities were more likely to receive positive support when they modified national policies in favor of their residents than when they rigorously enforced unpopular programs.

The central government, however, did not necessarily have to intervene on behalf of the exploited to enhance its image. As will be demonstrated, farmers' threats to take their complaints of local-level corruption to the central government ameliorated local corrupt practices. This was enough to give the central government a positive image for farmers even in instances in which high-level officials did not take action. What is important here are the perceptions of the rice farmers who develop a certain image of military leaders at the capital based on their daily experiences with various types of state authorities and the policies with which these are associated.

Burma in a comparative framework
The detailed accounts of local authorities' varying relationships with rice farmers in Burma represent a diverse array of state-societal interactions that can be found elsewhere in poor countries. They also provide a fine illustration of the complex nature of political legitimacy, and the existence of pockets, if not substantial, of societal support for authoritarian governments in poor countries. These varying levels of societal support for authoritarian governments do not emerge out of thin air. They are influenced by complex interactions between various parts of state and society, shaped by specific political and economic milieu, and molded by the nature of government's

economic and political practices. The last theme of this effort will demonstrate comparable patterns of state-societal interactions in other authoritarian countries, and discuss their broader theoretical relevance for political legitimacy.

Why the Agricultural Sector?
From 1962-1988, native and foreign scholars conducted few studies on Burma due to the government's isolationist policy and hostility toward academic researchers. With the exception of the capital city and small towns and villages in the border areas, the country was completely concealed by a thick teak curtain. Its citizens were largely isolated from the rest of the world, living through a dark period of fear, ignorance, and political and economic stagnation. Much of the scholarly work on Burma focused on a score of military leaders in the capital, relying on sources published by the government and analyzing official policies and rhetorical aspects of the military regime. Those who examined state-societal interactions emphasized urban groups, especially state-enterprise workers, students, and monks, who constituted a small segment of the population. A few works studied the role and activities of minority ethnic groups who denied the legitimacy of the military regime. Scant attention was paid to farmers, the bulk of the population, whose mere presence and contribution to the economy and foreign exchange have been fundamental and significant.

Burma has been predominantly an agricultural country. About 75 percent of the population, and 64.1 percent of the labor force still live in the countryside where farming is their main occupation. The agricultural sector constitutes between 37-49 percent of GDP and agricultural exports provide 25-45 percent of foreign exchange. Rice, which occupies half of the total sown acreage, is the main staple crop, the traditional major export item, and major foreign exchange earner in Burma.

Given the predominant role of agriculture in the economy, a few native and Japanese scholars have examined the peasant economy during the "socialist" periods (1974-88), but much of their analysis focused on the economic profile of a particular village, or the macroeconomic performance of the agricultural sector. Examples include the works of Mya Than, Myat Thein, Khin Maung Kyi, Mya Maung, and Teruko Saito.[6] None of these studies were devoted to the relationships between military authorities and villagers.

---

[6] Mya Than, "Little change in rural Burma: A case study of a Burmese village (1960-80)", Sojourn 2 (1) (1982): 55-87. Mya Than, "A Burmese village revisited", The South East Asian Review 2 (2) (February 1978): 1-15. Khin Maung Kyi and associates, "Process of communication in modernization of rural society: A survey report on two Burmese villages", The Malayan Economic

In consequence, the political activities of the countryside have remained scarcely explored or, for that matter, even visible for the past three decades. Scholars extrapolated from inadequate sources to argue that, unlike city dwellers who were hostile to the military government, the people who lived in the countryside had an amicable relationship with the military regime.[7] As evidence, some cited the relatively peaceful and quiescent nature of rural residents and the military's rhetoric that prioritized the interests and welfare of the peasants.

Others, however, have implied that rural people hold low regard for the military government due to the deleterious effects of agricultural policies.[8] Evidence for this thesis came mainly from national statistics and village studies showing slow agricultural growth and stagnant living conditions. Analyses of official policies, their impact on the rural economy, and the visible political aspects of the state-society relationship are necessary but not sufficient for determining the level of rural support for the military. The popularity of a particular agricultural policy as well as the support for authorities through their implementation of this policy are mediated by how the policy is implemented and the types of relationships the local state officials have with their local residents. It is difficult to build a convincing theory that focuses on the legitimacy of the state without a detailed understanding of the roles and practices of elite groups at various levels of the political and bureaucratic hierarchy, and how their respective constituencies perceive these practices.

After 1988, there was a slow but increasing flow of traffic of foreign scholars who were given visas to conduct research in Burma. In the agricultural sector in particular, the more "liberal" agricultural bureaucrats provided greater research opportunities and an enthusiastic welcome for foreign scholars. They began to accept "critical" evaluation of these studies, and acknowledged pitfalls and weaknesses within the system.[9] The increasing involvement of governmental (e.g. Food and Agriculture Organization of the United Nation Development Program) and non-governmental organizations in attempts to

---

Review 18 (1) (April 1973): 55-73. Teruko Saito, "Farm household economy under paddy delivery system in contemporary Burma", The Developing Economies 19 (4) (1981): 367-397.

7 See for example, John Badgley. "Burma: The nexus of socialism and two political traditions", Asian Survey 3 (2) (February, 1963): 89-95. Michael Aung-Thwin, "1948 and Burma's myth of independence", in Independent Burma at Forty Years: Six Assessments, ed. Josel Silverstein (Ithaca: Southeast Asian Program, 1989).

8 See for example, Mya Maung, The Burma Road to Poverty (New York: Praeger, 1991).

9 For further details, see Tin Htut Oo, "Myanmar agriculture under the economic transition: Present situation and emerging trends" (Tokyo: The Institute of Developing Economies, March 1996). Scott Sindeler, Agricultural Attache, United States Department of Agriculture, Bangkok, Thailand, interview by author, January 19, 1999.

eliminate poverty and promote a higher standard of living in rural areas has also spawned volumes of proposals, evaluations, and economic censuses on national as well as village level studies. Consultants and agricultural experts frequently visited Burma to propose strategies and to submit project evaluations for both private as well as governmental enterprises in agriculture. Disappointingly, however, much of this research continues to neglect the political aspect of life for the agrarian community.

This book has emerged out of my own frustration on the lack of research on local authorities' interactions with rice farmers.[10] To help fill this gap, it attempts to uncover these unexplored and generally ignored sides to the study of Burma by examining military-peasant relationships in the countryside. There are, in sum, two main reasons why this book focuses on rice farmers' sentiments toward the military regime. The first objective is mainly empirical; to unearth and capture aspects of agrarian relationships that in fact have never been studied in Burma, and to provide a case study for comparative agrarian politics. The second is value-based and, indeed morally based: to shed light on the existing agricultural problems and shortcomings. If silence is interpreted as a sign of acceptance and support for the military regime, there is a possibility that scholars and policy makers may continue to neglect the real problems that confront many agricultural producers. Instead of interpreting peasants' subservience to the state as unworthy of attention, one may be surprised to learn how a simple survey of peasant values and motivations can generate many interesting and ultimately revealing research agendas that deserve further analysis beneficial to the study of Burmese politics and peasant communities.

Outline of the chapters
Chapter one examines the Burmese farmers' conceptualization of political legitimacy. It offers a new approach to the study of political legitimacy in Burma and other Third World authoritarian countries through examining relations between local authorities and residents with particular attention to the material issues of everyday life.

Chapter two analyzes the relationships between state authorities and the Burmese rice farmers in pre-colonial, colonial, post-colonial Burma. It establishes the historical contexts within which

---

[10] I will use the terms "farmers" and "peasants" interchangeably in this book. According to Eric Wolf, peasants produce primarily for home consumption while farmers produce primarily for the market. Since the majority of Burmese farmers produce both for consumption as well as for the market, the distinction between "farmers" and "peasants" is considered irrelevant here. I will also occasionally and broadly refer to rice farmers, who are the focus of my study, as rural residents, agricultural producers, cultivators, or people from the countryside. Eric Wolf, Peasants Wars of the Twentieth Century (New York: Harper and Row, 1969).

contemporary rice farmers have come into contact with local and central authorities. This historical analysis of state-societal relationships will help us understand the origins of Burmese cultivators' different dispositions toward central and local authorities, the changing bases of political legitimacy, and the roots of cordiality and hostility between rice farmers and state authorities under the same political and economic milieu and across different points of time.

Chapter three focuses on local state agencies and departments (Myanma Agriculture Services, Irrigation Department, Land Record Office, the township and village Peace and Development Council) that implement agricultural policies in Burma. It analyzes a host of factors that affect relations between rice farmers and local officials.

Chapter four looks at responses to the local and central governments regarding the implementation of four different agricultural policies; the High-Yielding Variety Promotion (1976-82), the Partial Liberalization (1987-present), the Summer Paddy Program (1992-present), and Land Reclamation Policy (1991-present). It discusses situations in which both the local government and the central government were seen favorably, those in which both governments were seen unfavorably, and those in which there were mixed attitudes toward these two different levels of government.

Chapter five examines the question of political quiescence in the countryside. It highlights options available to farmers ("compliance," "exit," "passive resistance," "individual contacting," and "voice"), and demonstrates how farmers have used each of them under diverse circumstances to alleviate their grievances. This chapter will show that the existence of these options, along with fear of retaliation from the state and farmers' ambivalent attitudes toward authorities in power, explains why a collective peasant revolt has not taken place under the military regime.

Chapter six summarizes the arguments and draws out theoretical and empirical implications for developing authoritarian countries. It will also demonstrate comparable patterns of state-societal interactions in contemporary China and Vietnam, Marcos' martial law regime, Trujillo's Dominican Republic, India and Mexico, and discuss their broader theoretical relevance for political legitimacy.

Chapter 1
Authoritarianism and Political Legitimacy

How do Burmese farmers conceptualize political legitimacy? On what do these farmers base their support for the state authorities? Are the political values and attitudes of rural cultivators significantly different from those of their urban counterparts? To what extent do Burmese farmers share a common political outlook with cultivators from other developing countries? This chapter will address these questions by analyzing Burmese farmers' political values, orientations and the roots of their support for authority.

The first section of this chapter will provide a new conceptualization of political legitimacy within the context of the Burmese authoritarian regime. The second part will evaluate three schools of thought which have offered explanations for Burmese farmers' political behavior and practices. I will shed light on the limitations of these previous theories by looking at past and current agrarian practices and interactions that do not conform to them. I will show how the "process-oriented approach," which looks at agricultural cultivators' perceptions of the central government through their interactions with local authorities, explains not only the foundations of farmers' favorable attitudes towards the regime, but also the dynamics and degree of political legitimacy in Burmese rural areas and in other Third World authoritarian countries.

Defining Political Legitimacy in the Context of Authoritarian Regimes
Political legitimacy or "the belief in the rightfulness of a state, in its authority to issue commands," is a contextually specific, multifaceted, and highly dynamic concept.[1] The debate about what makes government "right," "just," "acceptable," and "proper" is age-old, and has generated many competing and contradictory definitions.[2] Most concepts, however, are drawn from the experiences of well-established democratic countries, where there are entrenched and accepted rules and regulations, and where public opinion can be easily discerned to identify the extent of shared

---

[1] Rodney Barker, *Political Legitimacy and the State* (Oxford: Claredon Press, 1990), 11.
[2] Robert Lane, "The Legitimacy in Bias", in *Legitimation of Regimes* (California: Sage Publication: 1979), 56.

beliefs and norms between the rulers and the ruled. Such a definition provides an inappropriate and misleading tool to apply in countries under different socio-political contexts.[3]

David Beetham, for instance, contends that for a government or political system to be considered legitimate, three conditions must be fulfilled. Most fundamental, power should be acquired and exercised according to established rules. Power is "illegitimate" where it is either acquired in contravention of the rules (expropriation, usurpation, coup d'état), or exercised in a manner that contravenes or exceeds them. To Beetham, the military government which takes over power through a coup d'état may over time achieve a degree of social support, and may enjoy a certain level of internal stability and economic progress, but "what it can *never* acquire is legitimacy," since it came to office through a breach of constitutional rule.[4] Second, established rules must be justified in terms of shared beliefs and values about the proper source of political authority as well as the ends and purposes that government should serve. These include the ability to satisfy society requirements and their own well-being. Third, citizens must express their consent through actions, either through entering into an agreement or contract with the state, swearing an oath of allegiance, or joining in acclamation, and/or voting in an election or plebiscite.[5] Beetham writes that "(a)ctions ranging from non-cooperation and passive resistance to open disobedience and militant opposition on the part of those qualified to give consent will in different measure erode legitimacy, and the larger the number involved, the greater this erosion will be. At this level, the opposite or negative of legitimacy can be called delegitimation."[6]

If we take Beetham's argument seriously, we must come to the conclusion that military governments in Asia, Africa, and Latin America are illegitimate (through the use of force to take over power) and are devoid of legitimation (by occasional public protests and demonstrations).

Such analysis of legitimacy, however, assumes an undifferentiated image of the military regime. Ron May, Stephanie Lawson and Viberto Selochan, for instance, point out that

---

[3] See, for example, Jan Pakulski, "Legitimacy and mass compliance: Reflections on Max Weber and Soviet type societies", *British Journal of Political Science* 16 (1986): 35-56.
[4] David Beetham, *The Legitimation of Power* (New Jersey: Humanities Press International, Inc., 1991), 233. Emphasis added.
[5] ibid., 132.
[6] ibid., 18.

> As more and more states came to experience periods of military rule it also became obvious that stereotypical models of military rule were inadequate. In some countries, the military, or factions within the military, had simply made a blatant grab for power; in others the military intervened to replace an ineffective or corrupt civilian government with the stated intention of handing power back to civilian rule; in still others the military and civilian authorities established a system of joint participation in government.[7]

Furthermore, the ways in which citizens behave do not always reflect what they think of the government, since political apathy or quiescence can be mistakenly interpreted as a sign of discontent. Likewise, popular mobilization in response to government's employment of a variety of incentives and coercion mechanisms, as occurred in communist societies, can be inappropriately labeled as acceptance of the regime.

The study of legitimacy is further complicated by the various components of state institutions whose legitimacy may vary from one to another; the legitimacy of an individual power-holder, or the legitimacy of the rules under which he or she holds power, or the legitimacy of a government, or the legitimacy of a political system.[8] Robert Lane argues that there are some components of state institutions that are more important in affecting the legitimacy of the state, and whether the government is in a legitimacy crisis or not depends on which parts of the state institutions create public dissatisfaction. Lane notes that a legitimacy crisis occurs only when critical views are mainly directed at the system and at the rationale or values underlying the system. Thus, citizens' dissatisfaction with the incumbents or policies or the system performance does not constitute a legitimacy crisis of government.[9] In a similar way, Beetham asserts that the system does not necessarily suffer from a legitimacy crisis if it fails to satisfy general interest requirements, whether through inability, incompetence or partiality, as long as the constitutions are "designed to allow for the replacement of governments or leaders who have lost confidence; and that the process of replacement enables alternative policies to be proposed by a different administration enjoying renewed authority."[10]

---

[7] May, Lawson, Selochan, "Introduction: Democracy and the military in comparative Perspective", in *The Military and Democracy in Asia and the Pacific,* eds. R.J. May, Lawson, and Viberto Selochan (London: Crawford House Publishing, C. Hurst & CO. LTD, 1998), 5.
[8] Ibid., 5.
[9] Robert Lane, "The Legitimacy in Bias", in *Legitimation of Regimes*, 63.
[10] Beetham, *The Legitimization of Power*, 146.

Lane's and Beetham's identification of the specific situations under which a legitimacy crisis takes place is worthy of attention. However, the relevance of their work for the analysis of other settings cannot be taken for granted. Especially in the Burmese rural areas and other Third World authoritarian countries, societal attitudes concerning the legitimacy of the state or government are more likely to be influenced by the behavior and practices of central and local authorities that impinge on the lives of rural populations. These values are less likely to be predicated upon the appropriate type of political system or the rationale and values underlying the system which bear little relevance to their daily concerns.[11]

It may be pragmatic for poor people to make judgments about government based on the actions of individual authorities who have contact with them. For it is easier to change and to exert control over an individual's behavior rather than to change the whole system. It may also be that the central governing authorities have played an insignificant role in the lives of those who live in peripheral areas. Lack of communication and transportation networks hinders the central governing authority's ability to establish direct contact with local residents, and empowers local authorities and native leaders with a higher degree of discretion and control over residents.

Thus, the study of legitimacy must not only be approached from the perspective of the governed, but also be "objectively" analyzed independent of a researcher's ethical or moral judgments and predispositions. In other words, a special conceptual apparatus must be formulated to reflect the political situations in non-democratic and poor countries.

I define political legitimacy in terms of 'the minimum level of acceptance of government authorities by a citizen.' This acceptance of authority is expressed through favorable views of state officials. Behavioral and verbal reaction indicating support for state leaders range from highly positive commentaries to satisfaction with the practices and actions of the relevant government authorities.

I will use the terms 'popularity' and 'political legitimacy' interchangeably to demonstrate the existence of rural support for state leaders. Popularity connotes 'the quality or state of being liked by many

---

[11] For instance, see Samuel P. Huntington and Joan M. Nelson, *No Easy Choice: Political Participation in Developing Countries* (Massachusetts: Harvard University Press, 1976). Here, I am not implying that other bases of legitimacy (such as shared norms and values) are unimportant in poor countries. They may still provide rationales for why citizens accept their governments as appropriate and legitimate.

people.[12] Legitimacy is 'belief in the legitimacy of the system of rule or command,' measured in terms of acceptable rules and practices underpinning the accession to and exercise of power.[13] Political legitimacy is a more enduring concept, and is sometimes used in reference to political institutions, or the requisite procedures for obtaining and exercising power, and fulfilling societal needs. Popularity, on the other hand, has a transitory character, and is directed toward individual power holders. Thus my definition of political legitimacy attempts to capture both terms by looking at 'popular acceptance for *individual power holders* and *their acceptable practices.*'

I will evaluate the legitimacy of the government by analyzing farmers' perceptions of central and local authorities who occupy the executive and administrative branches of the state and are responsible for policy making and policy implementation. I consider the legitimacy of the government to be synonymous with that of the state since it is almost impossible to distinguish the boundaries between the state, the government, or the regime in authoritarian countries.[14] Under an entrenched military rule like Burma's, military interests have captured the executive, judiciary, administrative, legislative and economic branches of the state and the military has complete control over the institutions of the state. Thus state, government, army, and military personnel are almost inseparable.

Burmese rice farmers' tendency to improve the conditions of their lives within a constrained political environment, and their periods of positive inclination towards the authorities do not necessarily deter them from challenging government authorities in a more open political system. Burmese farmers' support for certain authorities must be analyzed in the context of a military regime which has relied heavily on coercion and has limped along with little or no legitimacy. Thus a degree of satisfaction with state authorities has the effect of merely neutralizing rural opposition so that they are not willing to risk their lives overthrowing the regime.[15] Burmese peasants, in particular, have long been exposed to authoritarian rule and have been taught almost from birth that government is one of the five evils they must endure. Given their limited expectations,

---

[12] *American World Power Dictionary* (Oxford: Oxford University Press, 1998).

[13] C.K. Ansell, *"Legitimacy: Political"*, in *International encyclopedia of the Social and Behavior Sciences* (Oxford: Elsevier, 2001), 8704-8706.

[14] According to Max Weber, the state is a corporate group that has compulsory jurisdiction, exercises continuous organization, and claims a monopoly of force over a territory and its population, including all action taking place in the area of its jurisdiction.

[15] I am indebted to Professor James Scott for his comment on this important issue.

impoverished and destitute Burmese cultivators are likely to accept the government as long as their situations are relatively good or not too severe. Jonathan Fox, for instance, conceptualizes legitimacy in the context of the authoritarian regime in Mexico following the 1930s as follows: "Apparent political legitimacy in both city and countryside rested on widespread belief that life could be improved by working within the system. The lack of viable alternative channels of political expression for most people, most of the time, along with periodic partial reforms, has served to renew the basis of this belief." [16] Ben Kerkvliet's observation of the poor Bukiran peasants in Nueva Ecija province during Marcos' martial law periods also reveals that "modest" government actions that benefited the peasants were "suffice to prevent poor people from looking upon the government as an enemy and even to keep alive the belief that on occasion it can be a friend."[17]

Similarly, Kerkvliet demonstrates the limited expectations of the veterans of the *Huk* rebellion. They were satisfied that the Marcos government officially acknowledged them, for the first time in post war periods, as a guerrilla group which had "vigilantly resisted the Japanese." The Marcos government also promised them limited medical and education benefits. One veteran for instance remarked that he could be dead by the time the application forms for such entitlement benefits were ready, but what was more important was "the recognition, which we deserve, for what we did during the Japanese time." [18]

Throughout this book, I will also use the terms 'farmer' and 'peasant' interchangeably because Burmese farmers have overlapping identities as 'farmers' and 'peasants.' According to Eric Wolf, peasants keep "the market at arm's length, for unlimited involvement in the market threatens his hold on his source of livelihood...He favors production for sale only within the context of an assured production for subsistence."[19] Farmers, on the other hand, enter "the market fully, subjects his land and labor to open competition, explores alternative uses for the factors of production in the search for maximum returns, and favors the more profitable product over the one entailing the smaller risk."[20] Most Burmese farmers sell their surplus grain in the market, but their choices

---

[16] Jonathan Fox, *The Politics of Food in Mexico: State Power and Social Mobilization* (Ithaca: Cornell University Press, 1993), 3.
[17] Benedict Kerkvliet, "Martial law in Nueva Ecija village, the Philippines", *Bulletin of Concerned Asian Scholars* 14 (October/December 1982), 18.
[18] Quoted in B. Kerkvliet, "Martial law in a Nueva Ecija village, the Philippines", 7.
[19] Eric Wolf, *Peasant Wars of the Twentieth Century* (London: Faber and Faber 1971), xviii.
[20] Ibid., xix

over what to grow and how much to sell in the market and at what prices are largely determined by the government rather than by a profit-maximizing calculation. The government also prohibits the sale of land in Burma. Thus most Burmese farmers do not fit neatly into the category of "farmer" to the extent that a farmer subjects his land and labor to open competition, fully participates in the market, and maximizes his profits. Neither do Burmese farmers fit perfectly into the category of "peasant," to the extent that a peasant mainly produces for his own consumption.

Burmese Rice Farmers' Perspectives on Political Legitimacy
Michael Adas, a renowned historian on Burma's agrarian politics, argues that Burmese cultivators in the pre-colonial era had a clearly defined concept of legitimacy which was based on Buddhist religious principles and the values associated with the Burmese monarchical tradition. He contends that villagers in upper Burma accepted the monarchical rule as legitimate and divinely ordained and that was the reason peasant rebellions against Burmese kings were rare in pre-colonial periods.[21] Rebellions were, however, a common phenomenon in colonial periods. According to Adas, the British annexations of the *Irrawaddy* delta region in 1852 and the remaining portions of the *Konbaung* kingdom in 1886 were followed by nearly a decade of local uprisings and "bandit" attacks.[22] Adas writes that rebel leaders were able to generate popular support in the countryside due to *their elaborate use of kingly rituals and royal symbols* which gave credibility and legitimacy to their cause.

> Whether ex-officials, pongyis (monks), or professional bandits, all resistance leaders claimed to be commissioned by the Konbaung (the last Burmese dynasty) court, which in 1882 still ruled in Upper Burma to carry out on the struggle against the British. Leaders of the larger risings, like Gaung Gyi, wielded the ancient symbols of Burmese political authority: gilt umbrellas, royal elephants, and sacred gongs. Some rebel leaders claimed to be princes of the royal house. Widespread popular support for resistance groups, particularly in the form of food and shelter, demonstrates the strong hold these symbols and appeals continued to exercise over peasant communities despite the dynasty's setback.[23]

---

[21] Michael Adas, "Bandits, Monks, and Pretender Kings: Patterns of Peasant Resistance and Protest in Colonial Burma, 1826-1941", in *Power and Protest in the Countryside: Studies of Rural Unrest in Asia, Europe, and Latin American*, eds. Robert Waller and Scott Guggenheim (NC: Ruham, 1982), 76-105.
[22] Michael Adas, "Bandits, Monks, and Pretender Kings", 80.
[23] Ibid., 81.

Adas also contends that the Saya San peasant revolt, which took place during the British occupation of Burma in 1930, resembled many of the post-conquest rebellions against the British government in terms of *its emphasis on the restoration of the Burmese monarchy and the protection of Buddhist religion*. Adas admits that market fluctuation, economic distresses, abuses and exploitation by landlords were the main reasons for the outbreak of the Saya San rebellion. Nonetheless

> After over a hundred years of British rule in some areas and from fifty to eighty years in others, peasant rebels fought to restore Buddhism and the Burmese monarchy, rather than to win independence and gain government by parliaments and Western-educated lawyers and journalists. They rallied to monks and princely pretenders, rather than to nationalist agitators....The peasants' adherence to millenarian prophecies and their pervasive reliance on magical talismans (with disastrous results) further distanced them from the urban-based nationalists who would have little place in the new society which rebel leaders like Saya San envisioned.[24]

According to Adas, the Saya San rebellion in Lower Burma represents one form of social movements which "played out "hundreds of times" across different settings since the early nineteenth century. It is occasionally labeled as "millennial" or "revivalist" movement, characterized by organized effort of a society to reconstruct a more satisfying culture.[25]

Similarly, Michael Aung-Thwin emphasizes the culturally and traditionally based political legitimacy of Burma's countryside residents. He argues that the military takeover in 1962 was considered a legitimate act since it reintroduced the traditional values of most of the people.[26] He contends that the period immediately following independence in 1948 and until the military took over in 1962 cannot be considered a "watershed" in the history of Burma since it perpetuated Western values, such as the dominance of the Western-oriented elite and the Western political system. Thus for the majority of Burmese, "this independence was largely a meaningless (even if emotional) event, and for most Burmese it made very little difference to the primary concerns of their lives."[27] Aung-Thwin notes that

---

[24] Ibid, 103.
[25] Michael Adas, *Prophets of Rebellion: Millenarian Protest Movements Against the European Colonial Order* (Chapel Hill: the University of North Carolina Press: 1979), xvii.
[26] Michael Aung-Thwin, "1948 and Burma's Myth of Independence", in *Independence Burma at Forty Years; Six Assessments*, ed. Josef Silverstein (Ithaca: Southeast Asian Program, 1989).
[27] Ibid., 23.

Aside from the immediate historical reasons for the coup of 1962 (such as fear of secession from the Shans and Kayahs), there was a more fundamental cause: a collective psychological desire to establish "real" independence, which necessarily included purging one's colonial past....*Clearly, the majority of Burmese were more concerned originally with a meaningful and ordered society that preserved traditional patterns, and with finding some way to recover a lost identity than they were with economic development per se*, which is a more recent priority. In this sense, the coup and its immediate aftermath were less a reaction to the few years after colonial rule, than to many years of colonial rule.[28]

According to Aung-Thwin, some traditional values that had been upheld by the majority populations included (1) an isolationist policy, which helped strengthen the Burmese identity and traditional values; (2) the abolishment of parliamentary democracy which had "no real links" to Burma's social and economic realities; (3) the state role as the patron of *sangha*; (4) the composition of government with a predominantly military background; and (5) the priority of the agricultural sector in general and farmers in particular.[29]

The scholarly writings of the late 60s and early 70s echoed similar analysis. Jon Wiant and David Steinberg, for instance, wrote that "the keys to understanding the Burmese revolutionary experience and the place of the military in shaping that destiny are rooted deeply in Burmese culture and history. *Ideological contributions from a thousand years of Burmese politics provided the symbolic foundations of Ne Win's political authority and, in peculiar ways, gave it a legitimacy in Burmese eyes that was incomprehensible to many Western observers.*" [30]

The analysis of cultural and religious support bases for state authorities offers powerful insight into the political motivations and practices of Burmese peasants in pre-colonial societies. However, some peasants' movements that have these mere spiritual overtones are in fact caused by deep-seated economic grievances thinly covered by millenarian shell. In other words, the millenarian movement does not only provide a powerful appeal to the return of indigenous rule but also offers a better alternative to entrenched poverty, abuse and exploitation of peasants by local elites. The Saya San rebellion, in fact, occurred in the midst of rising tenancy, agricultural indebtedness, and socio-economic dislocations. Also,

---

[28] Ibid., 24-25. Emphasis added.

[29] Ibid.,

[30] Jon Wiant and David Steinberg, "Burma: the military and national development", in *Soldiers and Stability in Southeast Asia*, eds. J. Soedijati Dijiwandono and Yong Mun Cheong (Singapore: Institute of Southeast Asian Studies, 1988), 295. Emphasis added.

the argument for Burmese cultivators' overwhelming support for the military must be taken with careful consideration because it lacks evidence. Most writings repeatedly make reference to the "majority's views" and "beliefs" but they did not actually survey the population nor even cite events/anecdotes/ activities that would suggest the presence of the majority citizens' supports for the military.

Burma's current military regime, the State Law and Order Restoration Council (SLORC) or later referred to as the State Peace and Development Council (SPDC), in fact, has promoted Buddhism since its inception in 1988. The front pages of daily official newspapers and monthly magazines in Burma have been covered with pictures of military officials' offering gifts and money to Buddhist monks, visiting pagodas, and hosting the visits of Buddhist relics. Bruce Matthews, for instance, has written extensively on how the current Burmese military government (the SLORC and later the SPDC) has relied on the traditional appeal to Buddhism to legitimize its rule.[31] I remember residents of *Atek* village in *Alei* township in Upper Burma, flocking to watch television coverage of military's placing an umbrella on top of the pagoda. Although urban residents are skeptical about military gestures to Buddhist values, Buddhist cultivators nonetheless applauded them, and they did not hesitate to say so.[32] However, as yet, no systematic study has been conducted to examine Burmese rice farmers' attitudes toward the current junta's attempt to promote Buddhism.[33]

Nevertheless, there is little in the approach of culturally and religiously based political legitimacy to help us understand peasant behavior in the later part of the military regime. Specifically, these bases of support for the regime offer limited explanation for the 1988 nation-

---

[31] Bruce Matthews, "The present fortune of tradition-bound authoritarianism in Myanmar", in *Pacific Affairs* 71 (1) (Spring 1998), 7-23. Also see Michael Aung-Thwin, "1948 and Burma's Myth of Independence", in *Independent Burma at Forty Years: Six Assessments*, ed. Josef Silverstein (Ithaca, N.Y: Southeast Asian Program, 1989).

[32] Conversation with one villager in *Atek* township.

[33] Buddhist political ideology is rife with contradictions. On the one hand, Buddhist thought accords legitimacy to any ruler who promotes and protects Buddhism. The Burmese prophecies make reference to the emergence of great kings, whose descent to the throne was justified by their adherence to uphold and promote the welfare of Buddhism. These kings can either be royal descendants or usurpers. Whoever occupies the position of authority can justify his dominance in terms of good deeds from his past lives. Another aspect of Buddhist political thought, which can be traced to Indian Buddhist political theory, on the other hand, justifies the position of a king who is popularly elected. According to this concept, the people agreed to elect *Mahasammata* to provide order in a world filled with chaos and, in return, compensated with one-tenth of their produce. This legend contains the democratic principle or social contract stressed by European political thought, and has been used by the opposition parties in Burma to challenge the legitimacy of the regime.

wide pro-democracy demonstration. Although they did not initiate the popular uprising against the military dictatorship, Burmese farmers joined their urban counterparts in their call for the removal of the Burma Socialist Program Party (headed by military leaders), for the holding of multiparty election, and for the establishment of "democracy."[34] Why did the farmers, who supposedly shared the values that had been promoted by the military junta, rebel against government authorities? Why do they secretly admire Aung San Suu Kyi, the opposition leader who married a foreigner and spent most of her adult life outside Burma? Why did the rural population vote overwhelmingly for Suu Kyi in the 1990 election? It is not at all clear that the assumption of culturally-based political legitimacy can satisfactorily explain these puzzles. Traditional values and practices may continue to thrive in some societies, and may be utilized and manipulated to generate popular support, but it is dangerous to treat these values as unchanging sets of attitudes. As Alagappa points out, legitimacy is a "social practice, an outcome of the interaction between ruler and ruled; hence it must be framed in the sociopolitical and economic context of a specific society at a specified time."[35]

James Scott is another scholar who contends that the Burmese peasantry in the pre-colonial period had a clearly formulated view of legitimacy. However, this concept of political legitimacy is based on moral rather than cultural and religious principles. Scott argues that peasants in pre-colonial Southeast Asian societies developed their own concept of social justice and had certain expectations about the appropriate roles and obligations of the state. According to Scott, "the peasant is born into a society and culture that provide him with a fund of moral values, a set of concrete social relationships, a pattern of expectations about the behavior of others, and a sense of how those in his culture have proceeded to similar goals in the past."[36] *The legitimacy of the state depends on the state's ability to meet its minimum obligations as prescribed by the farmers:*

> Any balance of exchange above a certain minimum [i.e, norms of reciprocity] is likely to take on legitimacy over time, and even small movements away from a balance of reciprocity that will reduce peasant benefits are likely to give rise to a sense of exploitation which invokes

[34] See Bertil Lintner, *Outrage*. Also see chapter 5 of this book.
[35] M. Alagappa, "The Anatomy of Legitimacy", 11.
[36] James Scott, *The Moral Economy of the Peasant: Rebellion and Subsistence in Southeast Asia* (New Haven: Yale University Press, 1976), 166.

traditional on its behalf...The legitimacy of that authority is contingent upon the performance of obligations for which it is held responsible.[37]

The pre-colonial Southeast Asian peasants' view of the legitimacy of the state was predicated on whether the state could guarantee their right to subsistence, and fulfill its minimal obligation. In other words, the state must not demand so much from the peasants that it obviates subsistence, and it must provide some kind of safety net to shield farmers from the vagaries of natural disasters and market fluctuations. The strength of Scott's analysis lies in its parsimony: concepts which can be applied to different agrarian settings. Broadly speaking, Scott states that these minimum obligations include maintaining a fully functioning member of village society; resources to discharge one's necessary ceremonial and social obligations; and enough to feed oneself adequately and continue to cultivate. Scott's assessment, however, is problematic for several reasons.

First, even with their minimum requirements met, some contemporary Burmese farmers do not affirm the legitimacy of the government. In Burma, for instance, even the better-off farmers oftentimes develop hostility towards the government despite the fact that they have done comparatively better vis-à-vis the rest of the village. They have at least twenty acres of land, a tractor and/or television, enough food to eat, and surplus money to spend. However their status does not necessarily imply their satisfaction with the authorities. Like many ordinary farmers, they are equally exasperated by the state's imposition of various restrictions, frequent changes in agricultural policies, and local authorities' abuses and exploitation.

Thus the state's ability to fulfill its minimum level of obligation does not always promote its legitimacy among rural populations. Secondly, its failure to perform its minimum obligations does not necessarily lead to a legitimacy crisis, either. For instance, many rice farmers in Burma are positively disposed towards the local officials not so much because of the authorities' ability to improve rural welfare or eliminate farmers' difficulties, but because of their willingness to *alleviate* farmers' problems.

Thus, while Suharto believed that he could command popular support as long as there was sufficiency in rice, political leaders in middle Africa can be quite confident that they can still secure societal support as long as they do not "eat" (literally and metaphorically) excessively while

---

[37] Ibid., 180-181.

their citizens are hungry.[38] Among the Bukiran peasants in the
Philippines, the combination of a few people receiving favorable
responses from the government and the absence of drastically worse
economic conditions kept people to persevere and to continue with what
little they had or "at least not departing from their routine to challenge the
government or other parts of the social order."[39] By contrast, Kilimanjaro
peasants in Africa staged a protest against the British colonial government
simply because the government tried to impose a regulation which
required farmers to sell coffee to the co-operatives.[40]

Scott is therefore unable to provide quantitative and objective
guidelines to evaluate peasants' underlying perceptions of the state.
Michael Adas, in fact, contests Scott's basic argument by saying that
farmers in the Lower Burma revolted against the British authorities not
because they had shortages of rice and suffered from subsistence crisis,
but because they had surpluses of rice due to the drop in world prices and
the difficulty in exporting rice.[41]

While Adas and Scott offer religious and moral explanations for
political legitimacy in Burma's countryside, Manning Nash, an
anthropologist, offers one more, the instrumental basis of rural support for
political candidates.[42] Nash studied Burmese village culture in the
countryside in Upper Burma during the period of civilian rule in Burma in
the late 1950s and made the following observations. According to Nash
the Burmese villagers tended to disengage themselves from the conduct of
the government's affairs, to view authority with suspicion and mistrust,
and to regard government as one of the five traditional enemies (along
with fire, famine, flood, and plague). Nash implies that Burmese farmers
had no concept of political values in general and legitimacy in particular,

---

[38] Quoted in Tuong H. Vu, "Of rice and moral rule: The politics of Beras and State formation in
Indonesia, 1945-1949." Paper presented at the American Political Science Association Annual
Meeting, Boston, August 29-September 1, 2002. Michael Schatzberg, *Political Legitimacy in
Middle Africa: Father, Family, Food* (Bloomington and Indiana: Indiana University Press,
2001).

[39] Benedict Kerkvliet, "Martial law in Nueva Ecija village, the Philippines", 18.

[40] Goran Hyden, *Beyond Ujamaa in Tanzania: Underdevelopment and an Uncapatured
Peasantry* (London: Heinemann: 1980), 55.

[41] Adas, "Bandit, monks, and pretender kings: Patterns of peasant resistance and protest in
colonial Burma, 1826-1941." Samuel Popkins also questions Scott's romanticized description of
traditional communities in pre-colonial societies. He argues that the pre-colonial Vietnamese
peasants' political and social practices were based on rational calculations and local landlords
were not as benign, protective, and sympathetic as Scott portrayed. Samuel Popkins, *The
Rational Peasant: The Political Economy of Rural Society in Vietnam* (Berkeley: University of
California, 1979).

[42] Manning Nash, *The Golden Road to Modernity: Village Life in Contemporary Burma*
(Chicago: University of Chicago, 1965).

25

and he argues that they tended to support whoever was most likely to win the election: "not to participate in an election means to be outside of the potential benefits from a "successful" candidate, while to be on the losing side means to pay some price in favors, in government attention, and in services. To be on the winning side is to receive whatever small attentions and services the government can bestow on villages." [43]

In other words, peasants "tend in their relations with authority and political power to be self-seeking, to ask "what's in it for me?" and to bargain for short-run gains, and thus "the national issues are not relevant to them; they are trying to find an advantageous stance in a power struggle in which they believe their chances for being victims are much greater than those of being beneficiary."[44] The instrumental basis of rural support for political leaders is not typical of Burma; it can also be discerned across rich and poor countries.

Goran Hyden, for instance, shares the same perspectives about African peasants. He observed that candidates who ran for the 1965 parliamentary elections following Tanzanian independence had to resort to expensive patronage deals during the campaign. While those who failed to deliver goods or benefits to their home area lost the election, those who still managed to win used strategies such as hiring supporters "who would buy beer for prospective voters, usually influential people in their respective communities. That way some of the incumbents were able to compensate for failure to live up to past promises."[45]

Migdal emphasizes the same notion of material incentives motivating peasants' behavior; that is, peasants' participate in complex political organization to obtain material benefits that are offered to them. According to Migdal, peasants' initial aims in joining political movements "are not to implement a particular ideology. They do not even have such high hopes as to expect an influential role with the critical decision-makers at the locus of the new politics. Instead they seek immediately useful concessions that will aid them in navigating their social and economic environment."[46] The most simple tradeoff between peasants' support for the organization and the rewards offered to them in return can be discerned in Hsin Hsing, Taiwan in 1957-58, where "villagers received a few packs of cigarettes or some bath towels and soap in exchange for

---

[43] Ibid., 21.

[44] Ibid., 8, 87.

[45] Goran Hyden, *Beyong Ujamaa in Tanzania: Underdevelopment and an Uncaptured Peasantry* (London: Heinemann, 1980), 89.

[46] Joel Migdal, *Peasants, Politics, and Revolution: Pressure toward Political and Social Change in the Third World* (New Jersey: Princeton University Press: 1974), 212.

their votes for particular candidate of the hsen (county) assembly."[47] Exchanging votes for material items does not necessarily say anything about political legitimacy. But it illustrates one of the bases of rural support for particular state leaders and politicians.

Although Migdal, Nash, and Hyden describe different motivations behind peasants' alignment with particular candidates (material incentives in the case of Migdal and Hyden, and the most likely winner in the case of Nash), their basic assumptions about the peasants' political behavior are the same. That is, peasants search for immediate short-term gains, that they are self-seeking, and that they have no concept of political legitimacy. Of course, these attitudes are likely to be influenced by peasants' awareness of their vulnerability in respect to people in power. Hence, trying to see which way the political wind is blowing rather than trying to change its direction is often prudent for long-term survival of oneself, family, and community.

According to Alagappa, this type of support does not constitute a long-lasting and/ or a sufficiently reliable basis for legitimacy: "to give consent is to recognize the government's right to issue commands and to assume a duty to obey them. Duty-bound obedience should be distinguished from instrumental acceptance. The commitment to obey is based on allegiance; instrumental acceptance is based on rewards."[48]

Critiques of Culturalist, Moralist, Instrumentalist Approaches to Political Legitimacy
Although the three approaches have strong logical and empirical support, they are inadequate since they treat societal forces as operating in a political and social vacuum or within invariable sociopolitical atmospheres. The religiously and culturally based explanation of political legitimacy put forward that any government that promotes the values upheld by the majority of the indigenous population will enjoy popular support in the countryside. The morally based analysis presumes that state authorities will enjoy political legitimacy as long as they fulfill their "minimum level of obligation." The instrumental analysis forecasts a positive outcome for candidates who can provide material benefits to the rural constituencies. Thus these approaches account very little for varying local practices, interactions, and expectations which exist under particular situations. To perceive Burmese farmers as materially motivated or morally and religiously informed, with a fixed set of expectations and

---

[47] Ibid., 211
[48] M. Alagappa, "The Anatomy of Legitimacy", 23.

values, is to neglect specific socio-political contexts within which state-societal interactions take place. It is to miss one of the most important dynamics of local politics; that is the ways in which populations establish their ties to centrally appointed state authorities and native leaders. An examination of the instrumentalist approach is illustrative. If political legitimacy is defined in terms of farmers' favorable dispositions toward particular state authorities, instrumental analysis does not even cover farmers' perceptions of different authorities. The story begins and ends with peasants' exchange of vote for a particular short-term benefit. Nothing else.

A detailed examination of the interactions at the village level, however, uncovers a different story to Burmese farmers' political motivations and orientations. We can identify farmers' conceptualization of political legitimacy by looking at their relationship with *U Sein Ko*, the local strongman. Nash states that the village acted as a political unit, whose power structure revolved around a man of *pon* (glory, influence, charisma, power)."[49] In other words, a farmer's political activities do not extend beyond his association with man/men of *pon* in the community who can fulfill his basic social, economic and political needs: "people stay with the man of *pon* because he has power and because they derive something from his exercise of power. *U Sein Ko* lends money (a man of *pon* in *Nondwin* village), arranges for government loans, smoothes interaction between villagers and higher level politicians, and works out the ties between *Nonwin* and national political parties."[50]

Thus despite various appeals and campaigns made by the national rivalry parties, villagers took a cue from a man of *pon*, and "*Nondwin* people gravitates to *U Sein Ko* before expressing a political stand."[51] In fact, Nash recorded that half of the people he interviewed, when asked about politics, had "the standard reply of *na male bu,* or more specifically, 'I know nothing about it, and if I had my way, we would do without local elections; if we could get a decent headman, we should keep him and not put everybody to the trouble of choosing him, election after election.'"[52] A similar statement is echoed forty years later by a farmer's son who told me in 1999 that "peace and tranquility in our village depend on the type of headman (village chairman) we have. We are better off if we have a good headman, and worse off if we have a bad headman."

---

[49] Manning Nash, *The Golden Road to Modernity*, 272.
[50] Ibid., 85
[51] Ibid., 87.
[52] Ibid., 288.

Melford Spiro also wrote that Burmese villagers in *Yeig*yi in the late 1950s were divided between two rival factions, led respectively by U Lum Byei, a wealthy landowner and U Youn, a village chairman. The core members of U Lum Byei consisted of villagers who have only recently entered the upper class but who, "because of their wealth, have become serious contenders for the prestige normally accruing to the traditional upper-class elite," and tenants farmers and share croppers who suffered unfair treatment under U Youn.[53] The core members U Youn were mostly traditional elite and those who benefited from U Youn's power. Consequently, those who aligned with U Lum Byei, or the *Thamu-Hnamu* faction, voted for the more radical Anti-Facist People Freedom League (AFPFL), while those who supported U Youn, or the *Ayoundaw* faction, supported the more conservative Union Party.

These observations have far reaching implications for the study of farmers' behavior in Burma. They demonstrate that Burmese farmers, like the majority of poor peasants in Third World countries, are preoccupied with their local and immediate concerns, and that they are complacent as long as their needs are served by reliable local leaders and as long as the central authorities do not extensively and negatively interfere with their affairs. These attitudes are not so much different from that of many Bukiran peasants in the Philippines. They preferred peace if they had to choose between a peaceful barrio and elections that "divide people and cause confusion and violence."[54]

But a few problems remain unaddressed here. What do the farmers do in the absence of responsible and responsive local authorities? What if the central policies penetrate the village level to the extent that they impinge on farmers' lives? The moralist analysis addresses these issues to the extent that it highlights the obligations of state authorities at different territorial levels, but the culturalist and instrumentalist approaches rarely acknowledge the role and activities of local authorities. We must therefore disaggregate the state into different levels for analysis to understand the roots, variations, and dynamics of rural cultivators' support for different levels of authority.

---

[53] Melford Spiro, "Factionalism and Politics in Village Burma", in *Anthropological "Other" or Burmese "Brother"*?, p. 153.
[54] B. Kerkvliet, "Martial law in a Nueva Ecija village, the Philippines", 11.

Analyzing Political Legitimacy by Disaggregating the State: Hypotheses and Propositions

Thus far, two hypotheses can be drawn from the scholarly writings on how the interactions between local authorities and native populations affect the political legitimacy of local and central authorities. The first emphasizes how particular institutional environments influence state leaders and policy implementors' conducts and thus, in turn, affects state authorities' relationships with society, which then influences societal perception of different levels of government. The second hypothesis stresses the significant role of *native* local officials in shaping societal concepts about central and local leaderships.[55]

The first hypothesis implies that certain political institutions impose constraints on central authorities, promote flexibility at the local level, and facilitate societal favorable attitudes toward state authorities at both governmental levels. For instance, some scholars argue that pre-colonial political structures in Southeast Asia created fertile ground for protective and sympathetic local authorities as well as for a lenient monarch with constrained power and authority. Robert Taylor, Michael Adas, and James Scott argue that both the monarch who was the highest authority of the state, and the village headman, who occupied the lowest administrative position in pre-colonial society had personal and institutional interests to be accommodating toward the needs of local populations. Taylor, for instance, notes that

> Myothugyi (town headman) and thugyi (village headman), whose incomes came primarily from taking a percentage of tax collection, took a long term perspective on their positions, were loath to invoke extortionate demands on the population, and thus stood in protective stance vis-a-vis their transient superior who sometimes tried to quickly amass a personal fortune. Both states and thugyis sought to increase the manpower and resources at their disposal so as to maintain ongoing personal, familial and institutional interests.[56]

Scott sees the pre-colonial state as a "soft" state, which not only performed its culturally prescribed duties for its population, but also was hampered by physical and financial limitations to control and exact resources from its people. The local chiefs in traditional societies were equally "soft." Scott writes that local chiefs "had an interest in keeping their ears to the ground and adjusting their claims to the ability of their

---

[55] *Native* officials are authorities who were born and grew up in the areas they serve.
[56] Robert Taylor, *The State in Burma*, 36.

subjects to pay. So long as their local power rested on their ability to summon the necessary manpower in a conflict, they found it prudent to avoid excess that would provide potential rivals a base of recruitment."[57]

In line with the hypothesis that institutions constrain authorities, Adas finds that a king or emperor in a pre-industrial society or in a "contest state" attempted to claim a monopoly of power in a given society but was "in reality severely restricted by rival power centers among the elite, by weaknesses in administrative organization and institutional commitment on the part of state officials, by poor communications, and by a low population-to-land ratio that places a premium on man power retention and regulation."[58] These physical and administrative restraints, rather than the moral obligation of the kings, "provided numerous opportunities for peasants to defend themselves from excessive exactions by their overlords." [59]

The existence of protective authorities at the highest and lowest levels of power structures in pre-colonial societies tended to promote friendly state-societal relations and acceptance of both levels as "legitimate" and "acceptable." The colonial administrative system, however, transformed the previously accommodating king and *thugyi* into insensitive and impersonal forces. Taylor, for instance, writes that the village headmen were no longer seen as local representatives because they were now turned into salaried officials of the new state and subject to transfer from one place to another. They were appointed more for their knowledge of British procedures than for their vigilance protecting local interests. They were no longer the natural leaders of their communities, defending their clients' interests against a capricious state. Rather they became the salaried tax-collectors of that state providing the funds for the policies, police and courts which were unpopular amongst most of the people. The headmen also enhanced government's capacity to tax the land and people much more than the pre-colonial state. Increasingly, they had to rely on the use of force because their new position undermined their personal authority and ability to intercede between the demands of higher officials and the wishes of their residents.[60]

Scott concurs that colonial governments in Vietnam and Burma were stringent in their demands, and local authorities became relentless in enforcing the policies of the central government. Scott states that "the new

[57] James Scott, *The Moral Economy of the Peasant*, 53.

[58] Michael Adas, "From Avoidance to Confrontation: Peasant Protest in Pre-Colonial and Colonial Southeast Asia", 218.

[59] Ibid., 223.

[60] Robert Taylor, 83, 86, 90.

agents of the center, however, had far less interest in maintaining a local following... In revenues matters, especially, the satisfaction of the center with its agents tended to vary directly with the receipts they forwarded; short of provoking a rebellion, pleasing the center implied squeezing the local population."[61]

Likewise, Adas notes that village leaders, even though they were still chosen by peasants, were transformed into mere agents of the state, and "costly and time-consuming cadastral surveys, special training for revenue assessors, more sophisticated methods of record keeping, and more effective administrative surveillance greatly reduced opportunities for tax evasion or bribery of revenue officials." [62]

Scholars who stress the importance of political institutions in structuring state-societal relationships attribute the state's declining political legitimacy to more centralized and effective administrative practices, which allow no room for bargaining and flexibility at the local level.

While the first hypothesis emphasizes the significance of institutional structures in shaping policymakers' choices and constraining them to behave in certain ways, the second hypothesis paints undifferentiated images of central authorities and local authorities. Central authorities are always seen as rigid, capacious, unpredictable and illegitimate, while local authorities are frequently portrayed as flexible, sensitive, predictable, and legitimate.

One school of thought, for instance, asserts that native officials command a higher level of respect and authority among the native populations than non-native officials who are appointed from the capital. Daw Mya Sein, for instance, distinguishes local elites from centrally appointed officials in pre-colonial Burma

> The mothugyi (native headman) was the chief local authority who acquired a larger share of influence and following in the district than a Myowun (centrally appointed official) because he was a local man whose family had ruled for generations, the office being hereditary. Some of the English settlement officers described the Myothugyi as the most important man in the social organization of the districts."[63]

According to Daw Mya Sein,

[61]James Scott, 97.
[62] Adas, "From Avoidance to Confrontation", 241.
[63] Daw Mya Sein, *The Administration of Burma*, 41.

> The Myothugyis were really nonofficials in the sense that they were at first appointed by the people and that the people looked upon them as one of themselves and not as court official. The Burmese included government officials as one of the five enemies of mankind but the hereditary Myothgyi of their township was usually loved and respected by all. He guarded their interest against the avarice of the Government officials.[64]

The centrally appointed district governors or *wuns,* on the other hand, were exploitative and insensitive. Maung Maung Gyi, writes that

> The people would normally want to complain against extortion and misdeeds but before they complained to a higher authority they would have suffered at the hands of the local officers. *There is a saying in Burmese that nearer sword is sharper than the one at a distance* (nee-yar-dah-htet-the)...The poor people were not in a position to make a complaint against the local *wuns* (ministers) to the *Hluttaw* (central parliament or royal palace). It would have cost them time and expense that they could hardly afford. Communication was primitive, difficult, and time consuming. Besides, they were not sure whether the case had a chance of success at the capital. Even against a notorious *myowun* (governor of a town) who had been perpetuating a series of barbarities the people dare not complain, for he enjoyed the protection of the chief minister. It was only when his notoriety became so widespread, and the grievances of the people became so audible that he was arrested. [65]

Ting-tus Ch'u attributes the community-serving role of the Chinese local scholar gentry during the Ch'ing period to their close association with the native residents: "Because their tie with their native places were permanent ones that engendered a sentimental attachment, the gentry seem to have felt that it was their responsibility to guard and promote the welfare of these communities. This sentiment was lacking among the magistrates and other local officials who were nonnatives."[66]

Similar logic applies to scholarly studies on Mao's China. Vivienne Shue, for instance, writes that

> One of the most important elements in the success of the party's early rural reform efforts was the deliberate policy of recruiting local leaders from within the villages to carry out the land reform and the establishing

---

[64] Ibid., 67.

[65] Maung Maung Gyi, *Burmese Political Values: The Socio-Political Roots of Authoritarianism* (New York: Praeger Special Studies, 1983), 38-39. Emphasis added.

[66] Ch'u Ting-tus, *Local Government in China under the Ch'ing* (Stanford, California: Stanford University Press, 1962), 172-173.

of collectives. This technique often contrasted with the Bolshevik party's importation of urban outsiders to carry out similar tasks in Soviet Union, helped guarantee that, in China, that values and concerns of the original local community would be well reflected in the process of this reform and not stifled by the deluge of party rhetoric about the revolutionization of social relation.[67]

Shue notes that local cadres who identified closely with native populations are more protective of their residents or the people they had known for a long time. Local cadres "who stayed in their position for any length of time inevitably came to identify with and represent the interests of their localities and regions,"[68] and they were inclined "to pursue the interests of their own areas against other areas, when necessary, against the demands of the vertical state apparatus."[69]

Both the institutional analysis and the emphasis of the birthplace and residency of local state officials provide us with general understandings of the different foundations for political legitimacy at various levels of government. They are, however, incomplete since they can not account for diverse and complex patterns of state-societal interactions that vary under the same political and economic milieu. For example, few instances of hostile confrontation can be found in pre-colonial societies just as isolated cases of friendly relationships can be discerned under the colonial administration.

Furthermore, there are many cases of abuse and exploitation by native leaders and local officials. Those who study agrarian politics in the Philippines, India, and Latin American countries point out that the welfare of poor peasants has been obstructed by the local elite (large land owners, local bosses and politicians) through patron-client relationships and manipulation of electoral politics.[70]

States vary in their relationships to society. Their varying interactions have different consequences for societal perceptions of state authorities. A neat, compartmentalized portrayal of the differences between pre-colonial and colonial societies or between benign native local officials and insensitive central authorities or centrally appointed non-native officials becomes messy, when local variations are taken into account. Jonathan Unger's depiction of the variation of local officialdom's

---

[67] Vivienne Shue, *The Reach of the State: Sketches of the Chinese Body Politics* (Stanford: Stanford University Press, 1988), 66-67.
[68] Ibid., 56.
[69] Ibid., 56.
[70] See Jonathan Fox, ed, *The Challenge of rural democratization: Perspectives from Latin America and the Philippines* (Portland: Frank Cass, 1990).

performance in Deng's China is a prime example. Unger examines state-societal relationships in the prosperous coastal region, the impoverished regions of the western hinterlands, and the grain belts of central China and demonstrates how differences in rural administration, ecology, and economy differently influence local officials' relationships with villagers. Unger concludes that although it is generally true that corruption, overstaffing and undeserved benefits have become common in contemporary China, it is in the agricultural heartlands where villagers have the deepest cause for political discontent, and where peaceful protests involve appeals to the central government against local policies, even when central policies are in part the reason for disgruntlement.[71]

In conclusion, only studies that disaggregate the state into discrete levels of analysis and which account for local variations can show us how societal actors' relationships with local authorities have particular impact on the political legitimacy of the government. The instrumentalist, moralist, and culturalist approaches to Burmese farmers' conduct give us only a fixed set of explanations for the bases of rural support for governmental authorities. The institutional analysis and the emphasis on local authorities' permanent residency highlight farmers' different dispositions toward central and local authorities, but they hardly take into account the variations that exist within a particular sociopolitical context.

More comprehensively, the "process-oriented" approach takes into account local variations that are shaped by broader economic and political factors as well as actions of the local authorities which impinge on Burmese rice farmers.[72] The process-oriented approach identifies a combination of *the importance of material incentives and the nature of personal ties between local authorities and rural populations* as the foundation of rural support for state authorities. It also acknowledges the degree of political legitimacy due to changes in central government policies and the nature of state-societal relationships at the local level.

In his study on the voting behavior in Thailand, Anek Laothamatas, for instance, notes that "(v)oting in farming areas is not guided by political principles, policy issues, or what is perceived by the national

---

[71] Jonathan Unger, 13.

[72] Joel Migdal, who advocates for a "state-in-society" approach, provides a useful tool to analyze political legitimacy. Migdal does not discuss the issue of political legitimacy, but his "state-in-society" approach emphasizes the importance of looking at the "process" or interaction between various parts of state and society. See Joel Migdal, *Strong Societies and Weak States* (New Jersey: Princeton University Press, 1988). See Migdal, Kohli, and Shue, *State Power and Social Forces: Domination and Transformation in the Third World* (Cambridge: Cambridge University Press, 1994).

interest, all of which are regarded by urbanites as the only legitimate rationale for citizens casting their ballots in democratic election."[73] According to Laothamatas, rural residents' preference for a particular candidate is based on (1) the material benefits (loans, roads, bridges), and official attention he/she would be bringing to their village, and (2) the personality and performance of the candidate. Laothamatas thus observes that

> Most recent studies find that (rural) voters pick politicians who visit them regularly; who help them cope with different personal or family problem, often in collaboration with their canvassers; who regularly attend social functions at the village level; who make generous donations to neighborhood monasteries or school; and who bring in public programs that generate jobs, money, and reputation for their villages and provinces. Conversely, rural voters care very little about the election platform of the candidates, their party affiliation, or their integrity or work as members of the house or of the cabinet.[74]

Sally Moore's observation of the behavior of Tanzanian peasants also demonstrates how the rural population's attitudes toward state institutions, their personnel, and their auxiliary organizations are determined by their daily interactions with government authorities. Their views change depending on which components of state they deal with, and on changes in the relationship between cultivators and state officials. They are not guided by abstract ideologies nor culturally defined standards of roles and obligations. Moore, for example, states that

> For the rural cultivators, the powers and capacities of the state are conceived to have beneficent and protective potentialities as well as having invasive, punitive, and other undesirable possibilities. It is well known that government projects bring in piped water, public health workers, and sometimes even electricity. But the party government has also been associated with many shortages of commodities, from cooking to soap, for which there is daily need, and it has also been the source of many restrictions.....*for most Tazanians in 1984, the question of which sentiment, the positive or the negative, dominates depends on immediate*

---

[73] Anek Laothamatas, "A tale of two democracies: Conflicting perceptions of elections and democracy in Thailand", in *The Politics of Elections in Southeast Asia*, ed. Robert Taylor (Cambridge: Cambridge University Press, 1996), 203. Emphasis added.
[74] Ibid., 206-207.

> *circumstances rather than on any general stance of political support or opposition.*[75]

Thus farmers' positive inclination towards government are materially driven to the extent that their judgments are based on improved socio-economic conditions, and they are socially, culturally, and morally constructed to the extent that they define the legitimacy of the state in terms of acceptable behaviors. Cultivators' improved socio-economic conditions are measured not in terms of the government's short-term provision of goods or services in exchange for their supports or votes, but in terms of particular agricultural policies or infrastructural projects which have relatively broad-based positive impacts on farmers' lives. David Steinberg for instance contends that the people's uprising in 1988 was, relatively speaking, an urban phenomenon because of the positive results of "liberalization" policies in 1987 which "seemed to placate the peasantry."[76] He described the reform movement in the agricultural sector in 1987 as "rather a shrewd political move designed to alleviate pressure on the government from the rural sector, containing the bulk of the population."[77]   James Guyot agrees that the peasantry suffered the least from the economic reversal that ultimately led to urban protests in 1988 because they could provide food for themselves or could market it at the rising prices that plagued urban workers during the 1988.[78] In addition, farmers' expectations of state officials are not based on a fixed set of traditional values but on flexible responses specific to their daily interactions with these authorities.

The process-oriented approach to political legitimacy also suggests that it is misleading to treat the popularity of local government as synonymous with that of the central government. Sometimes, the popularity of one level of authority comes only at the expense of the other. For instance, local government popularity may increase only at the expense of the national government, especially when local officials are willing to shield their populations from the rigid demands of the capital. Conversely, widespread local corruption often turns citizens' attention

---

[75] Sally Moore, "Legitimation as a Process", in *State Formation and Political Legitimacy*, eds. Ronald Cohen and Judith Toland (New Brunswick: Transaction Books: 1988), 158. Emphasis added.

[76] David Steinberg, *The Future of Burma: Crisis and Choice in Burma* (New York: University Press of America, 1990), 21.

[77] David Steingberg, *Crisis in Burma: Stasis and Change in a Political Economy in Turmoil* (Bangkok, Thailand: Institute of Security and International Studies, 1989), 125.

[78] James Guyot, "Burma in 1988: Perestroika with a military face", *Southeast Asian Affairs* (1989): 107-136.

toward the central authority, whose legitimacy can be enhanced by its "perceived" ability to reduce local exploitation. A critical evaluation of the literature on peasants' behavior, and on analysis of the disaggregated state concludes that it is difficult to build a convincing theory of political legitimacy without a detailed understanding of local authority's role, and its relationship with residents. It is only through analysis of the disaggregated state that we will come to appreciate varying degrees of societal acceptance for authoritarian regimes, and the different foundations of political legitimacy.

The Process-Oriented Approach to Political Legitimacy
People in poor countries tend to attach great importance to social and economic security and, their support for the government will more likely be determined by the state's ability or inability to improve their situations rather than official emphasis on ideologies, shared norms and culture, which may or may not deal with the pressing issues of ordinary people. Thus Alagappa points out that "(i)n Myanmar, failure to perform deepened the legitimacy problem of the Ne Win government." [79]

Michael Schartzberg also depicts the image of acceptable political leadership in middle Africa as

> When political fathers care for, nurture, and provide wealth for their children, their political legitimacy is enhanced. When, on the other hand, economic conditions deteriorate and they are no longer able to nurture the population in this way, their political legitimacy will decline markedly. When harvests are poor, when the rains fail, when the livestock dies, when the state's revenues are not themselves used in creatively productive economic ventures, then political legitimacy will diminish. In other words, when political fathers see to it that their children have the resources to "eat" (both literally and figuratively), their political legitimacy tends to remain strong. [80]

Likewise, for authoritarian governments, whose values and procedures do not seem to be accepted by the society it governs, "performance" seems to be the only viable way to strengthen the state's legitimacy. David Beetham, for instance, argues that the legitimacy of every government rests on three legs. The first is the acknowledged source of authority underpinning the rules of appointment to the leading offices of state. The second is the capacity to facilitate economic achievement and to fulfill

[79] Muthiah Alagappa, "Seeking a more durable basis", in *Political Legitimacy*, 310.
[80] Michael G. Schatzberg, *Political Legitimacy in Middle Africa: Father, Family, Food* (Bloomington and Indianapolis: Indiana University Press: 2001), 24-25.

appropriate functions and objectives of government. The third is supported by popular expression of consent. According to Beetham "a military regime rests on the second of these alone; it is a tripod supported on one leg. To achieve this balancing feat at all, the leg has to become grossly enlarged. Performance is everything, and the achievements and capacities of the regime have to be disproportionately magnified." [81]

Nevertheless, although many authors agree that economic development can alleviate, if not eliminate, the legitimacy problems of governments, the extent to which positive economic performance enhances the citizens' perception of the government's right to rule remains an issue of scholarly debate. Alagappa, for instance, contends that economic performance is not a sufficient or durable basis for political authority. His argument is based on the history of Southeast Asian politics, where continued success in performance gave rise to a variety of unintended consequences, caused either by equity concerns of the lower class, or by the emergence of new forces (especially the middle class), that challenged the legitimacy of the state. Alagappa's findings have two important implications.

First, "performance" is often associated with the Gross Domestic Product (GDP) or per capita GDP growth, and it rarely addresses the relative gains and losses of each group as GDP grows. In other words, the aggregate data and development by no means reflects the type and level of popularity enjoyed by the government. Arjun Appadurai, for instance, cautions that we need to be careful in interpreting increases in certain aggregate measures, such as number of wells, number of electric pumps, acreage of irrigated land, or yields of commercial crops, as indicators of improved status of the agricultural producers. This is because such growth may disguise increases in the concentration of agricultural capital in the hands of a small rural elite, co-existing with a large number of small commercial farmers who eke out a precarious subsistence in a heavily monetized agrarian economy.[82]

Second, there are many different kinds of policies that can be implemented to promote "growth" or "equity," or both, and the contributions they make with regard to enhancing or undermining government's legitimacy are varied. Jonathan Fox, for instance, writes that it is easier for Mexican presidents to use subsidized loans, agricultural inputs, high procurement prices, food subsidies, and employment as

---

[81] David Beetham, *The Legitimation of Power*, 234-235.

[82] Arjun Appadurai, "Small-scale techniques and large-scale objectives", in *Conversations between Economists and Anthropologists: Methodological Issues in Measuring Economic Change in Rural India*, ed. Pranab Bardhan (Oxford: Oxford University Press, 1989), 257-258.

strategies to improve the conditions of poor peasants. Land redistribution, on the other hand, is harder to implement because it poses a threat to the entrenched interests of the rural elite. According to Fox, subsidies and market regulation "delivered substantive benefits at less political cost than land redistribution."[83] Thus "it was politically easier to isolate intermediaries than to confront agribusiness interests directly, leading to the official definition of inefficient and inequitable rural markets as a key obstacle limiting rural progress."[84] In addition, these various forms of subsidies, which are targeted at impoverished peasants, are more likely to be captured by the rural elites than to significantly benefit the rural poor. Thus the implementation of agricultural policies bears very little resemblance to what the policy makers in the capital city envisaged. Consequently, it is important to study how individuals who benefit or suffer from particular agricultural policies feel about the local elite as well as the central government. What sort of outlets do these disadvantaged people use to channel their grievances and what kind of authority do they approach for remedy?

This book aims to unearth the tensions embedded within four different agricultural policies attempted by the Burmese military government---HYV promotion, partial liberalization, summer paddy, and land reclamation---and examine their impacts on legitimacy and on state-societal relationships in the countryside. Admittedly, agricultural policies constitute only one of the bases of political legitimacy. I acknowledge that other non-agricultural issues are important. Burmese farmers' affirmation of particular agricultural policies may easily be outweighed by their despair emerging from the inhumane treatment of local police and military which require labor, take farmers' property and land, and imprison, torture, rape or kill local residents. However, such serious abuse and violation of human rights take place less frequently in the main rice growing areas, the main focus of this book. In poor and non-democratic countries, agricultural policies remain a crucial source of political legitimacy because they have tremendous effect on farmers' well-being and way of life.

Satumino Borras, for instance, writes that the struggles over control and ownership of land involved "life-and-death" issues for peasants in some parts of the world who "consider land not just a factor of economic production, but also as an integral part of their social and cultural being,

---

[83]Jonathan Fox, *The Politics of Food in Mexico: State Power and Social Mobilization* (Ithaca, Cornell University Press), 57.
[84] Ibid., 57.

as it is a political resource to many."[85] Ben Kerkvliet also observes that the basis of political legitimacy in the Philippines is different from Vietnam's to the extent that in the Philippines, the state's legitimacy and its right to set policy "has been linked more clearly to democratic processes and methods of deciding who has the right to govern."[86]

By contrast, in Vietnam, "such democratic institutions and processes have not been linked to the legitimacy of the Communist Party-dominated state...Overturning the pre-independence land regime in order to distribute more or less equally to all farming villagers has been a major source of legitimacy...in the eyes of rural Vietnamese."[87] Furthermore, the evaluation of different agricultural policies will remain the focal point, since these policies are formulated by top executive authorities in Rangoon, and are intended to have a uniform affect on agricultural producers across the country. Thus their impact on peasants' lives and their attitudes toward authority can be analyzed and compared in different rice villages. In other words, while all paddy farmers are subject to the same paddy-related policies, they may or may not be subject to the same degree of abuse and mistreatment by local civilian and military authorities. Thus to the extent that daily encounters between the local state authorities and the local farmers are taken into consideration, this approach does not totally neglect farmers' activities outside the realm of agriculture. Treating the centrally formulated policies as a 'constant' will give us a better understanding of the mediating role of local authorities in shaping farmers' attitudes toward different levels of authority.

---

[85] Satumino Borras, "The bibingka strategy to land reform implementation: Autonomous peasant mobilizations and state reformists in the Philippines", (The Hague: Institute of Social Studies, March 1998), 1.

[86] Benedict Kerkvliet, "Land regimes and state strengths and weaknesses in the Philippines and Vietnam", in *Weak and Strong States in Asia-Pacific Societies*, ed. Peter Dauvergne (Sydney: Allen & Unwin, 1998), 174.

[87] Ibid., 174.

Chapter 2

The Rise of Authoritarianism and the Foundations of Rural Support for the Revolutionary Council

When Ne Win first came to power in 1962, he held a Peasant's Conference…Thousands of peasant representatives from around the country attended. Ne Win gave speeches, shook hands with peasants, and promised that his government was the one which was going to work to improve peasants' lives. In the beginning, peasants were taken in, including my uncles and my father. They believed in Ne Win's propaganda. Not long after, they were ordered to sell the quotas and came to know they were being cheated.

A farmer's son from *Natalin* township, *Sagaing* division.

Introduction

On 2, March 1962, the Burmese military staged a *coup d'état*, ending civilian rule. Calling itself the Revolutionary Council (RC), the military moved swiftly to change the date of Peasants' Day from 1 January to 2 March in order to honor the Burmese peasantry on the anniversary of the military's seizure of power and to stress the common interests of the army and Burmese farmers. It held a series of seminars and meetings with peasant groups to encourage "open" communication between top-level military officials and peasants, concerning agrarian problems. However, the government's preoccupation with the "politics of survival," manifested in its tightening control over rural produce and labor, gradually alienated most of the people it once had tried to mobilize for support.

This chapter analyzes the relationships between state authorities and Burmese cultivators in pre-colonial, colonial, and post-colonial Burma. It establishes the historical context within which contemporary rice farmers have come into contact with local and central authorities. Special emphasis will be placed upon the rationales and strategies different governments have used to promote the agricultural sector, to maximize exaction from the countryside, and to exert control over rural populations. It will also discuss the specific ties the Revolutionary Council attempted to forge with the peasants upon its accession to power, and how these linkages, in some respects, represented a dramatic break with the past, and in others, perpetuated old patterns of state-societal interactions. An outline of the important features of Burmese cultivators' relationships with state authorities in different periods will help us understand: (1) the historical roots of Burmese cultivators' different attitudes toward central and local authorities; (2) rice farmers' concerns with good local leadership and governance structure; (3) the dynamic nature of political legitimacy; and (4) the varying state-societal interactions that occur under the same political and economic structure, and their different impacts on farmers' perceptions of different levels of authority.

The State-society relationships in Pre-colonial Burma

The majority area of what is now known as "Myanmar" or Burma was brought under a single political entity by King *Alaungpaya* in the eighteenth century.[1] Like many Burmese kings, King *Alaungpaya* and his successors were tyrannical. However, the king's power and influence were by no means uniformly felt across the country. His presence was most pronounced in the areas surrounding the royal capital in Upper Burma, but his reach to outlying regions and remote villages was tenuous.

In Upper Burma, most residents who lived adjacent to the royal capital belonged to the hereditary, the *ahmudan* class, and were given the right to live on royal land. They paid direct taxes to the king. As members of *ahmudan* class, they owed their services to the king, and these were allocated according to their specialized service units. However, no *ahmudan* counterparts existed in Lower Burma, since there was no royal land in that region. Most inhabitants in Lower Burma were regarded as *athi* population, who paid taxes to the king but owed him nothing. While most people in Upper Burma were pure Burman, those from Lower Burma were mostly non-Burman, including descendants of the earlier Pyu and Mon inhabitants as well as the Arakanese and hill tribesmen.[2] Both *ahmudan* and *athi* populations were under the authority of *myothugyi* or hereditary office-holders who governed small polities.[3]

In pre-colonial times, the delta region in lower Burma, the current rice producing region in Burma, was only sparsely populated. The region was endowed with regular and heavy rainfall and had the potential to yield vast quantities of rice. Devastated by previous wars between the Burmese and the Mons, most of its land was inaccessible and uninhabitable for immigrants because of the tremendous difficulties involved in clearing

---

[1] Pre-colonial Burma was unified by three great warriors under a unified political authority in three different periods of time. The kingdom of Pagan was founded in AD 849 and ended in 1287. The Restored *Toungoo* dynasty was founded in 1587 and collapsed in 1752. King Alaungpaya founded *Konbaung* dynasty in 1752, which was taken over by the invading British forces in 1885.

[2] John Cady, *A History of Modern Burma* (Ithaca: Cornell University Press, 1958), 27.

44

new lands, as well as the afflictions of malaria, flooding, wild animals, and insect crop pests. Thus individuals could establish their usufructuary rights simply by clearing or and cultivating land, which reverted to the community if it was abandoned, and it could be cultivated by new farmers with or without the permission of the original occupant. The delta region was a frontier of the wet-rice cultivation in the dry zone of Upper Burma.

Pre-colonial economic practices were based on self-sufficiency. Generally speaking, peasants in dry land Upper Burma grew cotton and oil seeds, and those in the delta plains engaged in the cultivation of rice, fishing, and salt-boiling.[4] In fact, the relatively small-scale rice cultivation in the fertile delta region produced enough surplus grain to meet demand from Upper Burma. Most of the produce from lower Burma was taken for consumption and sale to Upper Burma, and rarely exported. Official policies did not encourage agricultural expansion in the region, either. The regime banned rice export and used surplus rice to regulate and stabilize domestic grain prices.

Given the limited reach of the king, the Burmese monarchy operated under a dual authority, "with a purely official central element and hereditary local element."[5] J.S. Furnivall describes the administrative arrangements in pre-colonial societies as follows:

> The unit of social life was naturally the agricultural village or settlement, but the higher organization was partly tribal and partly territorial. Groups of ten or twenty villages up to fifty or more were governed by a hereditary local chieftain. But his authority was personal, not strictly local; the political organization was quasi-regimental, and within the territory of a local chieftain, there were people of another regiment or group, they were subject of the jurisdiction of their own leader and not to that of local chieftain. Above the local organization there was a central administrative system.........(A)lthough in theory absolute, and in practice often arbitrary, the king had no means to enforce orders that were not regarded as within his customary powers.[6]

Thus despite the monarch's claims to land and services, peasants had considerable flexibility in evading the demands of the court. The monarch's control over man power retention and regulation was restrained by weak administrative organization and institutional commitment, by poor communication, and by a low population-to-land ratio. The lack of

---

[4] J.S. Furnivall, *Colonial Policy and Practice: A Comparative Study of Burma and Netherlands India* (Cambridge: Cambridge University Press, 1948), 16.
[5] J.S. Furnivall, *Colonial Policy and Practice*, 14.
[6] Ibid., 14.

established rules and regulations over succession encouraged rivalries within the court and consumed a great deal of energy that might otherwise have been devoted to the development of an effective administrative system. There were also rivalries among regional administrators, as well as among local elites, since the king was unable to maintain control over more than just the capital city and the heartland areas of the kingdom which surrounded it. Michael Adas, for instance, notes that

> Regional administrators not only vied with the ruler in their attempts to build their own bases of power and wealth, they competed with other nobles and administrators for the loyalty of client-retainers and control over peasant producers. These lords were also locked in a ceaseless contest with their own retainers and subordinates as each strove to maximize the share of the collected revenue that he retained as the tribute passed upward through a complex hierarchy of administrators and tax collectors.[7]

To collect taxes and maintain order, pre-colonial rulers thus had to rely on patron-client networks extending from the court through local notables to village leaders, rather than on the use of force. This hierarchical system incubated village headmen, the most influential authorities in local areas. Michael Adas, for instance, writes that headmen's control over local affairs

> Rested on the extent of their holdings, the number of laborers and artisans dependent on the use of their land and their patronage, the wisdom they demonstrated village councils, and their ability to defend the interests of their communities in dealings with supra village officials and their agents. In contrast to the often short-lived careers of courtiers and tax farmers, the village gentry families frequently controlled local offices for generations and, in some cases, centuries.[8]

Scholarly writings on Burma portray these local hereditary leaders (the village headmen or local gentry) as having the natural tendency and institutional interest to protect their communities. Cady, for instance, remarked that "the myothugyi (the hereditary township chief), in tending to identify himself with the interests of his own people, contrasted with the essentially arbitrary and often predatory authority of the royal

---

[7] Michael Adas, "From avoidance to confrontation: Peasant protest in pre-colonial and colonial Southeast Asia", *Comparative Studies in Society and History* 23 (1981): 221-223.
[8] Michael Adas, "From avoidance to confrontation", 222.

officials...He thus constituted an indispensable bridge between the arbitrary authority of the king and the subject people." [9]

This does not, however, imply that *myothugyis'* behavior was based on pure altruism. As Cady notes, some *myothugyis'* were self-serving, and they rarely undertook actions that did not benefit themselves: "he customarily collected taxes from more households than he reported existing within his jurisdiction and pocketed the difference."[10] Like the officials within the state hierarchy, village headman underreported the number of households and cultivated acreage in their circles and pocketed as much as they were able to squeeze from their community members. Furthermore, not all hereditary leaders were concerned about their residents' welfare. A case in point here is from Michael Adas's article which suggests local-level exploitation: "If a thugyi's (village headman) demands became too oppressive, households or whole hamlets could move to the lands of a rival thugyi, who was happy to acquire the extra producers, particularly given the shortage of labor in the delta frontier areas."[11] The *myothugyi* thus had an ulterior motive to keep their constituents happy. Adas wrote that

> In Burma, the *myothugyi*, or township heads, also competed for peasants to reside in their villages and work their lands. In Lower Burma in particular, the low man-to-land ratio and the highly mobile nature of the peasant household forced the *myothugyi* to temper their revenue demands and foster the well-being of their peasant subjects or risk losing these to neighboring townships where taxes were lighter and the headmen's demands were more reasonable.[12]

A typical portrayal of rural populations' interactions with crown-appointed regional and local officials, on the other hand, suggests these authorities were insensitive and abusive. There were two different types of centrally appointed officials. The first were the appendage holders who were referred to as *myosas*. They resided in the provinces and districts and earned their living by retaining a certain percentage of their territory's taxes (basic household tax, and an exaction on annual crop output, fruit trees, fishing and timber operations, resin oils, brokerage, ferries, and

---

[9] John Cady, 29.

[10] John Cady, 31.

[11] Michael Adas, "The village and state in Vietnam and Burma: An Open and shut case?", First publication of the paper delivered at a workshop on "The Village Revisited: Community and Locality in Southeast Asia", Asian Studies Center, University of Amsterdam, April 1988, 19.

[12] Michael Adas, "From avoidance to confrontation", 230-231.

landing stages).[13] The second type of centrally appointed officials were the *myowun* or "minister-in-charge-of-town." *Myowun* conducted local administrative and judicial affairs in the various districts of the capital and were paid in bullion.[14] They had to supervise the local hereditary elite and they were allowed to appoint new sets of provincial officers to run local affairs.[15]

Scholars agree that there was a lack of intimacy and interaction between centrally appointed officials and their local residents. According to Adas, the appendage holders spent little or no time in their support areas. They preferred to reside in the capital, the center of "vastly superior social and cultural amenities and political excitement," and leave the day-to-day administration in the hands of subordinates. Even officials who governed in their home districts knew little about village conditions and relied on "poorly trained and self-serving subordinates" and village notables for the actual running of village affairs. These officials did not identify with local populations partly because of the limited time they spent in particular posts. Lack of permanency and a firm commitment to an accepted code of bureaucracy also propelled most officeholders to get all the material advantages they could before their tenure ended.[16]

John Cady, a renowned historian on Burma, also highlights the corrupt and exploitative nature of *myowuns* and *myosas*: "poor communications between the capital and outlying areas left open the possibility of considerable abuse of authority on the part of provincial governors (*myowuns*) and the parasitic overlords called *myosas*." [17]

Generally speaking, local populations in pre-colonial eras had distant and hostile relationships with royal appointed officials but mutually beneficial and amicable interactions with hereditary leaders (*myothugyi* and *ywathugyi*). However, one cannot dismiss the fact that the traditional leaders could be as manipulative and self-interested as their counterparts from the center and may also have ignited villagers' resentments. Nonetheless, the institutional and demographical environments within which these native leaders found themselves mitigated their objectionable behaviors.

---

[13] John Cady, *A History of Modern Burma*, 20.
[14] Cady, 20.
[15] Thant Myint-U, *The Making of Modern Burma* (Cambridge: Cambridge University Press: 2001), 75-76.
[16] Michael Adas, "From avoidance to confrontation", 224.
[17] John Cady, *A History of Modern Burma*, 21.

The Elite-Mass Distinction and Agrarian Situations in Colonial Burma

The British colonized Burma by engaging in three successive wars: the first in 1824-26; second in 1852-53; and the last in 1885. After the first Anglo-Burmese war, the British occupied Arakan and Tenasserim, the western-most and southern-most areas of Burma. There was very little resistance from the indigenous people who had long resented the king's aggressive and domineering behavior. The second annexation in 1852, which added 600,000 people and 32,000 square miles to British rule, however, sparked protests from the local population.[18] The entirety of lower Burma, including the current capital of Burma, Rangoon, Pegu, and Bassein, had been brought under the British rule, but it took the British approximately eight years to reestablish order and stability in the Pegu area.

After the second annexation, the Burmese kingdom was now deprived of regular food supplies (especially rice) and appendage revenues from the south. To make up for these losses, King Mindon, a reformist king who usurped power in 1853, attempted to restructure the existing economic, administrative, and political systems. Mindon modernized the military, oversaw the establishment of manufacturing industries, improved transportation and communication, and introduced western education to the Burmese ruling elites. He also centralized the administrative system by strengthening the power of centrally appointed officials vis-a-vis traditional local elites, and by increasing the power of the capital over these appointed officials. For instance, he dismissed a number of gentry office holders for practicing repressive policies (such as over-taxation) or engaging in criminal activities (such as running a distillery and a gambling center), and of being "unpopular" among their constituencies.[19] He further mandated royal sanction on the decision of local succession.

Measures to increase royal revenue were also designed to curb the power and influence of local ruling elites. The government, for instance, intervened directly in the economy by monopolizing and trading cotton, rubies, precious metals, and teak with Chinese, English, and other merchants. It also introduced a new *thathameda* tax, or a property tax, to replace all existing and customary fees and taxes. The new tax required the traditional rural chiefs to collect revenue within their villages, based mainly on the property and wealth of the particular household and to hand

---

[18] Mary Callahan, *The Origins of Military Rule in Burma*, A Ph.D. dissertation submitted to the faculty of the Graduate school of Cornell University (May, 1996), p. 46.
[19] Thant Myint-U, *The Making of Modern Burma*, 117.

over the sum to the provincial *myowon* in cash. It exempted destitute households or individuals from paying taxes. The rural chiefs were compensated for their work, but their new income was a pittance compared to their old one. These measures, however, failed to radically restructure the central-local governments' relationships, as many local leaders continued to ignore central demands and attempt to preserve their previous privileges. [20]

Mindon's reform, albeit unprecedented and exemplary, was a case of too late and too little. By the time king *Mindon* contracted dysentery in October 1877, Upper Burma was already mired in court intrigue, elite fiction, an ailing economy, and declining living standards. It also faced widespread armed resistance, including a revolt by the Shan from the east, and an attack by Chinese and Jingpaw freebooters from the west. King *Thibaw*'s accession to the throne and the following massacre of royal family members added further chaos to the collapsing state. King *Thibaw* desperately attempted to shore up state finances by regularizing the *thathameda* tax regime but this increased resentment and resistance from traditional local elites. The *Thatameda* tax, the poor rice harvest, and the increasing trade deficit of the late 1880s increased the populations' indebtedness. By 1885 as many as 50,000 people fled Upper Burma to Lower Burma, the British territory. In some places, local elites stopped paying revenue, and the break down of central authority was manifest in increasing banditry and millenarian figures.[21] According to Thant Myint-U, "revolts against the state also came under religious leadership…One such figure, named Buddha Thiwali, operated around Singu with 200 men and carried not only the red green and yellow flags of the nobility and the *Sangha* but also the white umbrella of royalty. In Mogaung, another similar figure appeared, calling himself Min Taya, or the 'Just Ruler.'"[22]

The British annexed the whole of Burma after the third Anglo-Burmese war in 1885. This invasion immediately sparked fierce resistance throughout the country, which came from a variety of local groups. Some of them were led by locally popular pretender kings, who promised to reestablish indigenous rule. Violence spread through every district of Upper Burma, and most of Lower Burma, and by February 1887, the British brought 40,500 troops to fight the rebels. Burma became the most dangerous place in the British empire. In some areas in Upper Burma, armed protestors were stationed every ten to fifteen miles, and

[20] Ibid., 105-129.
[21] Ibid., 154-185.
[22] Ibid., 174-175.

practically every household had a male family member fighting for resistance.[23] The British removed "suspected sympathizers" by burning whole villages suspected of sympathizing with the resistance, and executing suspected rebels. [24] By 1890, British-Indian troops were able to "pacify" most of the country.

The British occupation of Burma transformed not only the economic foundations of the agrarian structure, but also the nature of state-societal relationships in the countryside. In the delta region of Lower Burma, the colonial government developed the jungle and swamp region into cultivated land by encouraging migration, financing public networks and transportation, building railroads, canals, and irrigation, processing industries, and providing capital and tax exemption for the newly occupied lands.[25] These policies expanded sown areas and promoted agricultural production and growth, making Burma one of the largest rice exporters in the world. Throughout this period, it was not impossible for a tenant, through frugality and hard work, to become a large land owner. Low population density and large tracts of vacant land provided safeguards against landlessness, high land rents, and agrarian debts.

By the beginning of the twentieth century, however, the disappearance of available cropland (as most of the fertile lands in Lower Burma had been occupied) and the influx of Indian immigrants to the delta region led to increased competition for tenancy positions, and drove up the price of land, land rents, and the cost of living. Indebtedness and landlessness now became dominant features of agrarian Burma, since many cultivators who borrowed heavily from the *Chettiers* (the Indian moneylenders) and other Burmese money lenders could no longer repay their loans. This situation was exacerbated by the worldwide depression in 1929, when prices for agricultural crops dropped precipitously. Many farmers plunged into debt, and lost their land. Consequently, the proportion of land controlled by nonagriculturalists increased from 18 per cent in 1906 to 31 per cent in 1929-30.

Despite the positive developments of expanded agricultural production and trade, British colonial policy brought about the destruction of the self-reliant peasantry by subjecting it to market fluctuation, land taxation, competition for tenancy, indebtedness, and labor contracts.[26]

---

[23] Mary Callahan, 89-90.

[24] Than Myint-U, 201.

[25] Michael Adas, "The village and state in Vietnam and Burma: An open and shut case?", 19.

[26] W. Schendel, *Three Deltas: Accumulation and Poverty in Rural Burma, Bengal and South India* (New Delhi: Sage Publications, 1991).

The British government also instituted political and administrative reforms that changed the patterns of state-societal relationships in the countryside. Many scholars have observed that the relatively amicable interactions that marked relationships between the local leaders and their populations turned into hostile ones due to the British restructure of the administrative system. Immediately upon its conquest of Burma, the colonial government implemented the Indian system of local administration. Known as the Crosthwaite's Village Act, this new law broke up the *myo thugyiship* in pre-colonial Burma and replaced it with the village headmen "who now represented the government and managed his village according to the uniform and formalized village act which was enacted with the sole purpose of maintaining law and order."[27] Under this act, the entire village and the headman were jointly responsible for keeping and preventing crimes in their own locality. It demobilized resistance groups because each village was now responsible for what went on within its territory.

Another significant feature of village administrative reform which had far reaching consequences for villagers-headman relationships was the selection criteria for village leaders, which shifted from hereditary to skills-based requirements. Cady thus wrote that:

> After 1897, knowledge of land surveying became an essential qualification of the taikthugyi, who must also pass a simple test on revenue law. Under such rigorous surveillance from above, the circle headmen tended to lose the capacity to accept individual responsibility. They collected the taxes, but contributed very little else to public welfare and order. As the tool of an alien government, which was exacting in its demands and punitive in its sanctions, the taikthugyi lost face and popular prestige. The traditional link between government and people represented by the traditional myothugyi was clearly not reestablished through the artificially substituted circle headman set up under British rule.[28]

In other words, village leaders were turned into agents of the state, and the *myothugyi*, who used to represent the interest of his people, disappeared. Michael Adas highlights the changes in the nature of native leaders-villagers relationships by saying that "the frequency with which village headmen were the targets of peasant risings in the colonial period indicates the degree to which they became alienated from the village

---

[27] Khin Maung Kyi, "Pattern of accommodation and bureaucratic authority in a transitional culture." A Ph.D. thesis presented to the Faculty of the Graduate school of Cornell University (June 1966), 59.

[28] John Cady, 91.

population as a whole and to which they came to be perceived, usually quite justifiably, as tools of the European colonizers."[29] According to Adas, these new relationships emerged out of the more efficient and centralized administrative system, which was able to reach the remotest villages.

> Costly and time-consuming cadastral surveys, special training for revenue assessors, more sophisticated methods of record keeping, and more effective administrative surveillance greatly reduced opportunities for tax evasion or bribery of revenue officials....The more effective horizontal integration of the colonial bureaucracy rendered peasant transfers from one patron-official to another difficult, if not impossible. Greater uniformity to tax demands from one administrative division to another meant that there was little relief to be found in attaching oneself to another official because the new patron was obliged to follow the same rules and enforce the same policies as the one whose jurisdiction was abandoned.[30]

Thus, although mutually beneficial relationships between the native leaders and the peasants were possible in a few places, colonial societies in Burma saw the deterioration of local elite-peasant interactions in rural areas. Despite these local-level changes, certain features of the pre-colonial period remained. First, improved communication and transportation and the more centralized military and bureaucratic organizations now extended the state's reach to the remotest villages, but failed to foster better communications between centrally appointed state authorities and the majority populations. Villagers felt a greater state presence through the expansion of bureaucracy in the form of specialist departments at the grass-roots level. These specialist departments were created to deal with health, education, transport, public works, forests and agriculture, and they operated at the local level through their representatives. Furnivall notes that "even up to 1900 the people saw little of any Government officials, and very few ever caught more than a passing glimpse of a European official. By 1923 the Government was no longer remote from the people but, through various departmental subordinates, touched on almost every aspect of private life."[31]

This establishment of direct communication between centrally appointed authorities and local populations, however, did not necessarily

---

[29] Michael Adas, "From avoidance to confrontation: Peasant protest in pre-colonial and colonial Southeast Asia", 241.
[30] Adas, "From avoidance to confrontation", 241, 243.
[31] Furnivall, *Colonial Policy and Practice*, 77.

foster social and emotional ties between these two groups. Khin Maung Kyi, for instance, comments on the Burmese bureaucrats' tendency to distance themselves from ordinary peasants. He notes that Burmese bureaucrats "usually lived in separate quarters away from the common people in town, and also moved from place to place on government assignments, taking no organic root in any one community. They rarely had any social intercourse with the common people of the town and considered themselves superior to the common Burmese."[32] James Guyot adds that even a sympathetic officer had little time to develop an understanding of district problems because of "such rapid circulation of posts."[33] According to Khin Maung Kyi, these Burmese officials were never legitimate in the eyes of the peasants. Lacking the traditional authority of the *myothugyi*, they had to rely on coercion to command compliance. Local residents regarded them as agents of the foreign power, and detested their coercive roles as administrators of law and order, collectors of taxes and revenues, and dispensers of justice.[34] Guyot notes that despite the British government's attempt to institute a variety of welfare programs,

> government officials were perceived by the population and generally did behave more as coercive than as persuasive agents. The civil surgeon, for instance, was also superintendent of the district jail, and some public health practices such as vaccination of people and inoculation of cattle were sufficiently resented that officers were commonly bribed not to carry them out.[35]

The second pre-colonial legacy which survived colonial rule was Burmese cultivators' unwavering faith in the monarchical system. Khin Maung Kyi, for instance, notes that the British administration lacked legitimacy in rural society, and that evidence can be discerned in the prevalence of *minlong hmyaw*, the belief in the return of a legendary Burmese king.[36] In Kyi's words,

> The Burmese kings, however despotic, represented the symbol of Burmese identity and nationhood. Religious sanctification and charisma had been built into the kingship for centuries. Moreover as *thathana*

---

[32] Khin Maung Kyi, 66.
[33] James Guyot, "Bureaucratic transformation in Burma", in *Asian Bureaucratic Systems*, ed. Ralph Braibanti (NC: Duke University Press, 1966), 363.
[34] Khin Maung Kyi, 66.
[35] James Guyot, "Bureaucratic transformation in Burma", 363.
[36] Khin Maung Kyi, 74.

dayaca (first disciple of religion) the kings supported and promoted religion. The British government could neither fill the place that Burmese kings had occupied in the society nor enjoy any of their traditional prerogatives.[37]

The third feature which remained intact from pre-colonial times was the practice of docility and deference by subordinates towards their superiors, and the latter's ruthlessness and insensitivity toward the former. This deference towards authority demonstrated that Burmese status system did not disappear in the colonial period. Cady, for example, writes that under the Burmese monarchical system superior officials demanded subservience and payment of gratuities from their subordinates.[38]

This practice grew during the colonial period due to the impact of the colonial educational policy which widened the gap between educated indigenous elites and uneducated village headmen. Cady, for instance, explains "the semi-westernized Burman bureaucrat served the government and his family group and tended to look down on the village *thugyi* as an ignorant bumpkin. Many of them, but not all, became alienated from the interests or the view point of the people as a whole."[39] He also wrote that "the new headmen, like the old *kyedangyi*, was still at the beck and call of touring officials, subject to summons by overbearing *myooks* (parallel position to *myothugyi* under pre-colonial societies), and liable to official reprimand, fine, or dismissal for dereliction of duty."[40]

Thus, despite more frequent state-societal contact, Burmese peasants remained distrustful of centrally appointed officials in colonial times, much as they did in pre-colonial times. This was not surprising given the increasing socio-economic gap between these two groups and indigenous bureaucratic authorities' lack of interest in local affairs. Farmers' distrust of native bureaucrats was also compounded by their perception of the British colonial government, and its agencies and representatives as alien and illegitimate. Their memory of the brutality of British suppression of armed rebellion during its occupation was still fresh. Burmese kings in the pre-colonial Buddhist kingdom were also subject to local rebellion, but these revolts did not challenge the monarchical system. Michael Adas, for instance, nicely summarizes that peasants in pre-colonial societies rebelled

---

[37] Khin Maung Kyi, 75.
[38] John Cady, 21.
[39] Ibid., 151.
[40] Ibid., 144.

not to effect fundamental changes in sociopolitical order, which they accepted as legitimate and divinely ordained, but to back a lord or faction against rivals, to express displeasure with excessive demands of a particular lord or, in times of dynastic collapse, to influence the outcome of contests that would determine which family and factions of the nobility would control the throne.[41]

The centralized administrative system, which established more effective control over local populations, also intensified hostilities between villagers and village headmen, who came to be regarded as the mere agents of the foreign government, not their representatives.

The Nationalist Movements

During the British occupation, two types of indigenous elites emerged in Burma. Those who belong to the first group were Anglicized, with attitudes and behavior antithetical to traditional customs and values. Some of them were educated in England or India, most joined the British administration and worked their way up the ladder. Members of the second group were mostly local English language-educated individuals with little exposure to modern European ways of life, representing nationalists who were indignant about the alienation of traditional Burmese culture.

These nationalist leaders came into contact with Burmese cultivators through their shared grievances against the colonial government. The colonial state was by then collecting more revenue from the countryside and exerting greater control over farmers' lives. The farmers in lower Burma particularly disliked the imposition of capitation tax and land revenue. The capitation tax was levied on males between the ages of eighteen and sixty, at the rate of five rupees a year for a married and between two to eight rupees for a bachelor. It was highly regressive because a wealthy man or higher income earner paid no more than an ordinary man. It was also unpopular because it was collected immediately before harvest, when farmers were out of cash.[42] The land revenue system, introduced by the British, was calculated as a percentage of the net output of the cultivator's land, and adjusted for differences in soil type, water conditions, individual farmers' ownership, and annual

---

[41] Cited in Robert Taylor, *The State in Burma* (Hurst: London, 1987), 62.
[42] Ian Brown, "Tax Remission and tax burden in rural lower Burma during the economic crisis of the early 1930s", *Modern Asian Studies* 33, 2 (1999): 387. See James Scott, *The Moral Economy of the Peasant: Rebellion and Subsistence in Southeast Asia* (New Haven: Yale University Press, 1976).

production.[43] The land revenue was more flexible.[44] For a considerable time, farmers had called for a more lenient treatment of both capitation and land revenue taxes especially after the depression in 1929. Ian Brown contends that although the British administration in Burma did not ruthlessly enforce these tax demands in the rice delta through the depression years, "it was not until the administration year 1932/33 that land revenue rates were reduced throughout the rice delta" and "there was no cut in the rates of capitation tax until the year 1931/32.[45]

Thus indigenous nationalist leaders both responded to and took advantage of peasant discontent with colonial policies and economic problems. Initially they were able to channel farmers' grievances towards a nationalist cause and enlist their support. In 1921 when the British government agreed to institute dyarchy system of tutelary democracy in Burma, members of the central nationalist body, the General Council of Burmese Association (GCBA) were divided on the issue of cooperation with the colonial government and participation in the elections for the Legislative Council. The Twenty-One Party GCBA was willing to cooperate, while the Hlaing-Pu-Gyaw GCBA wanted a boycott. The latter, which not only favored non-cooperation in elections but also demanded home rule outside the empire, had the support of the peasantry.[46]

The fragile alliance between the nationalist elites and peasants began in the early 1920s after the two central nationalist associations, GCBA and General Council of *Sangha Samaggi* (GCSS), established *wunthanu athin* or village associations in rural areas.[47] By 1925 there were over 10,000 *wunthanu athins* throughout Burma, all linked to the central executive committee of the GCBA by an administrative structure of village, circle and district boards.[48] The GCBA leaders saw the *wunthanu athin* as organizers of peasants' support for the election, the boycott campaigns, and the demand for home rule. Through *wunthanu athins*, a link between the national political goals of the urban elite and the interests of the villagers was established.

---

[43] Ian Brown, "Tax Remission and tax burden in rural lower Burma during the economic crisis of the early 1930s", 385-386.

[44] See Michael Adas, *Prophets of Rebellion: Millenarian Protest Movements Against the European Colonial Order* (Chapel Hill: University of North Carolina Press, 1979).

[45] Ian Brown, 398.

[46] Robert Taylor, *The State in Burma*, 119, 185.

[47] The GCBA was a natural outgrowth of YMBA (Young Men's Buddhist Association) which was formed by a group of Burmese college students in 1906. The initial goal of YMBA was to promote Burmese culture and religion, and it had become totally dedicated to politics by 1920 under the new name of GCBA.

[48] Robert Taylor, *The State in Burma*, 194.

In 1921, the GCSS selected young, spirited, well-disciplined, and clever *rahan* (monks) to lead *wunthanu athin* to agitate for home rule and to engage in a non-cooperation campaign. At the village level, *wunthanu athin* encouraged people and monks to refuse giving their services, including food and religious ceremonies to non-European officials. Noticeably, village headmen were ostracized as government stooges and some were even killed. After 1923, GCSS and GCBA local branches organized *Bu* or "no" *athin* (organizations) to boycott the state's auctions of fisheries and fallow lands, and to refuse the state's right to control these resources. They also discouraged farmers from paying taxes and taking orders from village headmen. *Sibwayei athin* or village-level economic associations were also formed, and they occasionally used violence to persuade *chettiars* (Indian money lenders) to lower debt obligations. [49]

Wunthanu associations gave practical support to villagers who were imprisoned, fined, or had lost their possessions because they did not pay taxes. For instance, they helped a jailed member's family with ploughing and harvesting, and provided financial aid to the needy through a special contingency fund. At the central level, the GCBA held annual and regular regional conferences to keep close contact with local *wunthanu*. However leaders of GCBA later changed their minds and participated in the dyarchy elections and subsequently abandoned the boycott movement in the countryside. Growing friction within the central ranks of the GCBA and GCSS also reduced the organizations' capacity to provide leadership to peasant movements. Realizing the reluctance and inability of the central leadership, Saya San began to organize his *Galon* Association and recruit villagers.

Patricia Herbert therefore claims that the Saya San rebellion was a by-product of mass mobilization of the central level Burmese political associations of 1920s. [50] Even the most ardent boycotters of the early 1920s lost faith in their ideas and, one by one, negotiated with the British government. While young leaders from village associations continued to pursue the boycott, reject taxes, and oppose government with stern dedication, the management group in the central organs of GCBA and the GCSS began to get caught in the intriguing complexities of British-framed legislating politics. Herbert observes that by the time rebellion broke out, the villagers did not even bother questioning whether the GCBA was in

---

[49] Patricia Herbert, "The Hsaya San Rebellion (1930-1932) Reappraised", (Australia: Monash University, 1982), 1-12.
[50] Patricia Herbert, 2.

the rebellion, and that they were not surprised when they learned after the resistance that it had nothing to do with Saya San.[51]

Many nationalist leaders maintained their distance from the Saya San-led peasant rebellion which broke out in the *Tharrawaddy* district of lower Burma in 1930. While a few nationalists attributed the cause of the rebellion to the economic distresses (indebtedness and land alienation) of colonial economic policies, most of them saw it as a resurgence of traditional practice which was not well-received within the nationalist movement. The fact that Saya San, the leader of the peasant rebellion, claimed to be the *Setkya-min* (the avenging king of Burmese legend) and the *Buddha Yaza* (the divinely sent creator of a Buddhist utopia), and that the rebellion used oaths, amulets, and traditional methods to be invulnerable to modern arms caused uneasiness among the indigenous elites. In Robert Solomon's words, they were "surprised and perhaps embarrassed by the primitive uprising in the countryside"[52]

Solomon, however, argues that nationalist leaders' mass mobilization efforts at the village level failed from the beginning because "the rural Burmese of 1930 were more responsive to symbolic appeals than to programmatic designs for reform."[53] According to Solomon, the Burmese farmers were not persuaded by the "cosmopolitan tone and sophisticated proposals" of the western educated Burmese elites. They responded well to the Saya San's traditional appeal because "certain deep-seated values, such as the combination of respect for the monarchy and messianic expectations, which found their way into the myth of monarchic revival, were never conclusively displaced."[54] Aspects of Solomon and Herbert's analyses are contradictory. While Herbert emphasizes the nationalists' initial success in mobilizing Burmese farmers, Solomon stresses limited appeal of these leaders to Burmese farmers.

Regardless, both agree that urban elites abandoned the strategy of mobilizing the Burmese cultivators once they realized that Burmese peasants were more of a liability than an asset to their cause, and once they failed to adjust their values to those of the farmers. The alliance between indigenous nationalist leaders and the peasants was only short lived. This experience reinforced mutual suspicion between Burmese cultivators and urban nationalist leaders, who became removed from the

---

[51] Ibid., 5-8
[52] Robert Solomon, "Saya San and the Burmese Rebellion", *Modern Asian Studies*, 3 (3) (1969): 209. Some nationalist leaders, however, remained supportive of the Saya San's rebellion. This was the exception rather than the norm.
[53] Robert Solomon, "Saya San and the Burmese rebellion", 209.
[54] Robert Solomon, 217.

populations they claimed to represent. This did not, however, prevent Burmese nationalist leaders from further capitalizing on farmers' grievances. Solomon notes that "this is well illustrated in the subsequent careers of some of these Burmese politician figures whose lives came into contact with the martyred hero, Saya San, executed in late 1931."[55] He describes how Ba Maw, a young and struggling barrister, was urged by John Cunliffe, the President of the Burmese High Court, to be Saya San's defence lawyer because it would be Ba Maw's chance of a lifetime to start his political career. Cunliffe was right. Ba Maw later became the first Prime Minister of Burma. U Saw served as a defence counsel for Saya San's followers, and later joined Ba Maw in the Prime Minister's office. Ba U, who appeared for the British government as a prosecutor, played an instrumental role in securing leniency in some cases. He was promoted to the High court and eventually became the President of Burma. [56]

The Burmese peasantry's support was again tapped by the *thakin* nationalist leaders of the *Do Bama Asi-ayon* in the 1930s.[57] Unlike its predecessor, the *Do Bama Asi-ayon* advocated independence, self-determination and anti-imperialism but attempted to do so within the framework of British colonial law. The *thakin*'s central leadership opposed the old *wunthanu* methods, and urged peasants to abandon their non-payment of tax and to work through legal procedures towards a lowering of taxes and rents. Of course, this had very limited appeal to Burmese peasants and the local *thakins* who worked with the peasants. At that stage, *thakin*'s leadership focused on organizing industrial workers and laborers, convinced that "only industrial workers could lead a progressive movement."[58]

The Japanese Occupation

The period 1941-1944 can be characterized by the breakdown of law and order in Burma. The Japanese invasion of Burma in 1941 from southern Burma was accompanied by the Japanese-backed and trained Burma independence army (BIA). BIA was organized and led by the *thakins*. On hearing news of the Japanese bombing of Rangoon and the marching of Japanese troops toward the north, police officers, medical staff, school

---

[55] Ibid., 220.

[56] Soloman, 220.

[57] *Do Bama Asi-ayon*, formally organized in 1933, was an indigenous Burmese political organization that gave soon-to-be Burmese government leaders political experience at national level. Their members addressed themselves as *thakin*, meaning 'master,' the title addressed to Europeans by subordinates during the colonial period. Robert Taylor, 207.

[58] Robert Taylor, 213-214.

teachers, and administrators in Lower and Upper Burma deserted their offices. By May 1942, fewer than one quarter of pre-war district officials remained at their government posts. At the same time, there were already between 10,000 to 50,000 members of BIA units throughout Burma. *Thakins* took charge of the towns after the British bureaucracy collapsed. However in some areas, the *thakins* administration was marginalized by pre-war government officials.[59]

In the meantime, Burmese communist party members, who opposed collaboration with Japan, began their anti-Japanese campaign across Burma. *Thakin* Soe emerged as the party leader, and organized extensive network of underground cells. He began training peasant guerrilla units in the Delta area and sent them to other parts of Burma to mobilize farmers' support. *Thakin* Soe and his right-hand man, *Thakin* Tin Mya, also gave secret political training courses to educate peasants.[60] Thus, villages were now subject to different or overlapping authorities depending on the relative strength and mobilization skills of colonial state officials and anti-colonial or anti-Japanese forces. Scanty information tells us very little about farmers' perceptions of these different elite groups who were fighting for control during that period. We know, however, that the two communist leaders, *Thakin* Than Tun and *Thakin* Soe were able to draw on a mass following, most probably among the Burman, in their respective home base areas in *Pyinmana* and delta.[61] We also know that ethnic Karen agriculturalists, on the other hand, suffered badly at the hands of the BIA units especially in *Papun* and *Salween* in the east and in rural parts of the Delta. BIA units indiscriminately executed Karens regardless of their age and sex, and it is estimated that in the delta district of *Myaungmya* alone 1,800 Karens were killed and 400 Karen villages were destroyed.[62] This attempt to decimate the Karens ignited fierce resentment amongst them, and they would later in 1949 openly challenge the Burmese government demanding their own autonomous state.

The defeat of the Japanese forces by the British/allied forces/anti-fascist indigenous groups in 1945 did not necessarily ameliorate farmers' situations. Burmese cultivators were hit hardest by the British military administration's new policy of declaring Japanese currency valueless. By then, many agriculturalists had already sold their crops to the Japanese army and had no British or Indian currency to buy seed for the cultivating season. The administration immediately conducted a census of population,

---

[59] Mary Callahan, 138-139,150.
[60] Mary Callahan, 198.
[61] Ibid., 373.
[62] Mary Callahan, 204.

animals and crops, and conscripted labor to rebuild villages, roads, and communications. It also began the plan to collect land revenue. British treatment of peasant populations in the post-war era led Maung Maung to conclude that the return of the "liberators" did not transform the average Burman life, which was still subject to outsiders' strict regulation.[63]

The State-Peasantry Relations in the Independence Era
In January 1948, Burma gained independence from the British. The Burmese rejection of colonialism in general and "capitalism" in particular is manifest in the post-independence agrarian laws, especially the 1948 and 1953 Land Nationalization Acts. The purpose of the Land Nationalization Act of 1948, which was promulgated under the civilian government (1949-1962), for instance, was to limit private land ownership to fifty acres, to prohibit non-agriculturalists from owning land, and to redistribute land to qualified cultivator-applicants.[64] In the same manner, the 1953 Land Nationalization Act gave peasants "the right to cultivate land" with the authorization of the Village Land Committee, and prohibited cultivators from mortgaging, selling or renting land. Consequently, while tenants cultivated fifty per cent of total agricultural land in the colonial era, only 30 per cent of land was tenanted by 1962.

The civilian government also established the State Agricultural Marketing Board (SAMB) in 1948 to take over the rice-export marketing functions of various non-Burmese groups. It bought paddy from the cultivators at low and fixed prices (the prices for the paddy was kept constant between 1948 and 1955). It also provided agricultural loans to farmers, but they were insufficient to cover the total cost of production.

Both measures of agrarian reform, however, were abolished in 1958-59, mainly due to the lack of commitment at the higher levels of policymaking, as well as landowners' ability to skirt the intent of the laws (such as dividing land on paper among their close relatives), and failure to provide the continuing support and services to beneficiaries.[65] Widespread insurrection by minority ethnic groups and the communists against the ruling civilian party, or the AFPFL (Anti-Fascist People Freedom League), also proved to be a major impediment to implementing policies. Part of the failure to promote rural welfare can also be attributed to the state's inadequate attention to the agricultural sector. Sekhar

---

[63] Quoted in Mary Callahan, 239.
[64] Mya Than, "Burma's agricultural development since 1962", in *Unreal Growth: Critical Studies on Asian Development,* ed. Nyo Manh-Lah (Delhi: Hindustan Publishing Corporation, 1984), 743.
[65] Mya Than, "Burma's agricultural development since 1962", 744.

Bandyopadhyay, for example, observes that between 1948 and 1962, the "industrial sector received greater priority at the expense of agriculture, though the latter always remained the major sector in the economy."[66] Steinberg also agrees that "there was no priority given to agriculture, irrigation, forestry, or mining in the plan...(t)he plan stressed transportation, power, industry, and construction." [67]

In some areas the redistribution of land created animosity between those who benefited from the program (previous tenants), and those who were disadvantaged by the new system (previous large land owners).[68] Most of the time, the civilian government was unable to prevent the corruption, crimes, and murders that followed the implementation of the land redistribution program.

The first election in independent Burma was held in 1951, and U Nu led the Anti- Fascist People Freedom League (AFPFL) coalition came to power. The return of the power into the hands of indigenous elites, however, did very little to close the social gap between the indigenous politicians and most of the population. In fact, the nationalist elites deliberately abandoned the strategy of mobilizing peasants' support for other priorities. Mary Callahan, for instance, wrote that

> (t)he Burmese nationalist leaders who by 1948-49 had become the principle of the postwar Socialist Party had chosen deliberately to forego the cultivation of a mass base in favor of protecting these leaders from <u>Kempetai</u> investigation and torture so that they would be able to lead the Burmese to independence when the opportunity arose. This meant that after the war, these leaders—including Kyaw Nyein, Ba Swe, thakin Tin, etc—had escaped unscathed the wartime deprivations of the Japanese, but they also emerged with nothing like the mass following that communist leaders Thakin Than Tun had in his home base area in Pyinmana or Thakin Soe had in the Delta.[69]

Popular writing by educated native Burmese at that time, in fact, not only revealed the condescending attitudes of the urban elites toward the country folk, but also attributed the electoral victory of "undeserving" candidates to the inability of the peasantry to make appropriate choices. A

---

[66] Sekhar Bandyopadhyay, *Burma To-Day: Economic Development and Political Control Since 1962* (Calcutta: Papyrus, 1987), 32.

[67] David Steinberg, *Burma: A Socialist Nation of Southeast Asia* (Boulder: Westview Press, 1982), 67.

[68] See Manning Nash, *The Golden Road to Modernity: Village Life in Contemporary Burma* (Chicago: University of Chicago Press, 1965).

[69] Mary Callahan, 373.

renowned writer, Thein Pe Myint, who lost the election for parliament in his home district, for instance, wrote in 1962 that

> I campaigned in upwards to a hundred villages and encountered frequent attacks by opposition parties. One day an army officer lectured my audience about the evils of communism. After his speech a Stable AFPFL candidate gave a speech denouncing my party (Pamanyata or Myanmar Workers and Peasants Party, a Marxist Faction of National United Front generally following a Moscow line). Then two days later a monk from Mandalay spoke as follows: "If you vote for Pamanyata you will all go to hell, but if you vote for the Stable faction (AFPFL) you will enjoy a living hell, but if you do not vote for the Clean AFPFL faction your village will be boycotted by the Sangha...*How can the public distinguish between the good and the bad when they are not intellectuals. They lack enlightenment.*[70]

The rural population, on the other hand, were unconvinced by the appeals of nationalist leaders who were preoccupied with chronic factional struggles at the national level. According to Manning Nash, peasants participated in national elections, but their choices for particular candidates were determined not by abstract ideology and the various programs advocated by candidates, rather, they were based on the benefits attached to the possible winning candidates.[71] Obviously this voting rationale was not unique to post-colonial Burma. In most rich and poor countries, people rarely vote for candidates purely on "abstract ideology." Policies and the likely relevance of candidates to voters' own interests significantly influence people's choices. Self-serving Burmese politicians, attributes not uncommon in other countries, also used peasants to secure power, position, and material benefits. Moshe Lissak, for instance, states that although All Burma Peasants Organization (ABPO), one of the four affiliated associations of the AFPFL, was supposed to represent the interests of Burmese peasants, it tended to benefit the leaders of the organization. The relationship between peasants and the leaders of the ABPO was transient and mainly based on material exchange as the ABPO representatives failed to mobilize peasants on a more sustainable level. Lissak thus notes that

> The ABPO's broker activity was reflected in the peasants' exchange of political support for inexpensive---although insufficient---credit. Because

---

[70] Quoted in John Badgley, "Intellectuals and the national vision: The Burmese case", *Asian Survey* 9 (8) (August, 1969), 604. Emphasis added.
[71] Manning Nash, "Party building in Upper Burma", *Asian Survey* 3 (4) (April, 1963), 198-201.

of their control of manpower and financial resources, ABPO leaders probably held the strongest power position within the league (AFPFL). However, the strength of this organization did not reflect a political alertness and activism on the part of the peasantry. The focus of power lay in the hands of those who manipulated the ABPO bureaucracy.[72]

The Burmese election of 1951 also demonstrates the alienation of a large part of the rural population. Robert Taylor, for instance, notes that the turnout in the 1951 election was less than 20 per cent, with only 1.5 million voters out of an electorate of 8 million voting. Furthermore, although twice as many turned out in 1956 than in 1951, and the 1960 vote was 65 per cent above that of 1956, the elections were far from stable. As noted by Taylor, shooting, kidnapping of candidates, intimidation, falsification, and bribery were common features of elections under the civilian government.[73]

An examination of the Burmese cultivators' relationships with the nationalist indigenous elite until independence illustrates mutual suspicion, and lack of trust between these two groups. Farmers' trust in the nationalist leaders crumbled after they were abandoned by the GCBA in the late 1920s. Their mistrust of the indigenous elite grew as *thakins* were preoccupied with power struggles at the national level, and neglected farmers' problems. The civilian government also faced multiple challenges and armed resistance from ethnic and communist groups, which led to the break down of law and order in the countryside.

Perhaps, farmers' disillusionment with nationalist leaders may have reinforced and increased their reliance on the local leadership. Manning Nash, for instance, observed that villagers in Nondwin and Yagyaw were unconcerned about national issues and politics, and the village power structure revolved around a man of *pon* (glory, influence, charisma, power).[74] In other words, farmers' political activities did not extend beyond their association with man/men of *pon* in the community who fulfilled their basic social, economic and political needs.

[72] Moshe Lissak, *Military Roles in Modernization: Civil-Military Relations in Thailand and Burma* (London: Sage Publications, 1976), 149.
[73] Robert Taylor, "Elections in Burma/Myanmar", in *The Politics of Elections in Southeast Asia*, ed. Robert Taylor (Cambridge: Cambridge University Press, 1996), 173.
[74] Manning Nash, *The Golden Road to Modernity*, 272. *Pon*, a Burmese cultural concept, is defined by Nash as follows: it is a charisma (in the secular realm) and glory (in the sacred realm). A man with *pon* is a powerful man without any particular office or institutional locus. A man of *pon* does not need to try to dominate, for his power radiates, and people come to him to give allegiance and to offer up service and trust.

A few nationalist leaders like *Thakin* Soe and *Thakin* Than Tun were able to draw peasant support on a relatively larger scale, but they were the exception rather than the norm. As early as 1946 the Communist-led Peasants' Union in *Yamethin* district claimed to have 30,000 registered members, and its activities overwhelmed the efforts of peasants' groups which supported the AFPFL and its Socialist Party leader. The Socialists had lost support among peasants by advocating cooperation with landlords and payment of rents and taxes. The communist leaders, however, met a similar fate to their socialist counterparts when they were unable to provide protection for peasant families or implement policies in the face of the government's refusal to recognize their action.[75] Most leading *thakin*, who saw the rural population as backward and unenlightened, lost their appeal to the peasantry, and had to rely on various forms of patron-client linkages to obtain farmers' votes.

The Beginning of the Military Regime
In 1958, the ruling party, the Anti-Fascist People Freedom League (AFPFL), split into two factions; the "Clean AFPFL" led by Prime Minister U Nu and agriculture Minister *Thakin* Tun, and the "Stable AFPFL" led by U Ba Swe and U Kyaw Nyein. By then Burma had been through a series of open armed insurgences by the communist, Karen and many other ethnic groups who were demanding greater political and economic autonomy.

Many army leaders backed the Stable AFPFL because of their close association with U Kyaw Nyein and U Ba Swe.[76] The army became unpopular after pro-Stable army officers in field units in *Moulmein, Hanthawaddy*, and *Sandoway* districts were accused of favoring Stable politicians. Thus the delegates of Clean party in *Hanthawaddy* declared the army "Public enemy number one."[77] The military (led by War Office leaders) staged a coup in September 1958 on the basis of alleged rumors that Clean members were planning to assassinate army leaders, and that the field commanders were plotting a coup to move *tatmadaw* (army) more forcefully into civilian political roles. U Nu officially transferred power to General Ne Win's "caretaker government" on October 1958.[78] Ne Win publicly announced the transfer of power by citing

[75] Robert Taylor, *The State in Burma*, 242.
[76] Callahan, 469.
[77] Mary Callahan, 470.
[78] Mary Callahan, 476. For detailed information about the situations leading to the military coup detat in 1958, see Tin Maung Maung Than, "Neither inheritance nor legacy: Leading the Myanmar State since Independence", *Contemporary Southeast Asia* 15 (1) (1993): 35-38.

"misconstructed" constitutional provisions which guaranteed freedoms of speech and association, and the skillful exploitation of the apathetic electorate by rebel groups. Accordingly, the military was concerned that "unscrupulous politicians and deceitful communist rebels might take advantage of the inadequacies in the constitution", and create "gangster political movements, syndicalism, anarchism and a totalitarian regime."[79]

The *tatmadaw* then established security councils spanning the national and the local levels. The main purposes of the security councils were to establish law and order, to exert control over other governmental agencies, and to replace the Clean AFPFL's machinery of upcountry control. The army's establishment of law and order led to a steep decline in violent crimes from 1958 to 1960.[80] It deported or imprisoned most upcountry racketeers and gangsters. Some of the *tatmadaw*'s draconian measures, however, were heavily criticized by civilians. They included the conscription of students, civil servants, and teachers to clean up the streets, the creation of two new satellite towns, and the transfer of 25,000 settlers there, stricter control over the press, and imprisoning of numerous editors, publishers and reporters.

The caretaker government therefore became increasingly unpopular especially among many liberal-minded citizens who found the army's actions harsh and excessive.[81] Such attitudes were also shared by people from the countryside. Nash notes that villagers from Nondwin wanted the caretaker military government to transfer power back to the civilian government because the army made "too many demands (such as cleanliness, prohibition of betel nut sellers, replacement of rickshaws by pedicabs, dog poisoning, and elimination of beggars in larger towns) and had done its job of restoring security and relative peace in the countryside"[82] The *tatmataw* members were not unaware of their unpopularity. A public opinion survey carried out by the Pyswar Directorate, for instance, revealed the roots of public antagonism against the army. They included the army's favoritism toward Stable party, its engagement in illegal economic activities, its lack of respect for civilians and civil officers, and its narrow-mindedness.[83]

Despite its awareness of its own unpopularity, the military held elections in 1960. According to Callahan, public criticisms against the

---

[79] Mary Callahan, 478-479.
[80] Mary Callahan, 484-485.
[81] Mary Callahan, 486, 488-489,
[82] Manning Nash, *The Golden Road to Modernity*, 288.
[83] Mary Callahan, 492-493.

army may have weakened its enthusiasm to continue in office.[84] Thanks to the army, law and order were re-established, and 95 per cent of the country's electoral districts were able to carry out the February 1960 election. The elections were by no means fair; there were incidents of local units' stealing votes, condoned by Rangoon-based army leaders.[85] Callahan notes that "(i)n spite of (or perhaps because of) these machinations, Nu's Clean AFPFL won the election."[86] General Ne Win handed power back to U Nu. In the meantime, General Ne Win was "showered with praise and even awarded the Magsaysay Award" for guarding the constitutional Government and democratic principles in Burma through a period of national chaos.[87]

On 2 March, 1962, the military staged a second coup d'état. The army or the Revolutionary Council was particularly troubled by Nu's proclamation of Buddhism as the state religion, the organization of administrations for new Mon and Arakan States, and continuing negotiations with politicians from the Shan and Kayah States, and several other considerations which threatened the survival and independence of the new nation.[88] There was little or no resistance from Burmese society to the military take over. In Taylor's words, the coup d'état "evoked no outward manifestations of public opposition in either Rangoon or in the central and peripheral regions of the state."[89] This does not, however, imply support for the military's takeover. Scholarly accounts tend to portray enthusiastic welcoming for the army takeover in society, especially in the rural areas. Daw Mya Sein, for instance, emphasized that Burmese citizens were particularly satisfied with the army's promise to hand power back to the civilian government, and this enhanced the credibility of the military as the only institution that could redeem and reunite the country. Sein thus wrote that after the caretaker government handed power back to civilian government in 1960, "U Nu told how Bogyoke Ne Win had become a hero in the eyes of the people. The army won the respect and admiration of the people by its Defence of the Union not only against internal insurrections but also against the more dangerous threat of invasion by foreign troops."[90] Michael Aung-Thwin went further

---

[84] Mary Callahan, 494.
[85] Mary Callahan, 496.
[86] Ibid., 497.
[87] Ibid.,
[88] Robert Taylor, *The State in Burma,* 291.
[89] Ibid.,
[90] Daw Mya Sein, "The historical background of the new constitution", in *The Future of Burma in Perspective: A Symposium,* ed. Josef Silverstein (Ohio: Center for International Studies, Southeast Asia Series No. 35, Ohio University, 1974), 7.

to argue that the military takeover was considered a legitimate act since it reintroduced the traditional values of the majority people.[91]

It is difficult to discern Burmese cultivators' attitudes towards the military takeover because most writings on public perceptions of it were not based on surveys, nor did they provide events/anecdotes/activities as support. However we have many stories to demonstrate that the Revolutionary Council deliberately appealed to rural residents and that Burmese farmers cared very little about civilian politicians at the national level. Relatively speaking, the Burmese cultivators were able to identify themselves more closely with rank and file army personnel than they were with the urban westernized politicians. The AFPFL leadership represented and promoted western values that were not necessarily upheld by the military and the rural populations. John Badgley states that

> The strength (support for the military) flows from the Burmese rural ethnic group which numbers about 15,000,000 or three-fourths of the population. It is the culture of this Buddhist group that has dominated the nation in the face of militant minority opposition, and it is upon this culture that the military is attempting to found their own socialist revolution. The political process inherent in Burma rural life, and the values associated with that life, were the cause for the dysfunction of the western institutions utilized by the politicians...The military seeks to aggregate its power by utilizing non-western secular symbols and methods of rule.[92]

These "non-western Burmese values" that the *tatmadaw* emphasized to legitimize its regime included (1) the practice of governing reminiscent of the monarchical system; (2) the more autonomous authority (in comparison with civil service) given to army officers who served as chairmen of Security Committees at each level of government; (3) the diminished emphasis on the importance of non-scientific aspects in Burmese educational system; (4) the removal of foreigners from positions of influence in government and education; and (5) budget priority on agricultural rather than urban programs.[93]

The Revolutionary Council also attempted to justify its rule by associating itself with the great warrior Burmese kings in "golden days" of in pre-colonial periods. Jon Wiant and David Steinberg, for instance,

---

[91] Michal Aung-Thwin, "1948 and Burma's myth of independence", in *Independent Burma at Forty Years: Six Assessments*.
[92] John Badgley, "Burma: The nexus of socialism and two political traditions", *Asian Survey*, 3 (2) (February, 1965), 91.
[93] John Badgley, 91.

argued that "appeal to symbolic idea of unity have taken several forms. First is the symbolic identification of the revolutionary regime with the great dynastic king. The Ne Win revolution has been portrayed implicitly and explicitly as *the Fourth Great Unification of Burma*." [94]

Aside from their shared values and traditions, army personnel also shared social origins similar to those of Burmese peasants. According to Badgley, the relatively uneducated Burmese farmers can relate more immediately to military officials, the majority of whom were not educated beyond the district high schools. By contrast, the social gap between the peasants and civilian politicians, who held college degrees or went to college, was considerably wider. Burmese cultivators also developed friendships with military authorities during the insurrection years when the senior commanders (not to mention lower ranking soldiers) came to the district to fight insurgences. [95]

Given the many shared attributes and commonalities between the peasantry and the military, and the cultivators' negative experiences with the civilian politicians, it was possible that peasants may have preferred the military authorities to their civilian counterparts. The military itself wasted no time in mobilizing cultivators' support. It not only emphasized the importance of the role of peasantry in the national economy but also instituted a variety of reforms to promote the welfare of rural populations. John Badgley, for instance, notes that "It is from the peasants that the Revolutionary Council's most leftist *wungyis*, Brigadiers Tin Pe and Than Sein, seek their support. One observer noted that in 1962-63 the government loaned 700 million kyat to farmers so that they might have sufficient capital to pay for more fertilizer, better seeds, and the use of more government tractors." [96]

Silverstein agrees that "the military rulers sought to unite the people by mobilizing the peasants and workers....the government passed laws that freed the peasants from rent, provided new loans, and directed the peasants to create local land committees to reallocate land held by absentee landlords." [97] After the military government's takeover in 1962, it introduced the 1963 Tenancy Act to accomplish the "unfulfilled" mission of the Land Nationalization Act. The 1963 Tenancy Act transferred the landlord's right to the Village Land Committee to determine who the tenants would be, and prohibited the payment of tenancy rents in kind to

---

[94] Jon Wiant and David Steinberg, 298. Emphasis added.
[95] John Badgley, "Burma, The nexus of socialism and two political traditions", 91.
[96] John Badgley, "Burma's zealot wungyis: Maoists or St. Simonists", *Asian Survey* 5 (1) (January, 1965), 56.
[97] Josef Silverstein, *Burma: Military Rule and the Politics of Stagnation*, 52.

give tenants control over their produce. The *tatmadaw* also enacted a Peasant's Rights Protection Act to prevent creditors from seizing land and other peasant assets or from seeking peasants' punishment for non-payment through the civil courts. On the other hand, the military junta also immediately established the state monopoly over agricultural production, distribution, marketing, and exporting. It reorganized and renamed the State Agricultural Marketing Board (the agricultural marketing board created by the civilian government) into the Union of Burma Agricultural Product Marketing Board (UBAM) and began procuring rice from farmers by offering them low prices. Despite its emphasis upon socialism and cooperatives, the military, however, did not collectivize land. Farmers remain the largest bloc of private owners and producers in the country. It was the rigid imposition of government procurement practice that would soon generate resentment in the countryside.

To increase rural productivity, the Revolutionary Council implemented various programs designed to expand agricultural credit, improve rural health and social services, and broaden educational opportunities. Mya Than and Nobuyoshi Nishizawa, for instance, concluded that "as far as the agricultural credit policy was concerned, the amount of credit made available during the Revolutionary Council government was much more than that of the previous governments. It increased from K48 million in 1962/63 to K167 million in 1973/74." [98] The *tatmadaw* stressed the common interests between themselves and farmers by changing the date of Peasants' Day from January 1 to March 2 to tie the peasant celebration to the anniversary of the military's seizure of power.

The Revolutionary Council (RC), which in 1974 transformed itself into the Burma Socialist Program Party, attempted to establish a direct link between top-level executive authority and grassroots. This linkage was used by the GCBA leadership in rural areas in the 1920s but most Burmese peasants came in touch with the GCBA only through its auxiliary branches and representatives at the local level. The RC, on the other hand, utilized two different mechanisms to shorten the distance between top executive members and rural residents. The first channel was through the holding of annual peasant meetings where farmers were given the opportunity to have face-to-face interactions with highest ruling

---

[98] Mya Than and Nobuyoshi Nishizawa, "Agricultural policy reforms and agricultural development in Myanmar", in *Myanmar Dilemmas and Options*, 91.

officials. The second channel was through the formation of a variety of national and grassroots peasant organizations.

One outstanding feature of the early years of the Revolutionary Council was the promotion of "open" communication and exchange of opinion among the top level military officials and peasants. Silverstein wrote that "beginning within nine months of the coup, the military organized the first of several peasant seminars at *Ohndaw*. Here the leaders discussed both the technical and particular problems of the participants and the broad ideological goals of the government."[99] Through a variety of peasants' seminars in Lower and Upper Burma (such as the *Ohndaw* seminar, the *Duya* seminar, the *Popa* seminar, the *Kabaung* seminar) peasants presented their views "frankly and fearlessly," on issues ranging from favoritism, the corrupt behavior of local officials, to lack of water, flood prevention, insufficient supply of consumer goods, health services, and education, and the late arrival of agricultural loans.[100] These annual peasants' seminars served as official channels for them to express their grievances and make their demands.

A speech given by U Tha Din, a farmer delegate from *Ha-Nein* village, *Myingyan* district, at *Popa* Peasant Seminar, for instance, reveals that

> In our village, agricultural loans are not given in time. They came too late and we are again obliged to go to capitalists for cash. I suggest that these loans be disbursed before the month of Thadingyut (October). Again, in the case of village banks, let's not have a repetition of the same old state of affairs, like having an executive body as a family clique, with the father as president, the daughter as secretary and the son as committee member.[101]

U Ba Tin, another farmer representative from *Myeya-Chaung* village, *Natogyi* township, also remarked that "at some purchasing depots the sorting clerks had to be tipped about 2 and a half kyat to make them lenient when scrutinizing the cotton offered for sale. At these depots, the weighing machines were also defective."[102]

A close look at the Burmese cultivators' reports during the peasants' seminars in the early and late 1960s also portrayed the VSAC (Village Security and Administrative Council) and VLC (Village Land Committee)

---

[99] Siverstein, *Burma: Military Rule and the Politics of Stagnation*, 108.
[100] Selective issues from *Forward Magazine* and *Working People Daily News* in the periods of 1963-1973.
[101] *Forward*, 22 January, 1964.
[102] Ibid.

and VMAC (Village Multi-purpose and Agricultural Cooperatives) as "stooges" of rich cultivators, merchants, and village headmen, "obstructing the military's stated socialist goal of creating equality" in the countryside. The cultivators' complaints were mainly directed against "corrupt" local officials (who misused government power and authority, and practiced favoritism towards rich cultivators) and "rebels and insurgents" (who attempted to obstruct the construction of "socialism" in Burma). U Aung Din from *Natogyi* township, *Myin Kyan* district, for instance, complained that "there is a growing need for understanding between peasants and government service man, the latter responsible for wrongfully executing government policies."[103] Another farmer blurted out during one peasants' seminar that "annually subscription fees were collected from the members of Peasants' Council to enable the organization to stand on its own. Most peasants could not pay the lump sum in one year. Some collectors misappropriate the sums collected."[104]

The army also founded a nation-wide Peasant Organization, and a variety of other agricultural-related organizations to achieve its twin objectives of establishing both direct links with the peasant population and effective control over rural residents. The People's Peasants Council, for instance, was formed to mobilize agricultural producers and provide them with a forum and mechanism for exchange of ideas. At the same time, the Council was to act as a vehicle for supporting the military government. In the same manner, the Revolutionary Council created a number of rural organizational bodies (such as the Village Security and Administrative Council, the Village Land Committee, and the Village Multi-purpose and Agricultural Cooperatives, the Village Peasants Council, and the *Lanzin* socialist party). The objectives of these organizations were to provide a check on local initiatives, to control rural output and labor, and to ensure that central directives were followed. Aside from agriculture-related social and economic organizations, the military also maintained strict surveillance and monitoring of the rural population through formal political and administrative organizations. Badgley notes that

> Village, township, district and division Security and Administrative Councils form a hierarchy of communication and command which has proved effective thus far. The military has recruited influential rural leaders to serve on their local security, which are usually chaired by a military officer, or a police representative. The civil service has been

---

[103] *Working People's Daily*, 27 February 1968.
[104] *Working People's Daily*, 28 February 1975.

increasingly bypassed as specialized functions of government are turned over to "experts" directly responsible one of the councils. [105]

In addition to facilitating interaction with the rural masses through a variety of hierarchical organizations, the military promoted and sometimes forced contact between urban residents and the rural population. Silverstein, for instance, wrote in 1966 that

> Since it seized power, the Revolutionary Council has set the example of learning from the people--going to the villages and holding peasant seminars in order to hear complaints and suggestions. Last year, the government sent soldiers, bureaucrats, intellectuals and professionals to the villages and factories to live and work with the people. [106]

As will be discussed in a later chapter, this approach backfired and created antagonism between rural hosts and urban volunteers in some villages. The military regime also carried out a large-scale campaign to eliminate illiteracy by sending a massive force of educated urban residents to teach farmers how to read and write.

Interestingly, scholarly accounts on peasants during the initial period after the military's takeover tended to portray the relatively advantageous bargaining position enjoyed by peasants vis-a-vis the military. They emphasized the inability of the military to direct farmers' behavior into desirable outcomes, and to implement and enforce agricultural policies. Badgley, for instance, notes, that "(t)his year Ne Win castigated peasant leaders by repeating the old saw that every Burman would ride an elephant if he could borrow enough money to buy one. In 1963-64 the government loaned only 400 million kyat to the farmers, because of a significant proportion of the previous loans were defaulted."[107] Silverstein also notes that

> They (workers and peasants) have not become completely pliable and accommodating to the government. Both workers and peasants have demonstrated an ability to pursue their self-interest, and with the 1974 military-civilian government showing more interest in their grievances, the workers and peasants are beginning to use their potential power in the political arena. [108]

[105]Badgley,"Burma's zealot wungyis: Maoists or St. Simonists", 59.
[106] Silverstein, "Burma: Ne Win's revolution considered", 100.
[107] Badgley, "Burma's zealot wungyis", 59.
[108] Silverstein, "Burma: Ne Win's revolution considered", 52-53.

Especially in the agricultural sector,

> The efforts to eliminate private trades in paddy, and at the same time establish a government-operated system of purchases and sales with fixed nation-wide uniform low consumer prices, had a dual negative effect. They caused many peasants to act as "economic men" and shift from paddy to other grains which offered larger margins of profit, and caused the government to lose K70 million through its experiment in rigging prices, mainly because it set them too low to cover costs and made no allowances for differences in quality of product. Ne Win lamented the fact that 'some peasants replaced the cultivation of paddy with other crops in their selfish interests'...He implored them 'to resume paddy cultivation in the usual fields and stop such acts that would practically amount to exploiting our goodwill for the welfare of the masses'. [109]

Silverstein, in fact, goes even further implying that farmers took advantage of the good intentions of military government and abused the system that was designed to benefit them.

> The farmers accepted the security of their land, the easy loans, and other benefits bestowed upon them by the soldiers in power, but they did not change their outlook or life style. They farmed and marketed as before, and when consumer goods were not available or government demands seemed unacceptable they sold their produce on the black market, withheld their crops from the government buyers, and continued to live in their traditional unsocialistic ways. [110]

An analysis of the reports of official newspapers and journal magazines also sheds light on the willingness of the top-ranking officials to be attentive, to admit their financial, organizational, and personal limitations, and to correct or improve them. Ne Win, the leader of the Revolutionary Council and later chairman of the Burma Socialist Program Party, for instance, remarked during his speech at the Peasant seminar held at *Kabaung, Toungoo* district that

> I have heard that there are complaints against both sides (government paddy buying centers and the peasants). Among the paddy buying centers there are good ones as well as bad ones. If you come across any bad ones, report to us and we will take the necessary actions... On the other hand, inferior quality paddy and paddy containing dust, sand, and stones are brought for sale. [111]

---

[109] Silverstein, "Burma: Ne Win's revolution considered", 96-97.

[110] Silverstein, *Burma: Military Rule and the Politics of Stagnation*, 220.

[111] *Forward*, 22 March 1966.

During a speech at the ceremony of the establishment of the Amara co-operative village in *Dauk-U* township, Ne Win exhorted peasants while at the same time admitting the government was unable to provide sufficient loans "we have lent you money to give you a start. Use it as capital. Don't squander it. I am asking you to be frugal because I have heard that a shop which was opened here yesterday sold about kyat 4,000 worth of goods last evening. *Our loan is inefficient.* Work hard and put up with austerity for a couple of years." [112]

The chart below on production and procurement of rice in Burma shows that the level of government procurement in fact gradually declined (in spite of the absolute increases in production) after the military takeover in 1962. Furthermore, the chart on government procurement and free market prices of rice in Burma between 1948-87 also reveals that except for the period of 1968-69, the differences between government procurement prices and free market prices were relatively small until the early and mid 1970s. These statistics, crudely speaking, portray the military's leniency towards rural residents during the earlier years of its accession.

Chart on Production and Procurement of Rice (1948-87)

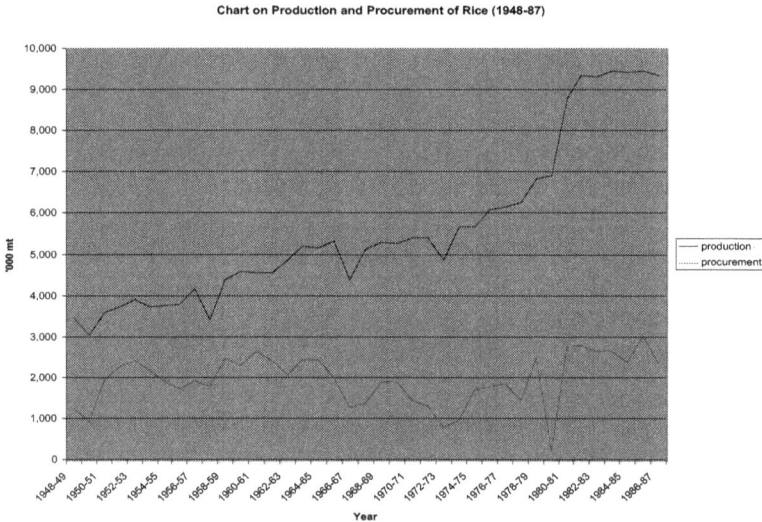

Source: Tin Soe and Brian Fisher, "An economic analysis of Burmese rice-price policies", in *Myanmar Dilemmas and Options: The Challenge of Economic Transition in the 1990s,*

---

[112] *Forward* 22 May 1963, 12-13. Emphasis added.

eds. Mya Than & Joseph Tan (Singapore: Institute of Southeast Asian Studies, 1990), 121-123. Soe and Fisher's data, however, are obtained from the Burmese official sources, whose reliability is subject to debate.

Government procurement and free market price (1961-87)

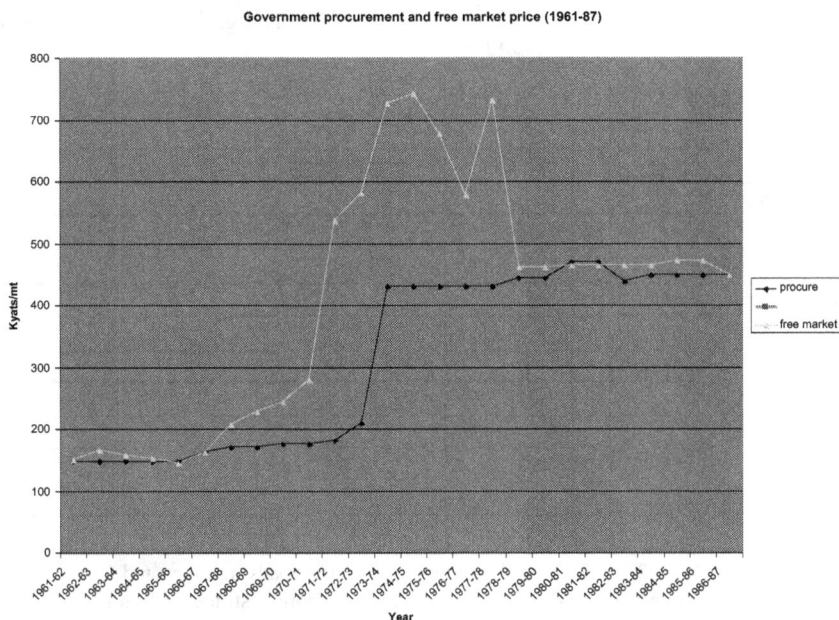

Source: Young, Cramer and Wailes, *Economic Assessment of the Myanmar Rice Sector* (Arkansas: University of Arkansas, 1998), 66.

The Military's Failures and Limitations

Over the long term, however, the military government could not meet its promises. The centralized economic system, poor management, and the closed-door policy discouraged private initiative and competition, decreased the quality and quantity of basic food and consumer product, and reduced reliance on foreign assistance, machinery, and technical know-how. These factors combined spelt economic disaster in Burma. From the very beginning the military regime was not financially capable of addressing farmers' economic problems on a large scale. It could not provide sufficient credit and capital investment in the agricultural sector which aggravated the decline in rural production and productivity. For instance, public expenditure on agriculture declined from 11.3 per cent of capital expenditure in 1964/65 to 4.4 per cent in 1970/71.[113] In 1972, only 1.8 million out of 4.4 million rural households in Burma had access to official credit, and only about 13 per cent of agricultural areas could be used for multiple cropping because of lack of irrigation. David Steinberg summarizes Ne Win's development strategy by saying, "(A)griculture had effectively been de-emphasized."[114]

Public investment by sector 1962/63-1986-87 (in percent of total)

Sectors	1962/63	1985/86	1986/87
Agriculture	13.0	12.0	9.2
Live stock/Fishery	2.0	5.0	3.8
Mining/ Processing	4.9	28.9	24.1
Manufacturing/power	4.2	10.3	8.8
construction	15.8	6.0	9.2
Transport/Communication	23.5	12.7	17.7
Trade	4.9	2.8	2.5
Social Services	4.5	9.2	8.0
Administrative Organization	26.0	6.2	8.0
Other	1.0	1.1	2.2

Source: U Tun Wai, "The Myanmar Economy at the Crossroads, Options and Constrains", in *Myanmar Dilemmas and Options* (Singapore: Singapore Institute of Southeast Asian Studies, 1990), 26.

Until the mid 1970s, the military regime toyed with small-scale approaches to increase agricultural production, including the expansion of cultivated lands, the subsidization of agricultural inputs, and the provision of low interest bearing agricultural loans. None of these activities succeeded because of insufficient capital investment. The declining agricultural production and growth rates during the first 10 years of the revolutionary government finally led the military to reconsider its planning and implement radical economic strategies. Promoting agriculture, in fact, was extremely important for the military, given the country's heavy reliance on agricultural produce as its major source of foreign exchange. A close examination of the military regime's formulation and handling of agricultural development programs since the mid 1970s demonstrates the government's concern with maintaining its

---

[113] David Steinberg, "Military rule in Burma since 1962", in *Military Rule in Burma: A Kaleidoscope of Views*, ed. F. Lehman (Singapore: Institute of Southeast Asian Studies, 1981), 32
[114] David Steinberg, 32.

grip on people from the countryside. This was manifest in its preference for strategies that increased agricultural growth and productivity and simultaneously strengthened the state's control over the rural production.

The first strategy of "high yielding variety promotion" (HYV) was employed in the mid 1970s and lasted for approximately 10 years, and can be described in terms of intensive use of fertilizers, chemical, pesticides, and high yielding seeds, and mass participation by a non-agricultural work force. Thanks to the application of new technology and labor inputs, there was a significant growth in rice production during 1975-1985, a period which has been referred to as the "third period of growth" of the last 150 years in Burma.

In retrospect, this strategy seemed to obtain the twin economic and political objectives of the military, for it not only increased agricultural growth and productivity, but also strictly monitored rural population and production. In particular, the military was able to procure greater amounts of grain from the countryside. Individual peasant households were now required to deliver a quota of paddy--as much as two third of the crop--to the paddy purchasing center at the end of the harvest. Failure to do so could lead to the loss of access to land and to limitations on state-provided credit. Since the low procurement prices and the high quota ratio were set without taking into account the increasing prices of the essential consumer goods and agricultural input, small farmers (farmers operating farms of less than five acres) often had to sell their *wunza* or personal consumption to the government for procurement during the bad harvest years. The benefits the state claimed were associated with the new agricultural assistance programs were, in fact, far outweighed by the costs to farmers due to the government pricing policies which were biased against the rural sector.

Nevertheless, the junta's ability to finance the program was soon undermined by a huge budget deficit and serious balance of payment problems in the mid-1980s. The socialist isolationist policy had created inefficient state-owned enterprises, reduced profits, and accumulated debt from foreign loans of the late seventies. The HYV strategy, which relied on a huge influx of capital (especially for chemical fertilizers and modern variety seeds), lost its momentum in the mid-1980s. No new large scale development strategy was instituted to improve the deteriorating agrarian situation until the late 1980s.

In September 1987, the government implemented a "partial liberalization program" in the agricultural sector by releasing its grip on trade in major crops, allowing farmers to sell some of their produce at market determined prices and to make decisions on the type of crops they could grow. It exempted nine grains, initially including rice, from government procurement, and encouraged private internal and external exports of rice and other crops. Nonetheless, the state's ambivalent attitude toward "raising agricultural productivity through the provision of economic incentives" became increasingly apparent in its "reimposition" of control over the private rice trade and the procurement system in 1989. The government nonetheless lowered the procurement quota (12 per cent of the total production), and offered higher prices for the procured products.

Gradually, the government shifted away from the open market approach to agriculture and forced farmers to grow more rice and to sell greater quantities of paddy to the state at prices increasingly below market.[115] The State Law and Order Restoration Council (SLORC) reimposed constraints on the use of designated paddy land during the dry season, and imposed export taxes and bans on the private export of some pulses.[116] In addition to the sale of grains to the government-owned MAPT (the Myanma Agricultural Product Trading or the agricultural marketing board), villages had to sell paddy to the military at low fixed prices, the quantities amounting to one-third as large as MAPT procurements in the rice-surplus regions.[117]

The unwillingness of the military to extend and experiment with the "liberal" approach in the agricultural sector, and the introduction of the summer paddy program and land reclamation highlight the military's intention to revert to its previous strategy of promoting agriculture without losing control over the sector. Although partial liberalization has significantly improved the lives of most peasants, it was too costly for the military to continue. Giving greater freedom and autonomy to agricultural producers and traders not only means exercising less control over the rural population, but also implies the loss of monopoly over the sector that had for centuries fueled the government's foreign reserves. In addition, the government has used compulsory procurement to sell rice at subsidized prices to insufficiently paid government employees and urban workers. It

---

[115] The US Embassy, *Country Commercial Guide: Burma, 1998*, 15
[116] Ibid., 16. The SLORC is the title of the military government which staged a coup detat after the 1988 popular demonstration against Ne Win's regime. The SLORC was dominated by most military officials who controlled the government in pre-1988 periods. The SLORC then changed its name into the State Peace and Development Council (SPDC) in 1997 to promote its softer development-oriented image.
[117] The US Embassy, *Country Commercial Guide: Burma*: 1996, 15.

is not a coincidence that urban riots broke out every time the government relaxed its control over the rice trade.

By the early 1990s, the government could no longer afford to import huge quantities of fertilizer. It shifted its focus from the intensive use of chemical fertilizers to sown area expansion through multiple cropping and land reclamation. Under the summer paddy program, the military regime has implemented different types of irrigation systems and remodeled the old ones. It was able to draft free labor for irrigation construction without relying heavily on foreign exchange. The summer paddy program has been considered successful because it has not only increased total annual paddy production, but also boosted the standard of living of many farmers. It is also popular in the countryside because, unlike the monsoon paddies, it does not require farmers to sell produce to the government. However, one major problem with summer paddy was the failure on the part of policy makers to take into consideration regional and climatic differences. Some paddy fields, especially the tail enders, were too far from the water tank to receive water, and many other areas are not suitable for summer paddies. Many farmers suffered badly from their involuntary practices of summer paddy.

The land reclamation policy was enforced soon after summer paddy program was instituted. The objective of land reclamation was to take advantage of and utilize the availability of cultivated land, which lies fallow, and covers almost the same area as the present net sown area. In addition, the government encouraged private entrepreneurs to launch paddy-fish farming schemes in deep water, where the cultivation of long strain paddy was risky. It provided many incentives to private business people to lure them into this new venture.

By December 1998, the Ministry of Agriculture had claimed that seventy six companies have claimed 1.2 million hectares, and most holdings were around 3,000 to 5,000 acres, though a few were much larger. Many experts on agriculture and economics, however, cautioned that the land expansion policy was uneconomical and inequitable. It was uneconomical because all the projects were heavily subsidized, and did not really reflect the market costs of the operation. The costs of the projects were even higher if the costs of environmental damage and local communities' loss were added. It was inequitable since the numbers of landless tenants continued to rise even as the government raced to open fallow land, which was ultimately reserved for the urban upper class businessmen. Some other farmers lost their lands to private entrepreneurs, because theirs were considered "fallow and uncultivated" and thus must be reclaimed by the government. Despite the loss and suffering of rural populations over land reclamation it is unlikely that the government, which measures the success of its policy in terms of the acreage that has been claimed and the total production, will halt this practice. Both the summer paddy program and land reclamation, in fact, are more desirable options for the government, since they enable the military to boost agricultural production without relinquishing its control over the rural population.

Along with the formulation and implementation of these policies, state-societal relationships have undergone some sharp reversals in a manner that contradicts the ideals of executive-peasant communication the military had when it came to power. The regime's previous efforts to establish a direct link between the highest executive authorities and that of the majority population gradually dwindled after the collapse of the HYV program. The optimism the military once had had with its specific relationship with the peasants in the heyday of the *coup d'état* were now exhausted. Specifically after 1988, the junta abolished the Peasant Organization, which had served as the vehicle for monitoring rural activities and transmitting the army's ideologies in the countryside, to maintain its distance from the past "socialist" practices. Peasant seminars or conferences, which were a common feature under the "socialist" government, were no longer held to promote exchanges between the elite leaders at the national levels and the grassroots population.

Changes in the nature of recruitment for military personnel have also reopened the social and political gap between central authorities and the farmers. Whereas the link between the military and the peasants during the initial years of the occupation may have been strengthened by the fact that approximately 70,000 soldiers were originally farmers, the majority of the present (second generation) high-ranking military officials can no longer trace their immediate background to rural communities. The recruitment network for the higher military institutions (such as Defense Service Academy and Officer Training Service) is confined to the families, relatives, and associates of the military who had already lost any understanding they may once have had of their social origins. The lack of communication and interaction between centrally appointed officials, who considered themselves socially superior, and the local population is also exacerbated by their frequent transfer and reshuffling. Thus the distance between the governing authorities and the peasantry that the military had attempted to close during its initial years of power has gradually widened as the military's tenure lengthened.

Conclusion

Four important lessons can be drawn from the analysis of state-societal relationships in pre-colonial, colonial, and post-colonial Burma. First, some Burmese opposition members in exile have argued that farmers' varying dispositions toward central and local authorities are the product of the manipulation of the top executive authorities.[118] According to this source, military officials have instilled ideas amongst Burmese cultivators that local authorities were to blame for farmers' problems. A close examination of farmers' relationships with various authorities over different periods of time, however, shows that Burmese cultivators' different attitudes toward central and local authorities have their historical roots in pre-colonial times, and are not simply a product of the military regime. These Burmese expatriates' argument assumes that Burmese farmers lack appropriate judgment of political realities. Burmese peasants' attitudes towards government authorities are based their past and present encounters with local leaders and supra-village authorities and their memories of the village and local affairs. Burmese farmers do not have blind faith in central or local authorities. As I have shown, they have taken various measures to show their dissatisfaction at the central as well as at the local level.

Burmese cultivators' support for the central authorities, on the other hand, has changed throughout the periods of different regimes. The second lesson that can be learned from this chapter is the dynamic nature of political legitimacy. Farmers accepted the Burmese monarchical system as legitimate and supported the king's role as the patron of the *sangha* and the upholder of religion. These culturally and traditionally ingrained concepts were shattered by the British occupation, which not only destroyed the monarchical system but also refused to play an active role in promoting the Buddhist religion. Therefore, from the farmers' perspective, the colonial government was illegitimate. Peasants resorted to rebellion and millenarian movements to resist British rule and to re-impose the indigenous rule. They threw their support behind nationalist leaders who challenged the legitimacy of the British government and stressed the importance of traditional culture and language. Burmese cultivators, however, gradually withdrew their support for the indigenous elite after their repeated failures to resolve farmers' problems.

When Burma gained independence in 1948, farmers remained detached or grew weary of national politics. They were happy to be ignored so long as they had a good local governing system. This was

---

[118] Conversations with Karen opposition members in Sydney, Australia, 19 August 2002.

partly because national political affairs had such little impact on their lives and partly because the less authoritative the state the fewer demands were placed upon them. U Nu was able to generate support from various parts of the countryside by promoting Buddhism. However poor economic conditions, the break-down of law and order, and the growing social and communication gap between national leaders and Burmese cultivators did very little to improve the image of the civilian politicians. Taylor asserts that the traditional concept of legitimacy based on monarchical institutions and the maintenance of the Buddhist religion lost its strength in the post-colonial period: "Nu's attempt to create state legitimacy on the basis of the symbols and beliefs of the Burmese monarchs failed partly because the society upon which he attempted to impose these ideas was much more religiously and educationally diverse and skeptical than that of the nineteenth century and before."[119] Improvement in economic conditions and the establishment of law and order was an important basis for popular support for the civilian government, and this was true for the military government as well.

Against this background of failed promises and patronizing civilian politicians, Burmese cultivators seemed to identify more closely with military personnel, with whom they shared many cultural and social traits. The military, in fact, was able to achieve what no other governments in Burmese history had been able to do; that is, to establish a direct link with the majority population. It was only under the early periods of military occupation that Burmese cultivators were given the opportunity to express their opinions, to shake hands and have dinner with General Ne Win, and to have direct contact with top executives and policy makers in the capital. Like its civilian counterpart, the military was unable to solve peasants' problems on a larger scale. This was manifest in its greater extraction of agricultural produce and tightening control over the rural population, which increasingly alienated the very people it had tried to mobilize for support. Once repressive state policies exerted too much control upon the countryside, as happened under the later periods of the military regime, Burmese cultivators could no longer remain detached from the national government. They jointed the pro-democracy movement in 1988, and voted willingly for the opposition party, the National League for Democracy, in the 1990 election.

Thirdly, the qualities of good local leaders are more or less the same in the minds or rural people, whether the leaders are "military" or "civilian," or "authoritarian" or "democratic." In the pre-colonial periods,

---

[119] Ibid., 208.

Burmese farmers placed great emphasis on having good native leaders, who would safeguard and promote their interests. They had very little direct contact with the King or his authorities, and they never cared much for these supra-village authorities. These attitudes were maintained, and reinforced by the broken promises and superior attitudes of the centrally appointed authorities and the urban elite in the colonial and post-colonial periods. Thus Burmese rice farmers are mainly interested in having good leaders and local governance structure. A "good leader" is someone who is reasonably honest, service oriented (responsive to rural people's interests, needs), who is not abusive nor arbitrarily uses force. Such qualities are favored and looked for in any central or local authorities, whether they are military or civilian, democratic or otherwise. This kind of orientation has little to do with "western" versus "non-western" values and seriously challenges the arguments of scholars who contend that the military's political legitimacy in the countryside rests on its emphasis on non-western values.

Melford Spiro, for instance, analyzed the motivations of villagers who supported the two contending candidates for a village headman in *Yeigyi* village in Upper Burma during civilian rule in the late 50s. Those who supported the incumbent consisted of those who benefited from his power, and those who supported the contender consisted of those who were harmed by the incumbent's activities.[120]

The fourth implication that can be drawn from this chapter is the need to acknowledge the varying local interactions and their impacts on societal perceptions of government. Throughout this chapter, I have shown the "general" patterns of state-societal interactions in pre-colonial, colonial, and post colonial civilian and military governments. I have also attempted to show the varying state-societal interactions that occur under the same political and economic structure, and demonstrate how they have different impacts on farmers' perceptions of different levels of authorities. For instance, I have shown the possibility of hostility between villagers and native leaders under the pre-colonial period, which the conventional understanding characterizes as dominated by sensitive and protective hereditary leaders. I have also shown farmers' relationships with the indigenous elite which went through various stages of transformation during the colonial periods.

During the later periods of military regime in Burma, pressure from the central authorities who not only had access to the use of force, but also

---

[120] Melford E. Spiro, *Anthropological Other or Burmese Brother* (New Brunswick: Transaction Publishers, 1992), 145-169.

had no scruple about using it, was immense enough to impair the village headmen's capacity to protect the interests of their communities. Peasants' ability to evade the demands of the state was also constrained by local-level networks of the state's multiple organizations that were all competing to extract resources from the agricultural producers. This definitely has weakened certain protective mechanisms that were once available to farmers under the pre-colonial state.

Given the fact that local officials are subject to frequent transfer, and that local headmen had relatively little autonomy and bargaining power vis-à-vis the state to protect the interests of their residents, the general pattern of state-societal interaction under the military regime bears a striking resemblance with the one under the colonial government. In other words, we are most likely to see local populations holding low regard for central authorities, local officials, and village headmen across Burma. Although the general depiction of the state-societal interaction under the Burmese military regime points to hostility at the grass-roots level, it does not reflect the significant cases that contradict the general pattern. It is necessary that we analyze the complex patterns of state-societal interaction that vary under the successive Burmese military regimes (the Revolutionary Council, 1962-74; the Burma Socialist Program Party, 1974-88; the State Law and Order Restoration Council, 1989-97; the State Peace and Development Council, 1997-present) to give us a better understanding of the roots of farmers' attitudes towards different levels of government authorities, and the existence of pockets of support for the military government.

In the next two chapters, I will address how different types of state-societal relationship have diverse impacts on societal perceptions of government authorities. Chapter three will look at relationships between rice farmers and various local agencies and departments that deal with agricultural issues. It will examine a host of factors that determines the degree of friendliness and hostility between local state authorities and Burmese cultivators. These varying local interactions provide a basis upon which farmers develop their attitudes toward central authorities. Chapter four treats local authorities as a unitary actor and examines the relationship between the popularity of the local government and that of the central government. It gives a detailed analysis of four different agricultural policies that have been implemented under the military regime, and examines various circumstances under which rural populations perceive the central and local authorities favorably and unfavorably.

Chapter 3
Local Administration: Understanding Divergences in Policies and Practices

Introduction

The Burmese military government is not a single entity. It has established a hierarchical chain of command, and has generally transmitted national policies through local state agencies and departments. Burmese rice farmers therefore deal with the various components of local state agencies and authorities on a regular basis, but the relationships between rice farmers and local authorities vary.

This chapter will analyze a number of institutional and organizational structures that influence the behaviour of local authorities and their relationships with rice farmers. First, I will give a brief description of the structure and organization of the current Burmese government as background to the environment in which the interaction between rural populations and local authority occurs. Second, I will examine a host of factors that determine the behaviour of local agricultural agents and government authorities, and affect their varying interactions with rice farmers. Third, I will analyse the problems inherent in agricultural implementation processes in Burma. Broadly speaking, I will look at the limitations arising from horizontal interdepartmental cooperation and the vertical gaps within the hierarchical line of the agricultural ministry.

The main purpose of this chapter is two-fold: to demonstrate the existence of varying local practices and to highlight cases of friendly interactions that contradict the general analysis of state-societal relationships in Burma's military state. I will show how the broader political and administrative environments within which the local civilian and military authorities operate constrain them to act in a manner that is not consistent with the collective welfare of rural society. This broad institutional milieu, however, fails to account for pockets of mutually beneficial relationships that defy the general depiction of hostile state-societal interactions in Burma. In particular, I will illustrate the Burmese rice farmers' conceptualization of what is meant by a "good village chairman" or "a good local government official," and their emphasis on responsive and sympathetic leaders in maintaining a good local governance structure. This chapter will analyse in some detail the actions of local authorities which not only have wide ranging consequences for their relationships with rice farmers, but also provide a foundation upon which farmers develop their particular attitudes toward the central authorities. For the Burmese cultivators' attitudes toward the central government are mainly determined by the practices of local authorities, which are manifested in their treatment of particular agricultural policies.

The structure and organization of the State Peace and Development Council (SPDC)

In Burma, political power is concentrated in the hands of the State Peace and Development Council (SPDC). The SPDC is dominated by a small group of senior military officers, and sits at the top of the power structure. A quite limited number of generals in Rangoon hold a monopoly over economic and political decision-making authority. There are no formal or informal procedures to provide checks and balances for this intensely concentrated nexus of power. The SPDC basically handles the security, political, and executive responsibilities of the government. The SPDC has also established and duplicated its subsidiary organizations from the capital down to the divisional, district, township, village tract, and village levels. The state and divisional Peace and Development Councils (PDCs), the township PDCs, the village tract PDCs, and the village PDCs are given political and economic discretion over their respective territories.[1]

Under the SPDC are several state ministries, departments, and agencies, with overlapping as well as separate jurisdictions over specific issue areas or programs. A typical ministry encompasses a number of related departments or directorates, each with its own field service. Their administrative hierarchies run parallel to the institution of government (SPDC).

The main responsibilities of the Peace and Development Councils (PDCs) at varying territorial and administrative levels are to enforce law and order, to pass on the directives of the central authorities to the subordinate organizations, and to coordinate activities among state

---

[1]Rural society, which forms the basic territorial and administrative unit in Burma, is referred to as "the village" in rural areas and the "ward" in urban areas. A number of villages/wards are grouped under a particular village tract/town, and a number of village tracts/towns are grouped to form townships. A number of townships and districts are then grouped into a state or division. There are seven states (Karen, Kayah, Shan, Mon, Rakhine, Chin, and Kachin), and seven divisions (Irrawady, Rangoon, Pegu, Mergui, Sagaing, Mandalay, Tenasserim).

departments and agencies. There are twelve regional military commanders, whose responsibilities include building infrastructure, developing industry and countering dissent. They are invested with administrative, political, and economic authority in each region alongside the performance of their military duties. All the regional commanders are chairmen of the state/divisional PDCs. They are the most senior military officers in their respective areas. This system operates almost like a "prefectoralism" where "the national government divides the country into areas and places a prefect in charge of each." [2] Here, a prefect represents the whole government, and supervises all specialized field agents under his jurisdiction. These military commanders, who are appointed by the central government, supervise and coordinate the activities of other ministries, departments, and state organizations in the same way as a prefect would supervise all specialized field agents under his area of responsibilities. Each national ministry and department has its function-based specialization, field staff of specialists, and duties to perform particular functions. However none of its subordinate organs can independently implement their policies without consulting and getting approval from the PDC at their parallel territorial levels.

Field Staff Ministries and Departments: The Ministry of Agriculture and Irrigation

Given that Burma is an agriculture-based country, the Ministry of Agriculture and Irrigation (MAI) has remained one of the most important ministries in Burma. The MAI has fourteen sub-divisional departments, all of which, except for the Minister's Office and Department of Agricultural Planning, have their own hierarchical organizations stretching from the centre down to the state and divisional, district, township, and village levels. They are: (1) the Minister's Office, (2) the Department of Agricultural Planning, (3) the Myanma Agriculture Service, (4) the Myanma Farm Enterprise, (5) the Myanma Cotton and Sericulture Enterprise, (6) the Myanma Sugarcane Enterprise, (7) the Myanma Jute Industries, (8) the Myanma Perennial Crops Enterprise, (9) the Irrigation Department, (10) the Water Resources Utilization Department, (11) the Settlement and Land Records Department, (12) the Agricultural Mechanization Department, (13) the Myanma Agricultural and Rural Development Bank, and (14) the Institute of Agriculture.

---

[2] James Fesler, "Centralization and Decentralization", International Encyclopedia of the Social Sciences, Vol. II, ed. David Sills (New York: MacMillan, 1968), 375.

The Myanma Agriculture Service (MAS) is the backbone of Burma's agriculture as a result of its role in extension works. There are approximately 8,881 officers and junior staff working for the Extension Department of the MAS, which employs a total of 13,098 officials and workers.[3] Like the SPDC in the capital, the MAS transmits orders and instructions through the central, state/divisional, district, township, village tract, and village managerial levels. The General Manager of the Agricultural Extension Division in Rangoon, who occupies the top administrative level of the Agricultural Extension Division, oversees the performances of the state and divisional managers, district managers, township managers, and village tract and village managers at their respective levels. A village extension manager oversees a few village tracts or a village with approximately 3,000 to 6,000 acres of cultivated land. A village tract extension manager (or worker) supervises the work of ten village extension managers who have direct communication with farmers.[4]

The primary duties of the Agricultural Extension Division at the township and village levels are to provide material (fertilizers, credits, seeds) and human support (extension agents), to educate farmers about new and modern technologies, to conduct demonstration farms, and to help implement and enforce government agricultural policies in the village. In fact, these lower administrative branches of the Ministry of Agriculture and Irrigation serve more as policy-implementing bodies than as policy- making or formulating bodies, as they seek to fulfill their assigned tasks and quotas. These include the acreage to be brought under monsoon and summer paddy fields, the paddy to be sold from each village or township, and the bags of chemical fertilizer to be distributed.

The Settlement and Land Records Department, on the other hand, is headed by the Director General in the capital, and assisted by a Deputy Director General in the Rangoon headquarters. Like other hierarchically structured departments, it carries out its duties through state/division, district, and township Settlement and Land Records Departments. A typical land record official at the village tract or village level institutes settlement work, collects agricultural statistics, assesses land revenue and land rent, registers deeds, and deals with other land administration duties.[5] The Irrigation Department, which has recently been incorporated into the Ministry of Agriculture, is also important in rural areas due to its role in

[3] *Information of Myanmar Agriculture: 1996*, 39.
[4] Ibid., 42-43.
[5] Ibid., 83.

water provision, maintenance, and quality control. The higher ranking irrigation officials, mostly civil engineers, supervise the construction of dams and irrigation facilities; they usually reside in the major towns and live temporarily in the construction sites. Junior irrigation officials are in charge of maintenance of the dams and irrigation networks and the timely provision of water to farmers. Headed and assisted by the Director General and the Deputy Director General, the Irrigation Department institutes new irrigation projects, deals with water-related issues, and passes down instructions through its subordinate branches at state and divisional, district, township, village tract, and village levels.

The Myanma Agricultural and Rural Development Bank (MARDB) serves as an instrument for rural savings and loan disbursement. It usually disburses its loans at the township level, either indirectly through farmers' representatives or directly through individual farmers. Although MARDB charges a very low interest rate (approximately 1.2 per cent per month), its loans cover only approximately ten percent of plantation and harvesting costs.[6] The procedures for obtaining a loan, and the amount allowed to individual farmers may vary from place to place. For instance, in some areas, eligibility for a loan is contingent on the output guaranteed by individual farmers. Farmers who pledge to produce 75-100 baskets per acre are favoured over those who produce less than 75 baskets per acre. Nonetheless, any loan hardly covers 15 per cent of production costs. Furthermore, the requirement to repay a loan immediately after harvest, and complicated bureaucratic red tape prevent many farmers from applying for a loan. For instance, in *Teik-Kyi* township, Rangoon Division, farmers must organize into a ten-member group, each headed by a designated leader. All group members are required to present themselves at the loan office on the assigned day; failure of even one member to show up will result in the delay of the loan. In addition, the group leader must guarantee the timely repayment of the loan by all his members and take responsibility for defaulting members.

A number of ministries, state departments and organizations share responsibilities with the Ministry of Agriculture and coordinate their activities with it. These include the Ministry of Forestry and the Ministry of Commerce. The Forestry department has become increasingly important in rural areas especially due to recent policy emphases on the reclamation of fallow and waste lands for agricultural expansion. The

---

[6] A monthly 1.2 per cent interest rate may be considered high from western industrialized countries' point of view, but it is relatively low given the fact that Burma has an annual inflation rate of approximately 50 per cent. In addition, a government loan is considered cheaper compared to private loan, which charges between 12-15 per cent per month.

main responsibilities of the Forestry Department include extension of reserved forest area, conservation of nature and wildlife sanctuaries, establishment of teak and other hardwood plantations, greening of the dry zone, planting of trees for industrial uses, and plantation for village wood lots and watersheds.[7] Like the Ministry of Agriculture, the Ministry of Forestry has branches and divisions at the state/divisional, district, township and village tract levels.

Myanma Agricultural Produce Trading (MAPT), one of the sub divisions of the Ministry of Commerce, procures crops, mainly paddy, from farmers through a network of buying depots in rural areas. MAPT and Myanma Export and Import Services (MEIS) are the two main state agencies with a near-monopoly over the buying and marketing of paddy in Burma. Before implementation of so-called "liberalization" policies in 1987, farmers had to sell as much as two third of their produce at below market prices to the Myanma Agriculture Produce Trading Corporation (currently the MAPT) and other state and cooperative enterprises. Since 1987, the military regime has reduced its rice procurement to twelve to thirteen baskets per acre (10-20 per cent of output per acre), and allowed private traders to engage in the internal marketing of rice. Rice export, however, remains a state monopoly.

Since 1988, the government has emphasized inter-departmental and inter-ministerial cooperation and coordination to implement agriculture policies. The Myanma Agriculture Service (MAS) cooperates with several other agencies under the Ministry of Agriculture and Irrigation (e.g. Land Records, Myanma Agriculture and Rural Development Bank, Irrigation department) or those from the Ministry of Forestry to implement specific agricultural policies. They are assisted, coordinated, or more accurately, headed by the Peace and Development Councils chairmen and secretaries at the respective territorial and administrative level.

With the exception of the chairmen and secretaries of the village tract and village PDCs, who are resident in the territory for which they are responsible, most civil servants and government officials are not native to the areas where they are assigned duties. Although some of them may stay in one place for lengthy periods, most are subject to transfer every two or three years. It is a common strategy of an authoritarian regime to regularly

[7] Forestry Department, "Country Profile for Forestry Sector Outlook in Myanmar" (Yangon: Ministry of Forestry, 1997), 4. Teak extraction, milling, and marketing are handled by a separate department, the Myanmar Timber Enterprise (MTE). Raymond Bryant, "The politics of forestry in Burma", in *The Politics of Environment in Southeast Asia: Resources and Resistance*, eds. Philip Hirsch and Carol Warren (London and New York: Routledge, 1998), 110.

rotate appointments in order to prevent state officials from becoming threatening centers of power.[8]

The Administrative and Territorial Aspects of Agricultural Policy Implementation

The Ministry of Agriculture			The SPDC
MAS	Irrigation Department	Land Record	PDCs
1. Director General	Director General	Director General	SPDC Chairman and Secretary
2. State/Divisional MAS State/Divisional Manager	Director	Director	State/Divisional PDC Chairman and Secretary Regional Commander
3. District MAS District Manager	Executive Engineer	Assistant Director	District PDC Chairman and Secretary
4. Township MAS Township Manager	Assistant Engineer Deputy Assistant Engineer	Head of Branch Deputy Head of Branch	Township PDC Chairman and Secretary
5. Village Tract MAS Village Tract Manager	Assistant Revenue Collector	Assistant Deputy Head of Branch	Village Tract PDC Chairman and Secretary
6. Village MAS Village Manager	Irrigation Bin Watcher	Land Record Clerk	Village PDC Chairman and Secretary

A sketch of the local military and civilian authorities

The local authorities in Burma include the PDC ruling officials as well as civilian field staff and administrative officers, who occupy positions at the district/township levels and below. While some of the chairmen and secretaries of the district/township PDC are military and police officers, others are former civilian officials with professional backgrounds in economics, management, and public administration. Almost all the village tract and village PDC authorities are civilians, and reside permanently in the villages where they are assigned responsibilities. Indeed, the overwhelming majority of government officials outside the PDC are civilians, although their respective national ministries and departments in

---

[8] See for example, Joel Migdal, *State in Society: Studying How States and Societies Transform and Constitute One Another* (Cambridge: Cambridge University Press, 2000), 71-84.

the capital tend to be headed by military generals or commanders. These local officials are centrally appointed and most of them are not native of the areas they represent. [9]

Thus generally speaking, Burmese cultivators have to deal with two different types of authorities on a daily basis: native leaders (village and village tract chairmen) and centrally appointed officials from outside the district. It should be noted here that the native leaders themselves are part of the government structure since they serve as members of the village tract and village PDC, the lowest administrative rung of government. Unlike the Philippines, India, and most Latin American countries, rural Burma has a relatively equal distribution of income due to land nationalization and redistribution by civilian (1948-1962) and military governments (1962-present). Burma has very few local "strongmen" (such as large landowners, money lenders, traders) who have accumulated sufficient power and wealth to compete with the state for control over human and material resources.

Chart on distribution of Land Holding

Size of land holding	Percent of peasant families	Percent of acreage
Under 5 acres	61.8 (2,7444,000)	26.7 (6,530, 000 acres)
5 to 10 acres	24.9 (1,105,000)	31.8 (7,791, 000 acres)
10 to 20 acres	11.0 (490,000)	27.5 (6,732, 000 acres)
20 to 50 acres	2.2 (100,000)	11.1 (2,720,000 acres)
50 to 100 acres	0.04 (2000)	0.4 (97,000 acres)
100 acres and above	0.02 (1000)	2.5 (608,000 acres)
Total	100 (4,442,000)	100 (24,478,000 acres)

Source: Young, Cramer, and Wailes, *An Economic Assessment of Myanmar Rice Sector*, 61.

The Township and Village PDCs

The PDC secretaries and chairmen at the state/divisional and township levels are appointed by the central government or by their immediate superiors. Those at the village tract and village levels, however, are handpicked by the township PDC chairmen or elected by their village community members. The tenure of a village tract or village headman varies depending on his popularity within the village as well as outside it. The appointment of a village chairman may be based on family

---

[9] Non-native authorities are those who were not born or raised in the areas they are assigned responsibilities. Native authorities are those who were born and raised in the areas they work.

connection or simply on merit. It is also based on his reputation as a fair, honest, and sensitive individual (if elected by his village), and on his economic status (if appointed by the township authorities). The chairman or secretary of the township PDC can demote or dismiss him if they dislike him. However, he is not subject to transfer as are other local government officials.

Rural residents are sometimes given the choice to select their own village headman (formally referred to as a chairman of the village PDC), especially if a newly appointed chairman or secretary of the district/township PDC lacks knowledge of local conditions and shows no particular preference. In the past, officials encouraged local people to replace an unpopular or corrupt leader who had been appointed previously by township authorities. Theoretically, a village chairman serves not only as a local leader, but also as the agent of the national government by occupying the lowest rung of the political and administrative system. Such leaders are regarded as administrators rather than decision makers. Their main task is to enforce the policies formulated by the central governing apparatus. They work cooperatively with other governmental agencies and ministries at the township and village levels, and report to the township or district PDCs.

A village chairman (or headman) may also run for election to become chairman, secretary, or member of a village tract PDC, the next highest local authority. Here, voters are drawn from the village chairmen of the surrounding villages, but their decision can be overruled by the township PDC chairman. The selection process and tenure of the village tract chairman and secretary vary from village to village. Some are handpicked by the township and district PDC authorities, others are voted into office by their peers; the choice depends on the preferences of the township authorities.

The village tract or village chairmen, who occupy the lowest rung of the PDC security, political, and administrative structure are the most hard-pressed authorities in the system. They are trapped between protecting the needs of the local population and fulfilling the demands of central and local governments. The pressure and workload involved in administering village communities can be extensive and overwhelming. Most potential leaders avoid the task of village government, except for those who see it as an opportunity for self-advancement and the accumulation of personal wealth. Of those leaders who are motivated to improve their local situations and serve their communities, most quit office when they can no longer handle unrealistic demands from the center, or harsh treatment from the political authorities in town.[10]

Consequently, while some of the village and village tract headmen assume their duties voluntarily, others have been forced into the job by their superiors at township level.

The preferences of the township PDCs and local farmers over the selection of village chairmen do not always coincide. Farmers want a chairman who represents and protects their interests, whereas the township and divisional PDC authorities prefer those who carry out central and regional orders without bending them. In fact, neither the village leaders who were overly protective of their communities nor those who tried to please their superiors at the expense of the local community remained long in office. They either left voluntarily or were fired because of their inability to manage heavy workloads. Very rarely, a village leader serves the role as mediator between his villagers and his superiors in town. This situation occurs where the village chairman is highly respected by both sides, due either to his status or his reputation as a fair individual, or to the personal relationship he enjoys with his township superior.

In one village in *Alei* township, *Sagaing* Division, for instance, a village chairman, *U Khant,* was able to work cooperatively with the chairman of the township PDC in favour of his local constituency due to his special personal relationship with the township chairman. The political environment was also important in shaping their unusual relationship. *U Khant* was elected by village residents following the 1988 students' pro-democracy demonstration in Rangoon. During this period, the military government tried very hard to improve its image by softening its grip on rural populations. Simply put, demands from the capital were more flexible and less coercive than usual. *U Khant* was presented with exceptional opportunities to openly consult and negotiate with an already accomodating chairman on the difficulties faced by farmers. This situation led to more lenient policies at the village level. *U Khant* quit his job, however, after the township chairman was transferred to another township.

A second example tells a similar story. In village in *Auk* township, Rangoon Division, village tract chairman, *U Kaung,* was popular with both the villagers and the township PDC authorities due to his status as a farming celebrity and his reputation as an even-handed and honest leader.

---

[10] This is different from the situation under the civilian government in the 1950s where there were election campaigns by serious contenders for a new headman position. See Melford Spiro, "Factionalism and politics in village Burma", in *Anthropological Other or Burmese Brother?* (New Brunswick: Transaction Publishers, 1992), 145-169.

An officially honoured model farmer, this sixty-eight-year old leader achieved fame as the inventor of *shwe-ta-soke* paddy (high yielding rice) in the late 1970s. He was awarded a gold medal for his discovery and multiplication of *shwe-ta-soke* seeds. Most villagers agreed that he never took bribes, was very disciplined and conscientiously enforced those agricultural practices which he considered beneficial to farmers in the long run.

U Kaung and his family knew many high ranking agricultural and military officials, including the Deputy Minister of Agriculture and Irrigation. The latter always stopped by *U Kaung*'s house whenever he visited his own farm near the chairman's village, bringing snacks, food, and gifts for the family. *U Kaung* said that he could discuss a wide variety of issues frankly and openly with the deputy minister.

U Kaung is one of the few elite farmers to establish a positive relationship with the military government. He has lived to see the ups and downs of individual ministers of agriculture and their staffs. He recalled how the current Managing Director of the Myanma Agriculture Service, U Tun Than, was once simply a "clerk" (in fact a junior officer), who carried suitcases and bags for his superiors when the agricultural team toured the chairman's village in the 1970s. *U Kaung* remarked that both U Tun Than and Dr. Mya Maung, the former Director General at the Department of Agricultural Planning, were "almost nothing back then."

A typical village chairman is a "generalist administrator" and is not paid a salary. He deals with local administrative matters, such as enforcing law and order, settling civil disputes, and keeping records of visitors from town or other villages. He also implements, monitors, and enforces distributive, regulative, and extractive policies assigned by his township PDC superiors and by government officials from other specialized agencies and ministries. Consequently, a village chairman spends most of his time on village administration, leaving personal business matters to family members. More often than not, it is beyond his capacity to perform the tasks expected of him, considering the fact that he is also a full-time farmer, and is not paid a salary. In addition, he is reprimanded, intimidated, and even imprisoned by the township authorities if he fails to implement and enforce policies. On one occasion, a secretary of one district PDC in Upper Burma threatened to arrest the village PDC chairmen for failing to take action against what he defined as "illegal" fishing. Many villagers recalled how the district secretary used phrases such as "I'll beat you up" or "I'll shoot you" to the chairmen. Villagers were not happy that their headmen dared not even "*maw kyii*" or look straight into the eyes of the township and district officials when they talked to them.[11]

The Burmese consider it is impolite for guests to leave the host's house without being served food or drink. One of the reasons why most able and qualified people refuse to become village chairmen is the financial burden involved in hosting officials from town. Obviously, serving urban guests with high socio-economic and political status places more financial strain on the host than serving ordinary village folk. It can easily lead to economic disaster if a headman is faced with up to five visits by at least five local officials from town per week. This does not include hosting hordes of local officials touring the village for national holidays, religious festivals, or promotional and propaganda purposes.

The wife of the chairman of *Taung* village tract in Rangoon Division, which was chosen as the first experimental site for high-yielding varieties (HYV) of rice in the late 1970s, remembered the constant flow of visitors to her house during the promotion. Visitors included high-ranking agriculture officials; central, regional, and local socialist party and council members; tourists, and scholars. Every day at least four cars visited and much of the chairman's income was spent on feeding and providing shelter for these 'VIP'. His family members prepared three meals a day for some visitors, and they always served the best food they had.

A former village chairman from the "socialist period" (1974-1988) also recalled that he raised hundreds of chickens and ducks just to feed the party, council, and agriculture officials from town, but these were never enough. The daughter of a former village tract chairman in an Upper Burma village also complained that such officials "devoured the food served to them like they had not eaten for days," and "left nothing but dirty plates whenever they visited" her house. I have seen officials demand certain kinds of food and drink during their visits to my host, who was a village tract chairman. To make matters worse, they concentrated their visits solely on the chairman's house, placing severe financial stress on a family that relied on paddy cultivation as its main source of income.

Although they are not paid a salary, there are many ways in which village chairmen can get reimbursed, depending on the local economy. A headman may earn money from imposing fines on law breakers, charging fees on land contracts, and on visitors' registration.[12] He can supplement his income by taking bribes from villagers in return for covering up their

---

[11] Accounts provided by farmers in *Sagaing* Division, March 1999.

[12] According to the existing law, all the visitors must inform their visit and duration of stay to the respective chairman of the village PDC.

"illegal" activities from the authorities (such as under-reporting cultivated acreage when selling the procurement quota). He can also recover expenses by passing on the costs to villagers, and get subsidized consumer products or agricultural implements and input with permission from the township authorities.[13]

But a chairman who takes excessive bribes, extorts too much, or makes corrupt judgments runs the risk of notoriety. He is coercive and relentless in imposing his own demands as well as those from above, and shows no sympathy for his villagers' plight. He embezzles local administrative and religious funds, and exempts farmers from the compulsory procurement quota not because they are financially inept, but because he has been paid to conceal or underreport their total cultivated acreage or yield.

A village tract chairman who exemplifies the "worst case scenario" from the farmers' perspectives is *U Pyet Cee*, who served as chairman of *Atek* village tract in *Sagaing* Division from 1996 until 1998. He was later found guilty of permitting a rice mill to operate during a prohibition period and was fired by the district PDC chairman (he was on good terms with the township PDC chairman).[14] During his tenure, villagers accused him of keeping part of the money donated for the funeral ceremony of the village abbot. *U Pyet Cee* exempted *Daw Waa Kyi*, one of the wealthiest farmers in the village, from selling procurement quota to the government because he owed her money. On the other hand, he reimbursed *Bo Kyi*, an eighty-six-year-old farmer, only one bag of chemical fertilizer, whereas *Bo Kyi* had paid for two bags.

Members of the village tract PDC also complained that *U Pyet Cee* failed to share money earned from fines, such as were levied against perpetrators of domestic violence and theft. Such fines must be shared equally among members of the village tract PDC. Although the chairman collected money from villagers to buy toddy trees from the monastery compound to build a bridge on the main street, he never paid the abbot, who owned of the trees. He was also hated for his relentless imposition of "*tamoe na thee*" or "double cropping in the monsoon," which farmers considered unprofitable at best, and a disaster at worst. He strictly supervised the recommended paddy planting methods, and ordered replanting of paddy that he considered substandard. He was said to live

---

[13] In a more remote or lower profile village, such opportunities were rare or non-existent.

[14] The government usually prohibits all rice mills, except for government owned, from operating immediately following paddy harvest. This is to make sure that all farmers sell their quota to the government before they sell to private merchants. Closing rice mills will deprive farmers of their chance to mill the paddy, and then sell to merchants at higher prices.

like "a king" during his tenure and had a "lavish" life style. He and his family were said to have dined on stir-fried noodles, a luxurious diet for Burmese farmers, bought large quantities of soda cans, hired a cook, and bought at least sixteen pairs of slippers for his daughter. And he asked his cousin to watch over the irrigation tank, and to release water to whomever offered a bribe.

Having said all this, it must be noted that this same corrupt chairman, vehemently disliked by his villagers, may be perceived very differently by the township authorities if they believe he performs his duties well.[15] They may in fact regard him as 'a go-getter,' 'efficient' leader to be praised for his relentless enforcement of unpopular policies, regardless of his insensitivity to their impact on his village's welfare and economy.

In total contrast, the more sympathetic or popular chairman acts very differently. While he informs his village about the prohibition on stealing water from the irrigation tank, at the same time, he warns his water-starved farmers to watch their step and beware of surprise-checks from the urban authorities. He is, to some degree, outspoken and is not afraid to reveal the plight of his fellow villagers to the authorities. He may sometimes "forget" to summon villagers to deliver their labour or financial contribution toward the construction of roads, bridges, or irrigation network, and he may fail to fulfill the quota requirement of his village. Not surprisingly, he is well-liked by his people.

A popular village headman need not always be moral, ethical, or honest. Sometimes his popularity within the village is based upon his deviant, defiant, and heroic behavior toward the authorities, even though this may be detrimental to the local economy in the long run. For example, he fails to enforce the "string-row transplanting method," which is time consuming, yet returns higher yields. He fails to mobilize villagers to contribute their labour for road and bridge construction, because he is too nice, too busy, too lazy, or too flexible to take action against them.

The grouping of several villages under one village tract often leads to problems of coordination and cooperation among the village chairmen. It is quite common for members of the tract administration (all of whom are headmen of their respective villages) to disagree over many issues, as they come from various backgrounds and hold different values and interests. Some are farmers, while others are military veterans or retired

---

[15] I say this because a village headman may be unpopular from the perspectives of both his villagers and his township superiors, when he not only exploits his village members but also is unable to enforce policies handed down by his superiors.

government employees. Whereas some are timid and easily intimidated by the township authorities, others are bold and outspoken.

Many village chairmen are caught between the excessive demands of the township authorities and the inability or refusal of farmers to comply. The only way to improve, if not escape, this situation is to establish amicable relationships with the authorities. Most of the time, however, tract and village chairmen are not that fortunate. The reality is that most officials are unwilling to acknowledge local difficulties or are simply ignorant of them. They are soldiers with a sense of loyalty and commitment only to the central government, partly because of their military training and partly because they see themselves as the ruling elite who have different interests and values from the majority peasant population. After all, these officials have very little social and personal connection with the communities in which they live.

It is difficult to systematically explain the causes of a wide spectrum of interactions between peasants and village leaders based on the limited cases available for analysis. Thus far, I propose two explanations for the kind of relationships observed, which are critical and conceptual rather than empirical. First, a village headman with higher socioeconomic status is less inclined to extort from villagers and to embezzle public money. He is more likely to develop an amicable relationship with his people. In fact, this is one of the main reasons why township authorities deliberately seek out better-off farmers to serve as village chairmen. In her study of *Layaintan* village in the Irrawaddy delta, Tin Thet Sann noted that "normally a chairman is a *well-to-do man* who is familiar with the history of the village and has an interest in the affairs of the villagers and in the solutions of problems, which might occur.... The chairman does not get salaries, but it is regarded as an honour to have this position."[16]

Two implications can be drawn from Tin Thet Sann's statement. First, a well-to-do-man has clearly prospered in his village setting and thus has fewer reasons to be corrupt. For instance, U Kaung and U Pwa Lay from Auk township, Rangoon Division, and U Khant from Alei township, Sagaing Division are well-off farmers who owned goods such as television sets and small tractors. They were all on relatively good terms with their residents. The corrupt U Pyet Cee from Alei township, Sagaing Division, on the other hand, was extremely poor, and did not even have a stable job. Secondly, because of their higher social and

---

[16] Naw Tin Thet Sann, "Life conditions of the rural population in the Ayeyarwady-Delta/Myanmar: Disadvantages and Remedies", English version of the thesis submitted to the Institute fur Regional Wissenschaft, Universitat karlsruhe for Postgraduate Degree of Licentiata in Regional Science, 23. Emphasis added.

economic status, the better-off farmers not only have more time to volunteer their services for the public good, but because of their better educational background, they also tend to possess leadership skills and a sense of public duty.

The second factor that influences the relationship between village headmen and farmers is the headmen's occupational status. Farmers commented that village chairmen who engaged in farming while in office were more likely to be sensitive to fellow farmers' problems and thus protective of them. For instance, while *U Kaung, U Pwa Lay, and U Khant* were farmers, *U Pyet Cee* had never owned land or worked on a farm. Admittedly, there are well-off headmen who are corrupt, and non-farmer leaders who are sensitive and sympathetic. A farmer from *Pegu* division, for instance, concluded that "most village leaders, whether they are farmers or non-farmers, are corrupt. First of all, it may be hard for them to speak out against outside authorities. Secondly, they got money from local authorities when they helped them implement unpopular policies."[17] Another farmer from Rangoon division at one point said that, "farmers with education tend to be even-handed," and yet at another point remarked that, "farmers with education are more corrupt, because they know how to manipulate the system for their own benefits."[18]

Agricultural Extension Workers and Their Relations with Rice Farmers
Newly appointed village tract and village agricultural managers at the township Myanma Agriculture Service (MAS or Township Extension Division) are typically holders of bachelor's degrees and diplomas in agriculture or graduates of agricultural high schools. The lowest starting position in the MAS, regardless of qualifications, is that of Assistant Deputy Head of Branch. Graduates begin their service as a village or village tract agricultural manager of a particular township. The activities of these extension workers are village-based and oriented toward practical field work.

The starting salary for an Assistant Deputy Head of Branch, also known as a village agricultural manager, is 950 kyat per month. He or she is also entitled to a benefit package containing twelve *pyi* of rice, and 100-250 kyat travel expenses (1999 data). The basic salary covers only eight meals for an ordinary Burmese citizen. The highest salary one can earn as a township manager is 1,500 to 2,000 kyat per month.

---

[17] Conversation with a farmer from *Pegu* division, December, 2002.
[18] Conversation with a farmer from Rangoon division, December, 2002.

Most township and village agricultural officials supplement their income by selling government subsidized chemical fertilizers, gasoline, and pesticides in the private market, products originally intended for distribution to farmers. Such activities drive up the prices of fertilizers and create shortages of subsidized agricultural input in the government's inventory. Junior agriculture officers may also over-report expenditures for visits by high-ranking officers from Rangoon. These expenses may include renting tables and chairs, buying food and drinks, and items such as towels. Although some of these items are provided free, either by private individuals or the public purse, agricultural extension workers often included them as part of their spending and submit these costs to the township office for compensation. The third major source of their supplementary income comes from taking bribes from farmers who want (or perhaps do not want) to be placed in a specific agricultural program. Their fourth and largest source of income derives from large agricultural experimentation projects (such as onions-growing), which involve managing huge sums of public money.

Workers with a bachelor's degree in agriculture can expect to be promoted to Deputy Head of Branch one year after beginning service, but promotion takes longer for those with lesser qualifications. The bachelor's degree is taken in the Institute of Agriculture in *Yezin, Pyin MaNarr* township, the only agricultural institute in Burma. Students attend the institute for five years after graduating from high school. Those seeking the three-year diploma of agriculture, on the other hand, attend one of the agriculture colleges located in many of Burma's major cities after graduating from high school. Others study for a diploma from one of Burma's many agricultural high schools for three years after graduating from eighth grade.

These extension workers are supervised by their township manager from the township MAS Extension Division. These managers, who are supervised by staff from the Myanma Agriculture Service at the central and state/divisional levels, cooperates with officials holding similar positions from other departments. These include township irrigation officers (Assistant Engineers), township land record officials (Head of Branch), and township PDC chairmen and secretaries.

The duties of agricultural extension workers include (1) implementing and monitoring agriculture projects and plans, (2) providing technical and professional assistance with tillage, and the use of pesticides and fertilizers, (3) collecting and summarizing economic census data in their area, and (4) organizing meetings to discuss farmers' problems.

Another responsibility, which strictly lies outside their professional realm yet proves very time-consuming and exhausting, involves arranging for the visits of high-ranking officials from the central, state/divisional, or district MAS and PDC. During the summer of 1999, for instance, at least five or six official visits were made to *Alei* township, *Sagaing* Division by the divisional agricultural manager, the chairman of the divisional PDC, and the managing director of the MAS in Rangoon. The extension camps near the township's main street are more likely to be visited by authorities than camps in the hinterland, and are more attractively constructed and decorated. During these official visits, junior officers would load piles of gifts into their guests' cars in expectation of future promotion or favours.

One task that must be carried by local agricultural officers prior to these official visits is to clean the billboards that decorate many rice farms, and clear away any obscuring foliage. These billboards are painted in white and green, the official colours of the MAS. Those rice farmers, whose properties lie along the main highways, come under pressure to produce high-yielding crops, and to practice officially recommended growing methods. These model farms were prime sites for the green MAS billboards. Rice farmers commented that agricultural extension workers were so keen to claim the credit for the accomplishments of local farmers that they would place billboards in any particularly green and attractive rice-fields in their area, the implication being that the farms looked so good because they had been groomed by the MAS. Rice farmers joked, "if the agricultural officials could, they would even put billboards on school teachers who wear green *longyi* (skirt) uniforms"!!

Needless to say, life as an extension manager is by no means predictable. Although extension workers in high-yield areas do not work full time, they can be called upon by their superiors at any time of the day, and any day of the week. They often have to travel to their office in town or even to Rangoon headquarters for emergency meetings, and find it difficult to plan their schedule ahead of time.

I found that very few extension workers visited paddy fields or gave professional and technical advice to farmers. Specifically, agricultural officials with bachelor's degrees have less interaction with farmers than those with the high school or 3-year-college diploma. This could be attributed to differences in curriculum: whereas the Institute of Agriculture is theoretically oriented, the other institutions emphasize technical and practical training in the fields. In addition, most graduates of the Institute come from urban middle-class families, and are more interested in career advancement and advanced study, than their less highly-trained counterparts.[19] They tend to consider themselves more as academics or members of the intelligentsia than as agricultural extension workers. The socio-economic gap between these elite graduates and farmers is wide, often resulting in misunderstanding and lack of communication. The graduates of the three-year- colleges and agriculture high schools, on the other hand, come from rural families, and their parents are mostly farmers and agricultural workers. They are more likely to identify themselves with farmers, and put their efforts into improving their relationships with cultivators rather than in exploring better career opportunities, which are usually beyond their reach anyway.

Let us take the example of *U Pein*, an extension worker and a graduate of a three-year-college. He preferred visiting farmers' rice-fields, and having heart-to-heart chats with them, to routine administrative work, such as record- keeping, attending meetings, and preparing for official visits. There seemed to be a deep understanding and mutual respect between *U Pein* and farmers under his supervision. *U Pein,* who has worked as an extension worker since the 1970s in one township in Lower Burma was also knowledgeable about farming practices, including the use of various cultivation methods for different types of soil. Such skills were in short supply among the staff with the bachelor's degree in *Alei* township, *Sagaing* Division. Similarly, *U Pein's* colleague, *Daw Sein*, who has a diploma in agriculture, made her home in the quarters attached to the extension camp, along with other daily agricultural workers. Like *U Pein*, she seemed to have connected well with local farmers, and they treated her with respect. Most bachelor's degree- holders were loathe to live in the village, and tended to reside in town.

Agricultural extension agents, especially degree-holders and non-local, enjoy the least power and prestige of any government employee in Burmese villages. Many farmers do not take these agricultural managers seriously, and they appear to lack professional and technical credibility as well as the means to enforce official agricultural policies. In rural provinces, the MAS thus has to rely on the township and district ruling authorities or even the local police to implement these policies. The inability of the MAS to provide sufficient assistance and the failure of extension workers to make regular visits to the rice-fields undermine the credibility of the MAS among rural residents.

---

[19] Approximately two hundred fifty students graduate each year from the Institute of Agriculture, which has recently been incorporated under the Ministry of Agriculture and Irrigation. The Institute ranks sixth in terms of the average grade earned by high school graduate students who enter universities and college each year. The Agricultural Institute is comparable to one of the top ten universities in the United States.

Farmers are convinced that junior agricultural officers, particularly the Institute graduates, have learned nothing but theory inside their brick-walled schools, and have nothing to teach farmers who have worked the land all their lives. Cultivators also complain about the lack of communication between themselves and the extension workers, who only go to the village chairman's house to discuss agricultural issues. U Kyi Win, a senior official at the Ministry of Agriculture, observed that "young and inexperienced, most of them were not happy with the uncomfortable life of the village. As they gained experience, they tried to move to urban areas. They realized that conditions prevailing at the Institute differed from those in the field."[20]

In addition, farmers were exasperated by the fact that extension workers visited their village (specifically the village chairman's house), only at the beginning of the cultivating season to ensure that project targets would be fully achieved. Cultivators felt the extension agents deserted them as soon as the latter achieved their project goals. They were more concerned with achieving their planned targets than with farmers' problems, such as lack of water and control of pest and plant diseases.

The following dialogue is based on my personal observation during an economic census conducted by a group of extension workers (assisted by the village tract PDC clerk and a volunteer from the government sponsored Union of Solidarity and Development Association, USDA) in *Alei* township in Upper Burma. [21]

> Extension worker..........."How many bicycles do you have?"
> Farmer's daughter......."Only one and it has only the front wheel. The back wheel is broken" (Laughter) (Of course, I knew they had at least three bicycles in good condition). The two young, inexperienced, female agriculture extension workers felt a little uneasy and their faces started to turn red.
> Extension worker...... "What was your average yield from *ta-moe-na-thee* (double-paddy- cropping in the monsoon)."?
> Village Tract PDC clerk.....Maybe we shouldn't bother asking them this question because they would definitely say the policy on *ta-moe-na-thee* was a failure."[22]

[20] Khin Win, *A Century of Rice Improvement in Burma*, (Manila, Philippines: IRRI, 1994), 84.

[21] The USDA is a government sponsored "social" organization, and it is currently the only legitimate political organization in the country which has taken a leading role in all high profile social, religious, cultural and political activities.

[22] This unpopular policy was introduced in 1998 in *Alei* township, where farmers were forced to plant two rice crops in one monsoon period. It was a failure due to intense cropping methods and lack of water in the region.

Farmer's daughter in-law.... Hey!!! that's the truth.....Let the truth be known!!

Village Tract PDC clerk.......*Ta-moe-na-thee* was a success!!!

Extension worker........Do you have a tractor?

Farmer's daughter......One, of course, in order to keep up with your intensive and unrealistic planning. With your fast-track schedule, the tractor did not till the soil adequately for broadcasting. We would have been even further behind if we'd used draught cattle.

Extension worker.....How many bags of fertilizer did you apply per acre?

Farmer's daughter......Three bags per acre.....Hey, but you guys didn't sell us enough fertilizer!

Village Tract PDC clerk.....Yes, we did!!! You just didn't come and buy from us.

Farmer's daughter........Please don't take my comments personally. We were always afraid to express our real feelings at the village meeting because the military and police were there.

Village Tract PDC clerk......We're going to provide you guys with enough water for summer paddies.

Farmer's daughter......No way!! We heard that the tank is already running out of water, and there will only be two more fill-up rounds!

Village Tract PDC clerk......The reason the tank is running out of water is that some people refused to cultivate the summer paddy we recommended IR 747, which uses less water. Instead, they planted long-maturing paddies such as *Manaw Thukha* which use more water.

Although the debate created hostile confrontation, there were jokes and bursts of laughter. The two female extension workers, degree-holders who had worked for the MAS extension services for two years, were rather quiet and interacted little with the host family. The conversation mainly took place between the PDC clerk and family members. The clerk, who was born and raised in the area, and worked for the village tract for a number of years, knew the size of land and types of property owned by each family. He did not record the deflated figures given by the family, but nor did he write down the actual statistics known to him. He skilfully made the necessary adjustment and recorded figures averaged out between the two sets of data. If the host told him they had only one bicycle and he knew they had three, the clerk recorded two.

PDC clerk..........What was your average yield per acre?

Farmer's daughter..... One hundred baskets from three acres of land.

PDC clerk.......No, I heard it was three hundred baskets from three acres land.

The clerk then asked the USDA volunteer to record sixty baskets per acre in the questionnaire. Before the survey team left to visit the neighboring family, the clerk confessed to the first family how he had been forced to pond an acre of his land as he too had had a bad harvest from *ta-moe-na-thee*. While the team were moving between the two houses, the farmer's daughter yelled across to her neighbour: "Hey!! don't tell them the truth!! Under-report your property and income."

The next farmer repeated similar responses, but more politely. She said she had ten acres of land when she actually had twenty. She also said she had a radio, but it was broken, seemingly oblivious to the strains of a classical Burmese song playing softly in the background. This did not seem to bother the survey team either.

Although this episode demonstrates a fundamental (if good-humoured) lack of respect by farmers for agriculture extension workers and the MAS, it is unclear to what extent it represents the larger pattern of relations between agricultural officials and farmers in rural Burma.[23] However, in contrast to their counterparts in *Alei* township in Upper Burma, farmers from *Auk* township, Rangoon Division were more likely to cooperate with government ministries and departments. One farmer from *Auk* was surprised that farmers in the dry zone tried to conceal their actual land-holding and yield. Living about forty miles north of Rangoon, and participants at the first experimental site for high-yielding rice varieties, farmers in *Auk* township said they were used to being observed, studied, and interviewed by foreigners as well as by Burmese scholars.

In fact, most of the time, agriculture extension workers "monitored" the projects they were involved in by delegating responsibility to local village headman without inspecting the fields themselves. They tended to accept the village chairman's words at face value, partly out of fear of reprisal by farmers who dislike close monitoring by officialdom, and partly because of their lack of commitment to the rural population. Yet agricultural workers are harshly criticized by their superiors if their projects fail and the expected yields are not achieved. Fear of criticism, transfer or dismissal causes many lower officials to report inflated data, in

---

[23] The survey was conducted in the first and second weeks of March 1999, and organized by the Ministry of Agriculture and Irrigation. Although the survey was supposed to be based on random sampling, the extension workers who knew nothing about the people and geography under which they were assigned responsibilities, followed the lead of the village PDC clerk, who took them to better-off farmers' homes. The questionnaires were fifteen pages long, ranging from educational level, personal property (tractor, television, radio, bicycle), average yield per acre, to usage of fertilizers.

terms of both achieving yields and acreage, or in their success in persuading farmers to practice recommended farming methods.

As a result of all these factors, there is a lack of understanding and communication among agriculture officials all along the hierarchical structure of the Ministry of Agriculture. For instance, divisional officers regularly refuse to acknowledge reports of failed crops or projects submitted by township or village officials. Likewise, headquarters staff in Rangoon want to read nothing but rosy news in the divisional and district agricultural reports. This leads to widespread inflation of performance figures in the agricultural sector. This in turn opens up an information gap between senior officials in the city and the lower-ranking officials in the provincial areas. Such a problem, however, is not unique to Burma. In 1972, Philip M. Raup described the limitations of agricultural development programs in Third World countries as follows: "There are few local signal stations to pass information up the channel of command when agricultural development programs are going badly......Hierarchies of control exist, but they were designed primarily to pass orders down, not to transmit grassroots information up."[24]

Obviously, farmers interact with many organizations in addition to the Myanma Agriculture Service. They must also deal with several other agencies under the Ministry of Agriculture and Irrigation, and other bodies (such as Ministry of Trade). Lack of time and access prevented me from exploring the impact of these other ministries and departments. However I will attempt to shed some light on farmers' interactions with other agricultural agencies by looking at how summer paddy programs are implemented in Upper Burma. Careful analysis of interdepartmental cooperation and the rigid hierarchical nature of the policy implementation process will reveal some problems inherent in the organizational structure of the military state.

The Horizontal Bases of Interdepartmental Conflicts
In implementing the summer paddy program, a number of agencies and departments at the township levels (i.e. the Irrigation Department, the MAS, the PDC, and the Land Record Department) are required to cooperate in realising state goals in terms of tasks and quotas, and in reassigning and finalizing these targets for each village and village tract. Those agencies operating at the local level, on the other hand, must

---

[24] Philip M. Raup, "Some interrelationships between Public Administration and Agricultural Development", in *Political Economy of Development,* ed. Charles Wilber (New York: Random House, 1988).

cooperate to carry out the tasks assigned by their respective township superiors. These local government authorities are assigned different responsibilities based on their area of expertise. The land record officials, who are familiar not only with the actual holdings of individual farmers but also the types and conditions of soil in each farm, are required to submit profiles on farmers who will be placed under each planned project. Their reports include the location of the farm (including its proximity to the irrigation tanks), soil-type, and size of land holding. With their detailed knowledge of the irrigation system, irrigation officials at the village levels are put in charge of water provision (i.e. turning the stopcock on and off on assigned days) and maintenance. At the township level, irrigation officers determine the numbers of farming households and the acreage eligible for water provision.

The chairmen of the village and village tract PDCs, on the other hand, are responsible for enforcing agricultural policies by exhorting, pressuring, or intimidating community members into meeting their household's agreed quota. In addition, they must organize residents to provide labour or financial contributions to the irrigation department or the agriculture department or the township PDC. The PDC authorities assist them with fining and imprisoning those who fail to comply with state orders. These same PDC authorities also oversee interdepartmental cooperation and draw up plans based on input from their civilian technocratic counterparts. Last but not least, agricultural officers provide support services, visiting the villages to encourage farmers to adopt modern technologies. They also cooperate with village and village tract headmen to implement specific rural policies and to assign quotas and tasks to individual household.

Horizontal conflicts--divisions between various ministries, departments, and other organizations involved--- emerged at specific territorial levels from the implementation of agricultural policies, requiring coordination among technocrats, civil servants, and officials from different departments and agencies. This situation created conflicts and disagreements among the agencies involved, and resulted in bureaucratic infighting as well as inertia due to the different goals and loyalties held by each department.

In the first place, the various departments concerned with agricultural production collect different data on acres cultivated, average output per acre, and total crop production depending on their particular interests. Generally speaking, agricultural officials have a tendency to inflate production figures, claiming credit for increases in yield and total cultivated acres and for transforming antiquated cultivation methods into modern and scientific ones. Similarly, irrigation officials are more likely to over-report cultivated acreage, attributing the increase to their efforts in expanding the irrigation network. Land record officials, on the other hand, with their accurate knowledge of land holdings tend to underestimate the extent of land owned or under cultivation in order to take a cut from the profits of unreported holdings and cultivations.[25]

Because the primary responsibilities of the Myanma Agriculture Service and the Irrigation Department are to promote higher yield, and increase the extent of land under cultivation, local agricultural and irrigation officials are under constant pressure to exaggerate their performance in order to impress their superiors. The land record officials' job is simply to keep track of land titles, their location, and the types of soil in each farm or village. They tend to under-report data partly because it has very little effect on their organization's integrity and partly because it is in the interest of farmers who are willing to offer bribes. Village and village tract chairmen, who have similar knowledge of actual landholdings in their area, naturally submit conservative reports, keeping quiet about the full extent of production. However, the military authorities from the township and district PDC, unlike their subordinates at the local level, bluntly emphasize the need for only "good news" about crops and acreage under cultivation. Higher yield and larger areas of cultivation translate into richer pickings for their pockets as well as filling local and national coffers.

A second source of conflict arises from the fact that the various agencies are equipped with different types of organizational resources (e.g. water, chemical fertilizers, and agricultural loan) and varying degrees of bargaining power (affecting their ability to determine the fate of farmers). With reference to the summer paddies project, the Irrigation Department is considered the most powerful organization of all those involved because of its control over vital water resources. The local irrigation department exerts a considerable influence over farmers' lives since it determines which farmers qualify for the program, and thus should be given water. Many local irrigation officers, from assistant engineers down to tank-watchers, have made quick money by accepting bribes from farmers who wanted to be part of summer paddy projects (especially in regions where summer paddy brought considerable return), and who were

---

[25] Government policy dictates that farmers must sell a certain percentage of their produce to the government at below market prices after the harvest, and their individual quota is determined by the numbers of cultivated acres. Farmers are left with larger amount of surplus if they can underreport their cultivated acres, and they must bribe the land record officials to help conceal their holdings or cultivated acres.

competing for the limited amount of water. As a result, tanks soon run out of water as the extent of the area cultivated surpassed what had been initially assigned by the agencies involved.

Other departments, such as the Land Record and MAS extension services, not only felt left out of the process of "sharing the pie," but also began to blame the irrigation department for the failure of summer paddy. Such resentments, however, were less likely to turn into official complaints as long as the aggrieved departments retained channels through which to supplement their income. For example, as a result of their access to peasants' landholding records, the Settlement and Land Record Department (SLRD) has been able to conduct illicit transactions for the benefit of both farmers and the agency, particularly since the Burmese government prohibits the sale and mortgaging of farm-lands. A widely circulated story within agricultural staff circles in Upper Burma tells how agricultural officials had to heavily intoxicate a land record officer in order to find out the true extent of farmers' land-holdings and productivity. Farmers are unlikely to misrepresent their holdings in order to gain benefits when dealing with this agency. Again, the township land record department may tolerate farmers both under-reporting and over-reporting their holdings (depending on the circumstances), help transfer land-ownership titles and misreport the quality and location of peasants' lands to the central authorities. However, the SLRD always has the upper hand in such illicit bargains and farmers do not always benefit since it will only facilitate these deals for a price.

One farmer from *Pyinmana* township, for instance, complained that he was "blackmailed" by a land record official, who refused to change the title of land ownership until the farmer paid him a certain amount of money. The farmer said he was required to sell the procurement quota from the rice farm he had already sold to another farmer. He finally paid 1,500 kyat to the land official, who then immediately transferred the title to the new owner. Junior agricultural staff in Upper Burma feel frustrated at their lack of knowledge about the true extent of cultivated acreage and crop-yield, and the secret dealings that go on between farmers and irrigation officers, land record officers, and township authorities. However, agriculture officials are not entirely toothless. They can influence decisions over who should be eligible for popular agriculture programs and determine which farmer is qualified for how many bags of chemical fertilizer.

Like the irrigation department, the township PDC has tremendous influence over the fate of summer paddy farmers. Although these township governing authorities lack the professional and technical expertise to determine the acreage to be brought under cultivation or the types of land that should be reclaimed as "fallow and uncultivated," they have ultimate control over interdepartmental decision-making. As a result, they tend to involve their associates and cronies, quite illicitly, in popular agricultural projects. On one occasion, an assistant engineer from the irrigation department expressed his concern over placing authority for water provision in the hands of non-expert township PDC officials. His concern was not unfounded; the PDC began selling water to farmers outside the project, which ultimately resulted in water shortages. (Of course, those who have professional expertise are not immune to corruption either).

Other incidents confirm the capacity of PDC officials for corruption. On at least one occasion, the township ruling authorities exacted a certain percentage of produce or income from farmers who were found to be cultivating outside the summer paddies program. In return, they promised that they would not report about the offenders to the state and divisional PDC authorities. Under the recent policy on land reclamation, the township and district PDC or the local military, in cooperation with the local forestry department, has the power to determine lands to be reclaimed as fallow or wasteland. On several occasions, PDC officials seized occupied farm-land under the pretext of the land reclamation policy, and sold it back to their cronies and associates. For instance, in *Auk* township, Rangoon Division, lands deemed to have been occupied by "trespassers" or "unlawful" residents were taken over under the new reclamation policy. The township PDC then sold each piece of land to disabled veterans at subsidized prices, who in turn sold the land on to private individuals for a profit. A rumour later spread that the beneficiaries of the new land policy, the disabled veterans, turned out to be physically and mentally healthy, young, military officials still on active service. And in *Alei* township, the township and district PDC seized plots of land and fish ponds from the local residents under the guise of land reclamation and sold them on to Indian businessmen.

Other agencies are also implicated in corrupt practices. The MAPT (Myanma Agriculture Produce Trading), a state agency under the Ministry of Commerce, has no role in implementing agricultural polices. It buys agricultural crops (quota) from farmers at low prices, and siphons off grain by under-weighing the crop at the purchase depot. Farmers from *Danupyu* township, *Irrawaddy* Division complained that they lost about ten percent of their produce through this practice--they were constantly told that their paddy was underweight, and so failed to meet standard measurements used at the depot. The farmers alleged that the standard measuring basket--claimed to hold 69 pounds of rice, in fact held 75 pounds. They needed a lot more rice to fill the new "standardized" bag. Sometimes, the MAPT would offer low prices for high quality rice by claiming that what they were offered was an adulterated crop. Both parties, in fact, preferred to deal in low- quality paddy, as the MAPT had to pay very little for poorer rice, and farmers could make more money by selling better-quality rice in the market. However, in *Alei* township in Upper Burma, farmers claimed that the township agricultural manager made a lucrative deal by colluding with the MAPT employees and the township PDC authorities to buy high-quality paddy from farmers at very low prices. They then bought low-quality paddy with these profits in the market. Finally, they sent the low-quality paddy to the capital as the farmers' procurement quota. The profits from this exercise were shared by the three parties involved: the PDC officials, the agricultural officer, and the trader.

In sum, the competing and overlapping claims, often involving a high degree of corruption, made by local branches of state departments and agencies on farmers and their produce have seriously undermined rural welfare. A notable example occurred in *Alei* township, where the township PDC authorities demanded that farmers pay a fine of 2,000 kyat per acre after finding out that sesame had been cultivated without their permission. These sesame farmers had in fact already bribed junior irrigation officers at 2,000 kyat per acre for water rights. The farmers were ultimately doubly taxed by authorities. Knowing that they could no longer trust the irrigation officers, the PDC authorities immediately ordered data to be collected on the extent of paddy and sesame cultivations. In the end, farmers must pay bribes to almost all the agricultural agencies with whom they have dealings, the irrigation department, the MAS extension service, the land record department and township and village PDCs.

These competing claims over farmers' produce also breed dissatisfaction and resentment among local civilian and military bureaucrats who are not in a position to make such claims; this in turn results in low levels of trust, communication, and interaction among the agencies involved. An example of such lack of trust can be observed from the reactions of irrigation officers in *Alei* township, who, after reading a report of crop failure made by land record officials, rushed to the local paddy field to double-check the condition of the crops.

A final cause of organizational conflict is seen in the involvement of a number of departments and agencies with separate and overlapping responsibilities and jurisdictions in the field of rural policy. This creates inefficiency and leads to a diffusion of accountability as well as blame-seeking for missed targets and failed projects. For example, in *Alei* township in Upper Burma, all the agencies involved (irrigation, agriculture, and land record departments) must carry out field inspections following reports of large-scale crop failure. The failure of staff from a particular agency to show up meant that the appointment had to be cancelled and rescheduled, and thus farmers' needs were neglected. Another case in point is the disagreement among the various agencies over water provision, which resulted in delays, and, eventually, crop failure. The divisional manager of the MAS in Upper Burma, for example, argued that summer irrigation could be reduced due to the drought-resistant quality of paddy that was grown in the area. Although the irrigation department did not agree with him, they eventually acceded to his advice, while the farmers were anxiously waiting for the release of water from the tank. It turned out that the divisional manager was wrong, and about ten percent of the cultivated acreage in the region failed as a result.

In *Alei* township, Upper Burma, it was quite common for civilian and military bureaucrats to hold one another accountable for the water-shortages, the failure of agricultural policies or the plight of farmers in general. While irrigation officials accused their agricultural counterparts of being negligent, irresponsible, and unreliable, the agricultural officials in turn complained that junior irrigation officers hardly ever attended extension camp meetings or visited the fields. The agriculture department occasionally pointed the finger at the irrigation department for water-shortages as a result of illegal sales or construction faults in the irrigation system caused by engineering errors, carelessness, theft of building materials, and dispensing of project funds for personal use. Likewise, in *Auk* township, Rangoon Division, the agriculture department blamed forestry officials for providing its headquarters with misleading information about the local situation. According to local agricultural officials, the forestry department had designated various plots of land, which were being worked by farmers as fallow and waste, and had driven out the occupants.

The Roots of the Vertical Gap in Policy-Making and implementation
The effective implementation of agricultural policies is constrained not only by conflicts arising from horizontal interdepartmental cooperation. It is also limited by miscommunications and misunderstandings within the hierarchical structure of government departments and agencies. These gaps, however, were observed less in terms of "passing down" rules, regulations, or policies to the least responsible bureaucracies, but rather in

terms of "passing up" the results of development programs or reports on rural conditions.

The chairmen and secretaries of the state/divisional Peace and Development council, for instance, have been misinformed and uninformed about the activities that took place under the jurisdiction of the township PDC chairman and secretary. Likewise, many activities that occurred at the village levels were concealed from the township political authorities. Not surprisingly, the ruling authorities in town are always suspicious of the motives and action of village and village tract chairmen, who themselves are the residents of the village or village tract they represent.

Due to the lack of exchange of information and interaction within the hierarchical structure of the PDC, it is possible, for instance, that the central military authorities in the capital were sometimes unaware of some "illegal" activities and violations of human rights that occurred at the local levels.[26] Thus, when the local military officials expropriated the lands and fish ponds of residents from *Ywa Ma* village, *Alei* township under the pretext of the new land reclamation policy, these residents threatened to take the case directly to General Khin Nyunt, the Secretary of the State Peace and Development Council. They got their lands back immediately from the local authorities. Some residents in *Taung* village tract, *Auk* township, Rangoon Division, who feared the imminent danger of their lands being taken over, complained to *Bogyoke* Tin Oo, the second secretary of the SPDC, when he visited the place. They got an oral assurance from *Bogyoke* Tin Oo to continue working the land, but the anxiety prevailed after *Bogyoke* left, as the local political officials were preparing to drive out the occupants.

A chairman from one of the villages in *Taung* village tract thus remarked that "nowadays, you do not have to be afraid of *atek lu*(meaning military authorities in Rangoon), but you definitely have to be afraid of *auk lu* (meaning township and district political and military officials)." Many rural residents, including local civilian officials, strongly believed that farmers must take their complaints directly to the capital. Going through the official channels (the processes of submitting grievances from the local office up the national office) will be inefficient and self-defeating since the local government whose interests are at stake is most likely to discard the case. For instance, in *Peace* township, *Irrawaddy*

---

[26] This does not imply that the central authorities are totally unaware of local corruption and abuses. Sometimes corruptions were condoned to buy off loyalty among subordinates. At the same time, there were frequent purges against those who had accumulated wealth and power and posed imminent danger to the central authorities' power.

division, the Christian residents appealed directly to the central government after the public high school repeatedly required Christian students to worship and offer flowers to the Buddha statue. This issue got the immediate attention of the central government, which reprimanded local township authorities and school officials.[27]

In similar manner, senior agriculture officials are frequently misled and misinformed by their junior staff in the provincial areas. This absence of vertical flow of information is caused and exacerbated by the existence of a high level of fear and respect towards the higher authorities, which is typical of any hierarchically structured organization in Burma. Lucian Pye, for instance, observed in the 1960s the behaviour of the civilian and political elite, which he strongly believed, bore resemblance to that of King's officials under the court politics: "A man acted with shameless servility before his superiors and poured out uninhibited contempt and disdain on inferiors."[28] Such norms are still in practice today.

It is not unusual to see junior officials fawning and showing abject obsequiousness towards their superiors. They carry their superiors' bags or suitcases (no matter how light or small the bags are), or serve them coffee and tea, or pose a docile manner and gesture whenever talking to senior officers. The senior officers, on the other hand, tend to take full advantage of their position by acting ruthlessly and insensitively towards their subordinates. A divisional Agriculture manager in Upper Burma, for instance, explicitly stated that he did not want to hear or read any seasonal and annual reports of bad harvest and crop failures. He threatened to transfer the extension worker under his supervision to a backward and remote area after the extension worker reported crop failure under his area of responsibility. In Peace township, *Irrawaddy* division, a local forestry official resigned from his post after being humiliated by the Minister of Forestry, who slapped his face in the presence of his colleagues and subordinates.[29]

Likewise, the township PDC authorities do not always treat the village PDC authorities with respect, despite the fact that the village chairmen help implement and enforce policies at the most basic village levels. These village chairmen were sometimes verbally harassed, physically abused, arrested, and imprisoned if they failed to collect targeted procurement quotas or to garner labour and financial contributions from their villages. In the remote areas, village chairmen

---

[27] Conversation with a pastor from *Tei- Kyi* township, Rangoon division, July 1999.

[28] Lucian Pye, *Politics, Personality, and Nation Building: Burma's Search for Identity* (New Haven: Yale University Press, 1962), 68.

[29] Accounts made by a junior forestry officer from *Peace* township, June 1999.

were either physically abused or were killed by the military authorities or police who accused them of supporting rebels and insurgents. Moreover, their position as the members of the village PDC, the lowest rung of the ruling administrative structure, does not necessarily guarantee them special rights and privileges. One village chairman in Lower Burma for instance said that part of his land was also taken over by the township military authorities under the guise of land reclamation policy.

In fact, many junior agriculture officers know very well that their tenure and future depend very much on the mood swings of the higher authorities, and they try very hard not to cause any problems or submit any bad news that would upset their superiors. It has thus become general practice among the junior agriculture officers to deliberately choose the words, phrases, statements, and news that would please their senior officials. Lies and sugar-coated reports and statements to the higher authorities become obvious to the extent that even outsiders are able to distinguish fact from fiction, though the superior officers remain oblivious to this. A joke circulated among the civilian officials outside the MAS is that a senior divisional agricultural manager in Upper Burma sincerely believed the words of his subordinate township agricultural officer, who presented him with string row-planting paddy field he called a broadcasting paddy field. "Any common person with a small knowledge," the joke goes "can tell the differences between row-planting fields and broadcasting fields!!!"

One reason behind high ranking authorities' ignorance and lack of understanding about their area of supervision (in addition to their adamant refusal to acknowledge any failed projects) is their narrowly specialized field of expertise. In addition, most of them are the graduates of Agricultural Institutes, and rarely have close association with the ordinary Burmese cultivators. Furthermore, the highest posts (the Minister and the deputy Minister) of the Ministry of Agriculture and Irrigation, have been predominantly occupied by military generals. Very few of them have technical expertise, professional knowledge, experiences and personal interest to learn and manage various aspects of rural development.

The discussion of the existence of the vertical gap within individual state departments and agencies is incomplete without reference to the rituals associated with the visits by high ranking officials to the peripheral areas. These high profile visits from the center, whether they are from the Ministry of Agriculture or from the state and divisional PDC, severely drain the financial and physical resources of the local government departments and agencies. Junior agricultural officers spent more time on preparation for the visits of high ranking officials (and their relatives) from the city, than on handling and resolving their department' issues and responsibilities. They prepared the best food, and organized the most variety of gifts, which were then piled into the back of the visiting officer' car, hoping that the favour would one day be returned to them through promotion and studies abroad. The most notorious and costly tour in the history of the Ministry of Agriculture was done by the former Minister of Agriculture, Lt. General Myint Aung, who consistently asked his hosts to provide millions in cash, and gold and jewelry for his grandchildren.

Sometimes, the visit was not confined to a specific department if it was intended to cover cross interdepartmental issues. Once in a while, the local farmers must involuntarily meet and welcome the visiting state officials, and yet they were not allowed to speak about their problems and difficulties during the visit. The village chairman or an outgoing person from the village may recite what he had been instructed by the local government officials. Those who blurted out their dissatisfaction at the current situation were reprimanded or threatened with arrest once the boss returned to his headquarters.

The Minister General
Aggravating this problem of continuously limited flow of upward information within the Ministry of Agriculture and Irrigation is also the appointment of a military officer as the head (or the minister) of the Ministry. The most memorable of these has been General Myint Aung who served from 1991 until 1997. Lt. General Myint Aung transferred the concept of military procedures into the daily operation of the agricultural ministry with strict hierarchical command and rigid discipline.

The Lt. General was given the minister's post in 1991 after serving as the chairman of the *Irrawaddy* divisional Law and Order Restoration Council (LORC) which earned him notoriety for relentlessly crushing, burning, and killing the Karen residents and villages from *Bogalay* township, *Irrawaddy* division, whom he believed to be aiding the Karen insurgents. Upon entering office, the General announced that he was willing to work only with hard working and dedicated agriculture staff, and that he would take strong action against those who failed to perform their duties. Thus one former agricultural officer told me that she quit her job after hearing the General's announcement, since she was a full-time mother and did not want to get fired from her job if she could not live up to the new standards.[30] The General meant it. He demoted and fired many junior and senior agricultural officers, whose performance did not satisfy

---

[30] Interview, Cat village, Henzada township, *Irrawaddy* division, June 1999.

his needs and preferences, and "jump-promoted" some junior officials who impressed him. One divisional agricultural manager in Upper Burma, for instance, was rumoured to be "jump-promoted" by the general. The General was immediately impressed upon seeing the demonstration farm in *Dream* township, and appointed the farm manager as a divisional agricultural manager, one of the most coveted positions in MAS.[31]

Some retired senior agriculture officers described the General, who never graduated from high school, as authoritative and patronizing. The General always took pride in reminding his subordinate professional technocrats at the headquarters about how "a person with sixth grade education is giving orders to those who hold PhDs and MAs' degrees."[32] Those who worked closely with him remarked that his decisions were based on his mood swings, but others said that he was a workaholic and disciplined.[33] Failure to enforce the General's orders meant dismissal from job or a slap in the face of the responsible staffs by the General. On the other hand, he initiated a number of high profile irrigation projects, and a considerable number of smaller ones, and was able to control the overall structure and staff of the agriculture institution by demanding loyalty and strict discipline from the subordinates within the organization.[34]

Talk about the personality and accomplishments of the General is controversial and inconsistent depending on the aspects of his career one looks at, and much of course depends upon the person one hears from. He was an ideal and exceptional minister from the eyes of farmers and students of the Institute of Agriculture. A lecturer at the Institute of Agriculture, *Yezin* town, for instance, lamented that the new generation of graduates from the Institute saw only the positive sides of the current government policies. She said that they were more or less "adopted" by the General as his "own children" and were given special treatment and opportunities in the form of foreign training and a Minister's scholarship.

---

[31] It was said that the current minister, Major General Nyunt Tin, who replaced General Myint Aung in 1997, reviewed and reevaluated the profile of agricultural staff who were unfairly fired by General Myint Aung. He also reoffered those staff their positions, and demoted those jump promoted by his predecessor.

[32] A former township agriculture officer, interviewed by author, Insein, Rangoon, 1999. It is rumored that the current minister (1999) shows greater respect toward academia and educated people, and relies much more heavily on professional and technocrats' advices.

[33] A retired professor of the Institute of Agriculture, interview by author, Insein, Rangoon, September, 1999.

[34] It was also said that the current minister does not exploit his position as much as the former minister, and thus much of the discretion and responsibilities over formulation and implementation of policies are now in the hands of the state/divisional agricultural managers, rather than that of the minister.

Once he assumed the position of the Minister, he incorporated the Institute of Agriculture under the Ministry of Agriculture, and set up a scholarship program for top-notch students. He also co-founded a "training program" with the Israel government under which approximately 70 to 100 graduates from the Institute of Agriculture were sent each year to Israel for on-the-job training for about eleven months.[35] Many prospective trainees competed for this limited space by bribing the interviewers. It was said that the General himself sometimes made the selection, and it was not always based on merits. He reportedly chose the most beautiful interviewees or any person who gave him amusing answers. One story reveals that when he asked a female graduate who specialized in insecticide whether she had seen any insect that can not be found on earth, the candidate replied that she could find one if he sent her to the outer space. She got chosen for the job training!

Consequently, those who obtained their bachelor's degree under the ministership of the General developed an extreme loyalty to him. They were then sent to different parts of the country, and served as the "eyes" of the General, and reported any improper and illegal activities committed by their local senior officers to the headquarters. The General thus used the "divide and rule" technique within the organization, and his protégés, newly graduated agricultural officers, posed a threat to senior staff members who had more experience and knowledge yet lacked direct contact with the Minister of Agriculture.

Likewise, farmers appreciated the General's effort to promote irrigation works and the introduction of the summer paddy. Thanks to the *Htee Dam* that was constructed under the supervision of the General, some villagers in *Alei* township in Upper Burma said they had been blessed with water for three consecutive years to cultivate summer paddy. Many farmers, in fact, seemed to recall and recognize his name more often than they do with the current Minister of Agriculture, who is said to be easy going. To some farmers, the General was their ally, who paid serious attention to their concern and complaints. Some local agriculture officers were fired by the General due to the complaints brought by farmers during his tour in the countryside.

---

[35] In reality, the training program turned out to be a menial labor contract where the holders of bachelor's degree in agriculture were asked to work in the farms (mostly the handling of crops such as packaging and cutting flowers), and to stay in cooperative dorms. They were not even taught the technology involved in the processes. The reason most ambitious and intelligent graduates were attracted to this program is because they could save at least one thousand dollars by the time they returned home. Some were even able to bring back up to US$ 4,000. It is considered quite a considerable amount of money for a typical government employee.

Undoubtedly, the General was a corrupt minister. He built extravagant mansions in every major city, including *Rangoon, Moulmein, MayMyo*, and *Mandalay*, and was rumoured to have a couple of mistresses. It was an apocryphal story that he owned too many houses to keep track of them. A rumour spread that he asked his subordinate officer to buy him a beautiful house he sighted while visiting the area. His subordinate had to remind him that the house he now coveted was already one of his!! He also created a tacit rule and informal set of rituals within the circle of local field authorities and department officials; for example, they had to prepare and stack up money (a minimum of 1,000,000 Kyat) and expensive items on each of his visits and present these to him as a gesture of courtesy. Oftentimes, he even demanded that the local staff from within or outside his department should adorn his grandchildren with jewelry when they accompanied him on a trip.

He was purged in 1997 by the central government because of corruption, along with several other ministers. His properties were expropriated, and his subordinates and associates were interrogated, demoted, dismissed, or imprisoned. He died in 1998 of a heart attack, although it is rumoured that he committed suicide. His legacy, however, will continue as he will be remembered as the general who introduced a "breakthrough technology" (summer paddy), implemented high profile rural development schemes, and who occasionally went out to meet with grassroots-level farmers, whose interests he claimed to represent. He will also be remembered as the first Minister who tried to restructure and reshape the framework of the ministry into a military, personalistic, and authoritative operation, earning him both notoriety and fame, which eventually led to his downfall.

The Bureaucrats under the Military Administration

A close observation of the implementation of agricultural policies in Burma first illustrates larger patterns at work within the administrative and political machinery of the military government. In other words, the broader political and administrative environments within which local civilian and military authorities find themselves constrain them to act in a manner that is not consistent with rural welfare. A number of institutional factors embedded within the military government operate against the interests of Burmese rice farmers. They included insufficient salaries, the creation of departments with overlapping responsibilities, appointment of military officers as the heads of civilian ministries and departments and the difficulties of passing up information within the hierarchical structure of agricultural administration.

First, many poorly compensated local officials regularly conduct illicit deals with the farmers to supplement their income, often to the detriment of farmers. Widespread corruption is a common feature of the military government, and the level of the corruption has increased to an unimaginable level, stretching from high ranking to the lowest positions of state institutions. Both high ranking and low ranking officials are under compensated under the military regime. A typical high ranking civilian official, for instance, earns about 2,500 kyat a month, equivalent to the prices of ten meals or a nice jacket.

Second, the central government's requirement for interdepartmental cooperation to implement agricultural policies also leads to illegitimate overlapping claims on farmers' limited produce. An example can be seen in the implementation of the summer paddy program which required the involvement of the irrigation, agricultural, land record departments and the township PDC. Farmers had to bribe the irrigation office as well as the PDC authorities to obtain water, provide a certain amount of produce to the PDC authorities for "local administrative fund," and pay a certain amount of cash to agricultural and land record officers to be included in the summer paddy project. Failure to cooperate horizontally among different departments and agencies has been a major barrier to implementing successful agriculture programs in Burma. This is partly due to the creation of new local offices and multiplication of organizations with overlapping responsibilities and jurisdiction.[36] The implementation of a particular rural development project therefore is prone to failure due to different orientations and outlooks held by the involved agencies, their lack of trust and cooperation towards each other, and diffusion of responsibilities and lack of accountability.

This is compounded by the difficulties in passing up bad reports (crop failures, bad harvest, etc) within a particular ministry, which lead to misrepresentation of the actual local situations. For instance, many local agricultural officials avoided reporting crop failures and bad harvests to their superior officials for fear of being transferred, slapped, or losing their jobs. Thus, junior officials make up rosy reports and conceal

---

[36] In November 1997, the SLORC restructured its government by reshuffling and reorganizing its cabinets, ministries, departments and their official personnel. There are now 28 Ministries, some are newly formed, some renamed, and some maintained from the pre-1997 periods. Some observers speculate that the establishment of new ministries, which are headed predominantly by military officials, and their redundant and overlapping jurisdiction, is a sign of reassertion of control and predominance over the society by the military. Others see this move as the creation of new jobs for military personnel, and thereby allow them to extract natural resources and privileged access through their control over ministries.

farmers' plights. Last but not least, the appointment of military officers to head civilian ministries also adds barriers to upward information flow because most military officials lack technical and managerial expertise to formulate appropriate agricultural policies, and many are rigid and unrealistic in their demands and planning.[37] The practices of Lt. General Myint Aung during his tenure at the Ministry of Agriculture exemplify this. Many skilled and qualified personnel were eliminated due to his quick and irrational actions. Pressure from military-cum-administrator is passed on within the vertical ladder of the civil agencies where superiors at varying stages make unrealistic demands upon subordinates. This is reinforced by the hierarchical nature of policy implementation coupled with existing cultural practices to show extreme deference toward higher ranking authorities.

However, this broad institutional milieu alone cannot explain the existence of a range of practices and varying state-societal interactions at the local level. There are a host of factors that affect the relative cordiality and hostility between rice farmers and local officials. Three cautionary notes must first be emphasized, however. First, like the hypothesis on village headmen-villagers interaction, my conclusion of local officials-villagers relations is based on my limited observation. Second, the fact that the salary of lower level officials is not commensurate with their power and position implies that corruption would be endemic at the local levels, and even a well-liked official cannot be expected to be impeccable and uncorrupt. Third, the "character" and "personality" of state officials play a significant role in influencing their interaction with farmers. Infrequently, there may be township military authorities who are flexible and sympathetic. Again, this is a residual factor, since the nature, orientation, and organizational resources of the department the official represents largely determine the practices of local officials. There are certain sets of parameters within which local officials are allowed to act in certain ways, and they vary across the departments, and across the region. For instance, an official whose department lacks distributional resources or coercive mechanisms and therefore exerts a minimum impact upon

---

[37] This of course is not unique to the administration of military government. There were barriers to communication and effective cooperation which separated superior and subordinate during the British periods. However these barriers were "social barriers" characterized in terms of ethnic and class composition of membership of the services, and thus did not significantly interfere with the formal operation of bureaucratic machinery. See James Guyot, "Bureaucratic Transformation in Burma", in *Asian Bureaucratic Systems*, ed. Ralph Braibanti (NC: Duke University Press, 1966).

farmers' lives has little reason to be corrupt, no matter how immoral he/she is.

First, agricultural officials with college degrees and those with diploma degrees tend to have different attitudes towards paddy producers. Rice farmers often have closer and friendlier interactions with diploma degree holders, who, because of their similar personal and socioeconomic background, demonstrate better understanding of farmers' plight and problems. These officials also tend to reside in their native place and they or their parents rely on farming as their main or partial source of income.

Second, the greater the leverage the agency has over farmers' lives, or the more indispensable and scarce the agency's distributional resources are to farmers, the more intense is the relationship. For instance, paddy farmers in Upper Burma developed greater resentment against irrigation officers than other agricultural officials although officials in all agencies were corrupt. The reason is that irrigation is crucial to summer paddies, and he who controls water, controls the livelihood of summer paddy cultivators. Rural resentments thus focus on irrigation officers and township ruling authorities (Peace and Development Council) who sell water illegally. The resources that the agricultural extension office has to offer, by contrast, are neither scarce nor indispensable. Farmers need chemical fertilizers, but they would rather buy them outside the agriculture department since they have to go through complex bureaucratic procedures to obtain government subsidized fertilizers. After all, there is little difference in price between government and free market fertilizer. In *Auk* township in Lower Burma, on the other hand, farmers did not develop hostile attitudes toward the irrigation department, for there was enough water for everybody who wanted to cultivate dry rice. Thus they did not need to bribe the irrigation officials to obtain water.

Third, farmers tend to have more open communication, if not always friendlier communication, with civilian departments than their political (military) counterparts. Specifically, agricultural extension workers are both the least feared and least powerful government agents due to their lack of access to the use of force and their low position in the political hierarchy. Consequently, farmers are not afraid to reveal their problems toward them nor to openly resist their demands. This type of resistance and open confrontation is less likely to occur between the military officers and paddy farmers. This does not mean, however, that township military officials, who have access to the use of force and to whom farmers could not openly express their opinion, are the most respected agency. They may be the most feared organization because they have access to the use of force. They are not the most respected agency because of their insensitivity to local plight and their rigid and forceful demands.

Fourth, paddy producers tend to have positive views of the department whose orientation and agenda are consistent with their interests. They resent the agricultural department's tendency to over report their crop output, but applaud the work of the land record office that tends to under report output and harvested acres.

It is possible that each local department and agency could incorporate both positive and negative features, which affect the nature of the relationship between its staff and the farmers. For instance, the positive image of the irrigation department as water provider can be mitigated by misusing its organizational resources to the detriment of farmers' welfare. Whether positive factors will dominate the negative ones depends on the degree of severity affecting farmers' well being. For instance, paddy cultivators may resent the agriculture department's tendency to over report their crop yield and production. Yet they may be neutral to the extent that the department has relatively little or no organizational resources to exert much (negative) impact on their lives, and therefore to alter their status significantly.

In sum, farmers' overall attitudes toward the highest authorities are an amalgam depending on their varying relationships with diverse local departments and authorities. Ultimately, however, farmers' attitudes toward the central government are determined by their relationship with local agencies that have the most direct and most significant impact on their lives. For instance, as noted above, the attitudes of summer paddy farmers in *Atek* township toward the central authorities were heavily shaped by the actions of irrigation and the township PDC officials. On the other hand, rice farmers in *Auk* township were preoccupied with the activities of forestry officials and the township PDC authorities. The forestry and the PDC officials reclaim virgin lands for agricultural expansion. However, some took farmers' lands, claiming them as "virgin" or "uncultivated." Therefore, *Auk*'s farmers' attitudes toward the central authorities were heavily influenced by practices of the forestry and the township PDC officials. They had no reason to come into conflict with the irrigation office because there was plentiful water in *Auk*, a township in lower Burma. Whether *Auk* and *Atek* farmers develop favourable or unfavourable attitudes toward the national government depends on the extent to which they think the central authorities are responsible for these various practices of corruption and exploitation. (Given the closed door nature of the policymaking and lack of media coverage in Burma, even scholars, not to mention Burmese farmers, have a hard time accurately capturing the central authorities' positions on these issues.)

Conclusion

This chapter reinforces the core argument of this book: it highlights the dynamic nature of the state-societal interactions at the local level and challenges the misconception of a singular governmental structure in Burma. I have shown how the broader political and administrative environments within which local civilian and military authorities find themselves create the incentive structure that guides their choices on how to relate to the villagers. In other words, the bureaucracy under the military state in Burma is replete with public officials who are preoccupied with advancing their personal interests at the expense of rural welfare. This is due to a number of factors that are embedded within the organizational structure of the military government. They include insufficient salaries, appointment of military generals as the heads of civilian ministers and departments, the creation of departments with overlapping responsibilities, and the vertical gap within the hierarchical structure of administration.

However, this broad institutional milieu alone cannot explain the existence of different practices and varying state-societal interactions at the local level. The Burmese rice farmers' relationships with local authorities vary depending on a variety of circumstances. I have demonstrated a host of factors that determine the relative cordiality or hostility between paddy farmers and local officials by looking at (1) the nature and objectives of individual local government agencies, (2) the type of their organizational resources, and (3) educational and socioeconomic status of local authorities. A detailed examination of the roots of a wide range of state-societal relationships in the countryside tells us what type of authorities are more likely to be sensitive to the needs of farmers and to share similar interests with farmers, and what are the institutional, organizational, personality and socio-economic factors that influence this sensitivity. It thus sheds light on isolated cases of friendly interactions between farmers and some components of state agencies and authorities, which contradict the dominant pattern of hostile state-societal interactions in Burma. Again, farmers particularly value village chairmen and local authorities who are impartial, honest, responsive to their needs, sympathetic to their plight, shield residents from the vagaries of the capital, and who are not too corrupt and abusive of their power and authority. The rice farmers are complacent as long as these qualities are present in local leaders, be they military or civilian officials.

A case in point here is farmers' favourable recollection of the township PDC official (a military officer) in *Alei* township, Upper Burma, who worked cooperatively in 1988 with the village tract chairman, *U Khant*. The PDC official relied on negotiation and bargaining method rather than on the use of sheer force to gain consensus from farmers on the amounts of grain they were willing to sell to the central government. Most officials are expected to engage in illicit deals among themselves and with farmers, but they do not necessarily create negative repercussions unless these activities take place at farmers' tremendous loss and suffering. Farmers prefer local officials who share similar interests with them (in terms of underreporting their outputs and cultivated acres), who dispense distributional resources (chemical fertilizer, water, seeds) with a minimum level of corruption, who do not rigidly enforce central policies that are inimical to their interests, and to whom farmers can openly and frankly express their problems (civilian rather than military officials).

The analysis of paddy farmers' varying relationships with local authorities is also crucial in understanding the relationship between economic policies and political legitimacy. For the behaviour and practices of the local officials, which are influenced by a number of institutional, political, organizational, and personality factors, are mainly manifested in their treatments of particular agricultural policies or packages. Different local authorities implement the same agricultural policy in slightly different manners, and their different treatments have varying implications on farmers' perception of central and local authorities. In the next chapter, I will look at farmers' responses to local and central governments in response to the implementation of four different agricultural policies.

Chapter 4

A View from Below: Who is Responsible for Our Sufferings?: "*Atek-lu*" (those from above) or "*Auk-Lu*" (those from below)?

Nowadays, you do not have to be afraid of atek-lu, *but you definitely have to be afraid of* auk-lu.

A Karen farmer from Rangoon division.

Democracy is coming and we do not have to string row plant anymore!!!

Joyful shouting of agricultural laborers from Rangoon division upon hearing the news about pro-democracy demonstration in 1988.

Introduction

The military governments in Burma have implemented four major agricultural projects: the High Yielding Variety Promotion (1976-82), the Partial Liberalization (1987-present), the Summer Paddy Program (1992-present), and Land Reclamation Policy (1991-present). Some of these policies are welcomed by farmers from different parts of the country, while other policies generate negative repercussions in the rural areas. Farmers' supports for central and local authorities also vary depending on how these agricultural policies are implemented at the grass roots level.

This chapter will depict the multiple images of the Burmese military regime by looking at how the types of agricultural policies and the ways in which they are implemented influence farmers' perceptions of the central and local authorities.[1] First, I will provide a detailed analysis of four different agricultural policies that have been implemented under the military regime, and will identify Burmese farmers' attitudes regarding each of these. Second, I will examine the specific situations under which the military elite in the capital and the local authorities in the provincial areas were perceived favorably and unfavorably because of these various policies.[2]

---

[1] Here, I will omit or change the names of people, villages, and townships, and the specific location of various places to protect the safety of those who assisted me or came into contact with me. I will underline specific persons or places to indicate that their names have been changed.

[2] I define local and central authorities from rice farmers' perspectives. Most farmers generally referred to General Ne Win, the leader of the Revolutionary Council and the Chairman of the Burma Socialist Program Party, who exercised unrestrained authority during the periods from 1962-

While chapter three emphasizes divergences in local practices, this chapter focuses on particular local agencies that have the most direct and drastic impacts on farmers' lives. In this chapter by doing so, I will treat local authorities at each village or township as a unitary actor, occasionally refer to them as a particular "local government," to illustrate the relationships between the popularity of the local government and that of the central government.[3] To many farmers, in fact, there is very little difference between local agencies (departments and the field staff of ministers) on the one hand, and local government (village heads, military officers, and township administrators), on the other. They see the military and civilian officials and traditional leaders at township levels and below, who have actual contact with them, as part of the local authority structure.

The findings of this chapter are based on my conversations with and observations of Burmese rice farmers' behavior and practices. Admittedly, the numbers of villages I visited were not "large" enough to warrant statistically significant or geographically representative results. My findings could have been different if I concentrated on peripheral villages under the control of minority ethnic insurgent groups, but they are not my focus.

Based on my study of villages that are within the perimeter of the central government's control and authority, I propose four different scenarios. They are, scenario (1) both governments are popular, scenario (2) local popular/center unpopular, scenario (3) local unpopular/center popular, scenario (4) both governments unpopular. I plot my findings from a number of rice villages from four major administrative divisions (*Henzada* township and *Bassein* township, *Irrawaddy* division; *Mawbi* township and *Teik-kyi* township, Rangoon division; *Tharawaddy* township and *Pyinmana* township, *Pegu* division; *Shwebo* township, *Sagaing* division) into four different ideal situations. I acknowledge that my project could not provide the exact frequency of occurrence of different types of interactions.

1988, and the secretary and chairman of the State Peace and Development Council, Major General Khin Nyunt and General Than Shwe as the central state authorities. They also consider the Minister of Agriculture part of the central circle, and usually approach him with complaints and requests during his tour in the countryside. On the other hand, they see military and civilian officials and local leaders at township levels and below, who have actual contact with them, as part of the local authority structure. They range from the secretary and chairman of township Peace and Development Council, township land record, agricultural, and irrigation officers, to secretary and chairman of the village Peace and Development Council, and village extension workers.
[3] Given the constrained political atmosphere under which I conducted my research, I define "legitimacy" or "popularity" loosely in terms of the minimum level of acceptance of state authorities by a particular segment of the population. Behavioral and verbal reaction indicating support for the state leaders ranges from highly positive commentaries to satisfaction about the practices and actions of concerned authorities.

Nevertheless, my major concern is to canvas the diverse reactions farmers have shown toward state authorities in the course of the implementation of various agricultural programs. If a very limited number of cases of paddy farmers-state authorities' interactions indicate complex and varying societal views of the state, one should expect an even wider range of state-societal interactions had more cases been incorporated into the analysis.

Approaches to Agricultural Promotion: Policies and Practices
Generally speaking, there are three main ways in which agricultural production can be increased.[4] They are: (1) vertical expansion or "intensification," which emphasizes an increase in output per acre through the intensive use of inputs such as chemical fertilizers, pesticides, insecticides, and high-yielding seeds; (2) horizontal expansion or "extensification," which promotes total agricultural output through the expansion of sown areas, such as land reclamation or multiple cropping; and (3) the creation of a market-oriented economy, which includes the privatization of inputs and trade in agriculture, the determination of prices by supply and demand, and the elimination of the procurement system. The military government has, at different times, tried each of these strategies, either fully or partially, and it has, to some extent, succeeded in achieving its goals of increasing agricultural output and productivity. Nevertheless, such an improvement in agricultural production and productivity does not necessarily have a uniform positive impact on the image of the military.

(1) High-Yielding Varieties (HYV) Promotion (1976-1982)
The Burma Socialist Program Party (BSPP), the only legitimate, military-dominated party organization in Burma in the period 1974-1988, first employed the HYV promotion in the mid 1970's. The major components of this program involved intensive use of chemical fertilizers, pesticides, and high-yield variety seeds, as well as the utilization of string-row planting methods.[5] Emphasis was placed on vertical expansion, or an increase in the yield per acre, rather than on

---

[4] I omit land redistribution as one critical element to improving agricultural production, since its impact on agricultural growth and productivity is ambiguous. Both the civilian and military governments instituted land reform with varying successes. Some authors attribute the cause of slow and stagnant agricultural situations in military-ruled Burma to "fragmented" lands from land redistribution and population growth. See Khin Maung Kyi, Myo Nyunt, and Mya Than, "Economics of production and farm size in Burmese agriculture with reference to paddy farming". Yangon: Department of Research Institute of Economics, 1975.

[5] Tin Maung Maung Than, "Burma in 1983: From Recovery to Growth?" in *Southeast Asian Affairs* (1984): 89-122. Lanzin youth is the youth organization of the socialist cadre party.

horizontal expansion, namely, sown area expansion. Also known internationally as the Green Revolution, this strategy required a huge influx of capital (especially for chemical fertilizers and modern variety seeds) and labor input (trans-planters, harvesters, and extension workers). The government responded to this challenge by subsidizing fertilizers and high-yield rice varieties, and sending out extension workers to help farmers adjust to modern technologies and practices. Farmers were reluctant to use fertilizers at first, and abhorred string-row planting, which was time and labor consuming.[6] However, they soon found out that the high-yielding potential of modern varieties could not be realized without chemical fertilizers.[7] Gradually, a new dynamic extension program promoted fertilizer utilization, and the application of new technology led to a significant growth in rice production during 1975-1985. This period has been referred to as the "third period of growth" of the last 150 years in Burma.[8] Burma's rice production increased from nine million metric tons in 1976/77 to 14.3 million metric tons in 1985/86.[9] The paddy area in high yield varieties (HYVs) increased from 4.3 percent in 1972-73, to over half of all paddy in 1986-87, and average fertilizer use per hectare rose from about 5 kg in 1970 to 49 kg in 1983.[10]

This spectacular achievement in agriculture, however, was followed by a forced and extensive output mandated for the benefit of the central government. Farmers were allowed to keep certain amounts

---

[6] During the monsoon season, paddy farmers transplant their month-old nurseries from a small plot into a bigger field. The traditional practice involves a group of female transplanters, ranging from ten to twenty, putting the young plants into a knee-deep water level field. Each woman has her own pace of planting, and consequently the spaces between each plant or each row are uneven. Most of the time, small spaces were left unplanted, and the field tended to have fewer numbers of plants than it could accommodate, and thus produced fewer grains. The string- row transplanting method aimed to maximize the number of plants in each field by requiring two additional people to hold the string from each end of the field. A group of transplanters would then plant along the string at the same pace. The string was moved to the next row only after everybody finished planting. Since all the transplanters worked at the same pace on the same row, each row tended to be filled completely and there were even spaces between each row. Theoretically speaking, each field is utilized fully, and thus produces a higher level of output. Both farmers and agriculture extension workers, however, remained unsure about whether the string- row method was superior to the conventional one in raising output.

[7] U Khin Win, *A Century o f Rice Improvement in Burma* (Manila: International Rice Research Institute, 1991), 68.

[8] The first period of growth occurred between 1885 and 1910 due to the rapid expansion of the rice area when the British government opened the "frontiers" to immigrants from Upper Burma, and the second took place between 1955-1965 as the rice land abandoned during World War II was brought back into production . Khin Win and Kyi Win, *Burma's Experience in Rice Improvement*: 1830-1985 (Manila: IRRI, 1990), 1.

[9] Dephane Khin Shwe Shwe Aye, "The Rice Situation in Myanmar", unpublished paper, 1998, 5.

[10] Young, Cramer and Wailes, *An Economic Assessment of the Burma Rice Sector: Current Developments and Prospects* (Arkansas: Arkansas Agricultural Experiment Station, University of Arkansas, 1998), 19.

of paddy for their family consumption (12 bags of rice per person annually), and were required to sell (usually sixty to seventy per cent of their produce) the rest to the government at below-market prices. Consequently, farmers were left with almost nothing to sell on the market. The government's emphasis on a rice priority strategy also led to a prohibition on the cultivation of non-paddy crops (such as mungbeans and pulses). The punishment for violating these rules was death. A farmer's son from *Natalin* township, *Sagaing* division, also notes that,

> Depending on what kind of rice was in demand on the world market, peasants were ordered by BSPP (Burma Socialist Program Party) local officials and Peoples' Councils to grow a particular kind of rice. For instance, my township's soil is of mediocre quality. So, we were ordered to produce mid-class rice for domestic consumption such as *Nga-sein* and *Yar-kyaw*. In the delta areas and other regions endowed with rich soil, peasants were ordered to grow high-class export quality rice such as *Pathein Zabanit*. If a peasant did not grow what the authorities asked, he was quickly prosecuted with fines and or would have to buy the kind of paddy the government wanted from other peasants and resell it to the government-monopolized Trade Corporation One's purchase centers.[11]

Thus, the impressive growth from High-Yield Variety Promotion has not translated to improved welfare for individual farmers at the grassroots levels. Furthermore, the strict enforcement of cultivation practices and the sale of crops were accompanied by mass mobilization, which was unpopular in the rural areas. Under a variety of banners such as "Operation *Shwewamyay*" (The Golden Land Operation) and "Operation *Myaseinyaung*," (The Emerald Operation), the government sent hundreds and thousands of military officers, soldiers and urban "volunteers" to the countryside to help farmers in planting, harvesting, and transporting paddy produce. The government also held competitions promoting higher output and higher sale of output to the government. Whoever produced the highest amount of grain per acre, and whoever sold the highest amount of grain to the government were honored in newspapers and special local political events. There were also contests on string-row transplanting, aiming to "promote the productive force among peasants and farmers and to produce socialist worker heroes."[12]

---

[11] Ye Myint, personal correspondence with author, April 11, 1997.
[12] *Forward*, November 1979, 3-7.

Rice Yield and Production 1966-88

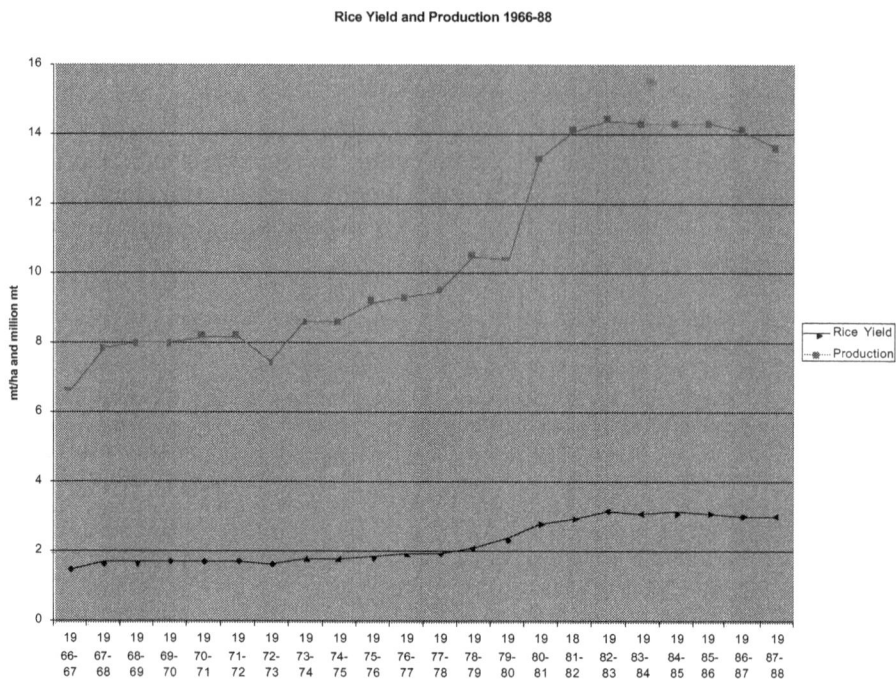

Fertilizer Application in Burma (Kg/ha)

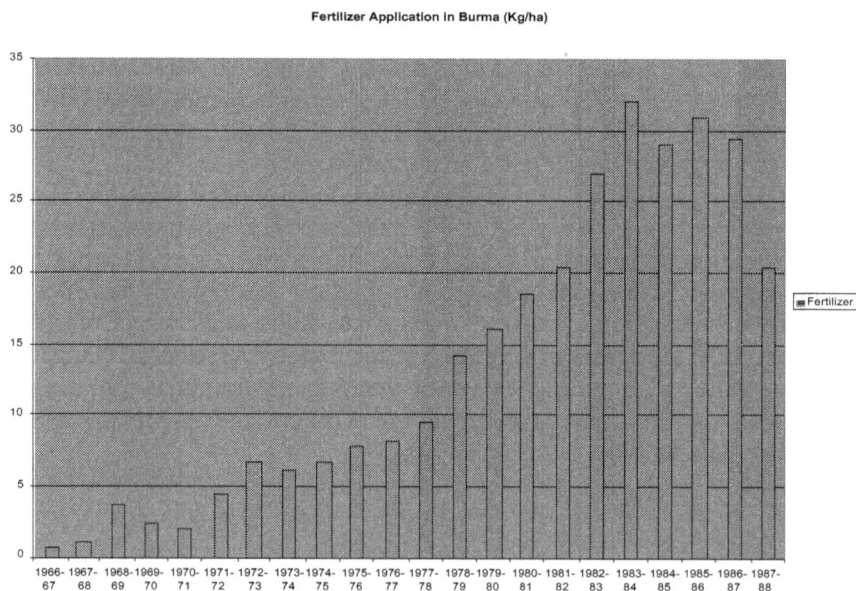

Source: Kenneth Young, Gail Cramer, and Eric Wailes, *An Economic Analysis of the Myanmar Rice Sector*, 66.

134

Many farmers, however, viewed the military's "volunteerism" in the field as "an extension of the more coercive side of military rule."[13] Some paddy cultivators also felt that they had been doubly squeezed by the responsibility to provide food and shelter to hundreds of volunteer workers, a double burden given the poor performances of military personnel and urban dwellers who had never cultivated land before.[14]

Furthermore, although rice yield and production increased in some regions, it was hardly universal. Worse still was the widespread practice of local government reporting highly inflated data. This was partly because the national government used extremely powerful mobilization mechanisms to drive up the output of crops per acre, which pressured and motivated policy implementors, as well as the model farmers (or the early adopters) to lie about yields. The higher the total production and output per acre on paper, the better the image of the local party, council, and agricultural officials or the village chairmen, and the more opportunities there were for career advancement, material rewards and socio-political recognition. Consequently, almost everybody manipulated the data on crop output. One ordinary farmer from *Tharrawaddy* township, in fact, recalled that the overwhelming pressure to win the prize for the "highest yielding field" led many farmers to cheat: "some of them would place a bunch of ripened paddy plants into the model field that was up for competition a night before the contest, and yet they still could not win, since everybody cheated!"

Scanning through a book on *Model Farmers in Burma: 1978*, one former model farmer recalled that it was a common reaction by farmers whose farms were put under experimentation to over-report their production, and that the formulas used by the MAS (Myanma Agriculture Service) to measure yield were inaccurate and unreliable.[15] The book provided a list of farmers who produced the highest output per acre in the nation. Their yield ranged incredibly from as high as 250-300 baskets per acre, whereas the average output in Burma today is approximately 60 baskets per acre!! One ordinary farmer remembered the visit of General Ne Win to his village during the HYV period. The General was greeted by a model farmer, who then bragged about his record-breaking yield to impress him. According to the story, General Ne Win exclaimed, "(c)ould that be possible? I have never heard something like that in my lifetime as a farmer's son!"

---

[13] Jon Wiant, "The political symbolism of Taw-Hlan-Ye-Khit", in *Military Rule in Burma Since 1962*, ed. F.K. Lehman (Singapore: Institute of Southeast Asian Studies, 1981), 69.

[14] Charlie, interview by author, Washington D.C, May 30, 1998.

[15] Agricultural Corporation, "Farmers with Production over 150 baskets per acre in 1978/79", (in Burmese). Yangon: 1980.

In fact, many model farmers also over-reported their production by borrowing produce from their neighbors to impress the visiting ruling authorities or agricultural officials.[16]   Model farmers were touted and given awards, honors, and political offices. Such action and practice misled the central government, specifically General Ne Win, leading to the expansion of the government's paddy procurement quota on ordinary farmers. In addition, ordinary as well as model farmers were subjected to abuse and harassment by officials at the government buying depot, who asked for additional amounts of product based on the argument that what was brought to them had been under-weighed, wet, low quality, or impure. This practice of officials mistreating or aggravating farmers, nevertheless, is not typical only of the HYV period: it has persisted throughout the entire period of military rule in Burma.[17]

General views on the HYV program
The High-Yielding Variety Promotion provides an example in which increases in agricultural production do not correlate very well with a corresponding high level of government popularity in the countryside. There were three reasons for the lack of support for the HYV strategy. First, a closer observation of growth and productivity in the paddy sector demonstrates that these increases were not directly translated into equivalent surges in farmers' living conditions.   This cautions us that the economic situation of individual farmers must be measured in terms of their net earnings (disposable income) rather than the gross amount of their yield, production or sown areas.

Second, Burmese farmers abhorred rigorous enforcement, close monitoring and supervision. During the HYV periods, government provided substantial human resources to accomplish the HYV program; there were three agricultural extension workers for every HYV model village (whereas the current ratio is 1:5).[18] Male agricultural officials were stationed in the villages to educate farmers about new technology. They conducted demonstrations, supervised farmers in the field every morning, held formal and informal meetings, and had "open" and "intimate" discussions with farmers every evening. Female extension workers, on the other hand, had to get up at six o'clock every morning. They boarded a big truck parked in front of the MAS

[16] A comment made by a farmer from *Alei* township, *Sagaing* division, March 1999.
[17] See Mya Maung, "The Burmese approach to development: Economic growth without democratization", *Journal of Asian Economics* 7 (1) (1995): 105-107.
[18] In the first experimental township like *Auk* township, Rangoon division, forty-two extension workers were assigned to forty-two model farmers.

(Myanma Agriculture Service) office, and then rode to their assigned villages where they spent the whole day.

Model farmers from the HYV townships vividly remembered how they were forced to attend a meeting every night at the extension camp for appropriate technical and political training. In addition to putting in extra labor and applying new technology in the fields, much of their time was spent hosting the urban voluntary work force, agricultural extension workers, and the local and national high ranking officials. They also needed to prepare for string-row transplanting and harvesting contests. Associated closely with this period was the compulsory requirement to match and attend a mass meeting held in the city on every national holiday, especially on Peasants' Day on March 2. Here they had to listen to tedious speeches by high-ranking party and council members.

Thus the HYV promotion, which was closely associated with mass mobilization, strict surveillance and intensive training courses, was disliked by many farmers. In fact, one extension worker from Auk township, Rangoon division, witnessed cries of joy from transplanters in his village during the outbreak of the pro-democracy movement in Rangoon in 1988. They exuberantly shouted "democracy is coming, and we do not have to string row-plant anymore!"

Third, many cultivators tend to have a higher level of tolerance for a policy package that fails to provide sufficient financial, technical and human assistance, but only claims a small proportion of produce from the farmers. A development strategy with a higher level of support from the central and local government, on the other hand, may not be appreciated much if it is followed by a higher level of extraction from the cultivators. Such nature of expectation is not unique to Burma. Joan Nelson and Samuel Huntington, for instance, observe that "in many developing countries increased government regulation and activity [usually in the name of broader public welfare] have prompted a good deal of participation aimed not at extracting benefits, but at avoiding burdens."[19] In authoritarian and poor countries, cultivators do not expect so much from the government since they are not used to being offered material incentives or sufficient financial and physical support. These low expectations can be attributed to farmers' awareness of lack of government revenues or the absence of competing political parties to mobilize them. Although there were differences in expectation between villages close to the center and those in the peripheral areas, Burmese rice farmers tended

[19] Joan Nelson and Samuel Huntington, *No Easy Choice: Political Participation in Developing Countries* (Massachusetts: Harvard University Press, 1976), 130.

to complain less about insufficient loans and support from the government, and more about the excessive demands and controls by the state. Nonetheless, the tarnished image of the national government was either minimized or worsened depending on the specific types of relationships local authorities had with their constituencies.

The Varying Regards for Central and Local Authorities
Many farmers blamed local authorities, who generally withheld information from the central government about their misery and hardship. In some farmers' minds, those from atek (officials from the capital) could have been much more lenient on poor farmers had they been informed about their actual situation. For instance, the central government policy required farmers to keep a certain amount of their produce (twelve bags of rice per person per year), and sell the remaining crops to the government. This meant that the more paddy cultivators produced, the higher the percentage of output they had to sell to the government at an artificially low price, given the fixed numbers of family members. Thus, the grave distortions of official figures on a certain village, due either to over-reporting by a few elite farmers or by the local authorities, led to a higher procurement quota on ordinary and poor farmers within a village and worsened their living conditions. Karen residents from the surrounding areas of an HYV model village in <u>Auk</u> township, for instance, complained that they had to sell a higher proportion of their output due to the reports of exaggerated yield by their neighboring counties, despite the fact that the Karen yields were extremely low. A farmer from Tharrawaddy township also complained that

> The person (turned out to be the *Pegu* divisional manager of the Myanma Agriculture Service) who was in charge of estimating our "expected" yield and output was not from our area. He was from *Pegu* city. He had his own formula on how to estimate the potential yield from our field. He took into consideration the expected production costs, including wastes, and the costs of agricultural inputs and hiring labor, and he came up with the average yield expected from our village. Based on his calculation, the concerned authorities announced that the average yield of our village was 70 baskets per acre, whereas most of us can barely produce 50 baskets per acre. Consequently, we were required to sell all of our paddy to the government (both Corporation One and Cooperatives or *Tha-ma-wa-ya-ma*).[20]

[20] Conversation with farmers from <u>*Lucky*</u> village, *Tharrawaddy* township, *Pegu* division, July 1994.

Coupled with the highly inaccurate performance reporting of ordinary farmers, the rampant corruption at the local paddy buying center did not help improve the state-societal relationship at the local levels. This type of interaction (quadrant 3; local unpopular/central popular) in Chart 1 improved the image of the national authorities, who were thought to be misled and misinformed. This tarnished the image and legitimacy of the local party, the council officials, and professional bureaucrats. Accounts by farmers from _Lucky_ village, _Love_ township, Pegu division and an ordinary Karen village located adjacent to a model village in _Auk_ township confirmed that they had experienced a situation similar to the scenario described in quadrant three.

Even if the reported economic figures of a particular region were real, rural support for the local governing authorities was limited as long as practices were enforced so strictly. The state had imposed irrational policies from above and farmers still had little or nothing left to sell on the market. In the situation described in quadrant four, the national leaders were held as equally responsible as the local officials for asking too much from the peasants, because they were assumed to be correctly informed about the grain output. Consequently, both types of governments failed to generate popular acceptance for their practices, despite their successful effort in boosting rural growth and productivity. Rigid imposition from the center, and the potential punishment for failure to enforce the policy prevented most local officials from being too lenient toward the local population. A farmer's son from *Natalin* township, *Sagaing* Division, for instance, remarked that

> I saw some instances in which local (village) officials covered up things from township officials who are city-dwellers. But in the case of quota, *they were under pressure from the township officials and they could not help but pressed other farmers*.....It is hard for peasants to get around the system when they did not meet the quota. Village councilmen were under pressure from the higher authorities to make sure that the peasants met the quota. Also, the local purchase center had the list of who met the quota and who did not. Township authorities could themselves ask police or the local councilmen to take action.[21]

Consequently, all the farmers' memories about the HYV periods were overshadowed by the negative opinions about both governments, who were insensitive to their problems, and attempted to get as much as they could from them. Stories about excessive quotas and complaints

[21] Ye Myint, personal correspondence with author, April 11, 1997.

against both levels of government were found almost everywhere in the country.

Cultivators' support for the local governing authorities was likely to be strong, however, when there was leniency on the part of local officials, either in terms of under reporting their residents' output or of imposing less severe penalties on those who failed to comply with the quota system (quadrant 2: local popular/central unpopular). Here, the image of prominent figures in Rangoon was likely to be severely tarnished because of both their policies and the willingness of particular local state departments or agencies to protect their constituencies' welfare.

Finally, very few farmers, specifically model farmers, who were given material incentives, political office, awards and honors, were supportive of both the local and national government. Quota demand was high, and pressures to produce higher levels of paddy output were endless. Nonetheless, nothing was more satisfying for these elite farmers than having the opportunity to shake hands with high-ranking officials from the capital, to attend dinner at the President's residence in Rangoon, or to receive awards, honors, and gifts from the Central Party and Council Organizations as well as from the Minister of Agriculture. One model farmer, who was well known for his innovation of a particular type of high-yielding rice varieties, for instance, was given VIP treatment at the military hospital in *Mingaladon* when he suffered from malaria. He was visited by the minister and other high ranking officials from the Ministry of Agriculture, and the authorities from Central Party and Council Organizations.

Circumstances under quadrant three (local unpopular/central popular) and four (both governments unpopular) were the predominant trends of the HYV periods. Interestingly, however, none of the interviews and conversations with farmers from different parts of the country uncovered stories or activities that might suggest the possibility of the situation in quadrant 2 (local popular/central unpopular). It is still possible that conditions of local government popularity and central government unpopularity existed in remote areas where the government's reach was tenuous. In the same manner, the type-one situation (wherein both governments enjoyed popularity) hardly ever occurred, except among very small numbers of model farmers from High-Yielding Varieties village, specifically from *Taung* village, *Auk* township in Lower Burma.

However, there were approximately 42 model farmers in *Taung* village, who may or may not necessarily share the views of the few model farmers with whom I have spoken, who had a relatively amicable relationship and close ties with the central and local authorities. Nonetheless, the fact that most farmers from the village avoided joining the demonstration of the farmers from the surrounding villages in 1988 demonstrates their indifference or unwillingness toward changes in political system. (Admittedly, this could have involved some political farsightedness on their part). The recurring themes and stories about the intense pressure on local officials to fulfill their assignments, and the overall policy of extracting high levels of peasants' produce therefore show that both types of governments enjoyed little or no legitimacy in promoting the HYV promotion.

(2) Halting steps toward Liberalization (1987-present)
The first major step toward "partial market oriented reforms" in Burma came in September 1987 when the military government allowed farmers to make decisions on the type of crops they should grow. [22] It exempted nine grains, originally including rice, from the government procurement, and encouraged private internal and external exports of these crops.[23] The former state buying agency, State Corporation No. 1, which was later renamed the Myanma Agricultural Produce Trading (MAPT), began to offer higher procurement prices of paddy to farmers, although the official offered prices remained as low as 20 per cent of the unofficial/black market rate.[24] The government also abolished price controls, reduced subsidies on agricultural inputs, and allowed direct foreign investment in the agricultural sector. Although rice exporting was still a state monopoly, the government reduced the compulsory delivery quota from approximately 50 baskets per acre to 12 baskets per acre (1 basket equals to 46 pounds).[25]

---

[22] The UNDP, *Agricultural Sector Development in Burma: A Trend Analysis of Published Statistics*, 1987/88-1996/97 (Yangon: UNDP, 1998), ii.
[23] D. Steinberg, *The Future of Burma: Crisis and Choice in Burma* (New York: University Press of America, 1990), 21.
[24] Mya Maung, op.cit. , 106.
[25] According Myat Thein and Maung Maung Soe, those who grow traditional varieties are required to sell five baskets per acre and those who grow high-yielding varieties are required to sell eleven baskets per acre to the government. Myat Thein and Maung Maung Soe, "Economic reform and agricultural development in Myanmar", *ASEAN Economic Bulletin* 15 (1) (April 1998): 16.

Chart (1)

The basis of popularity/unpopularity of the local authorities and central government in HYV promotion

		Central Government	
		Popular	Unpopular
Local Government	*Popular*	A small minority "model farmers" who were given awards, honors, and prizes (1) e.g. *Taung* village, *Auk* township, Rangoon division.	Local officials lenient on quota demands; no exaggerated economic figures; less abuse at the buying depots. (2) (unobserved).
	Unpopular	Local government exaggerated yields, leading to the higher demand for quota, which in turn was strictly enforced by local authorities; strictly enforced cultivation practices; widespread abuses at the local buying centers. Farmers assumed the central government was unaware of these corrupt practices and the grave distortion of official figures. (3) e.g. Lucky village, Love township, and surrounding villages of model village in *Auk* township.	No exaggerated economic figures, but relentless enforcement of procurement quota by the local officials; strictly enforced cultivation practices; widespread abuse at the buying depots. (4) e.g. *Natalin* township, *Sagaing* division.

At first glance, these partial market-oriented policies seem to demonstrate a classic example of development strategies enjoying widespread popularity. Farmers could now sell most of their produce in the market and thus earn higher income. Previously under the "socialist government (1972-88)," the cultivation of pulses and beans meant the death penalty or life imprisonment. Thanks to the new policies, the sown area for pulses increased 85 per cent from 1984/85 to 1995/96. Since 1990-91 pulses and beans have taken over the top list of all other items of agricultural export, including rice and rice products, both in terms of value and volume.[26] Rice farmers' economic conditions have improved to the extent that they can now practice double or multiple cropping patterns (rice-pulse, rice-beans, or rice-beans/pulses-rice) as opposed to only being able to grow one crop.

Although the aggregate and disaggregate data on rural income are not available, the U.S Embassy in Rangoon wrote that "real disposable farm incomes have been clearly rising since 1989 in most of Burma's villages in response to the partial liberalization of agricultural production and marketing of the late 1980s."[27] The increasing use of radios and bicycles in the countryside demonstrates improvements in living conditions in the agricultural sector over the past eight years. In addition, "many villages enjoy privately-owned generator-powered VCR/television facilities that serve as community theaters. Diesel-fueled irrigation pumps have widely replaced traditional animal- and human-powered alternatives." [28]

What is unpopular is not the market-oriented policy, but the frequency with which policy makers have vacillated between the elimination, and the reimposition of control over rice farmers, as well as the failure to provide stable and predictable policy outcomes. For instance, the rice procurement system, supposedly officially eliminated in 1987, was reintroduced in 1989. *The Far Eastern Economic Review* reported in 1989 that liberalization of the private trade in paddy "had disastrous results. Official rice exports, the country's major foreign-exchange earner, fell to just 50,000 tons in 1988....urban rice supplies dwindled, prices rocketed in July and August last year, and political tension mounted...At the end of last year, the government reinstituted central collection." [29]

Again in 1997, the military government announced that the existing paddy procurement system would be replaced by a more

---

[26] The UNDP, *Agricultural Sector Development in Burma*, 13.

[27] The US embassy, *Country Commercial Guide: Burma* (Rangoon: 1998), 8.

[28] The US embassy, 18.

[29] Bertil Lintner and Paul Handley, "Rancor over Rice", *Far Eastern Economic Review* (10 August, 1989): 58.

competitive method of selling stock for the best price. Unable to compete with merchants and traders who offered higher prices, this policy was soon eliminated in March 1998.[30] Confused and frustrated, some farmers said they had already sold most of their produce when the rice procurement system was reimposed.[31] They were then forced to buy paddies at higher prices in the market to comply with the central government. One farmer from *Pegu* division complained in 1999 that "you can never predict what the government's next move is, and I am worried about the likelihood of government's restriction on free marketing of beans and pulses which could re-empower the local police to interfere in our life...You just cannot tell!!"[32]

Added to the already confused and complex structure of policy formulation and implementation was the gradual movement toward the old practices of strict control. The following data on the percentage share of the procurement over the last five years, for instance, indicates the gradual increase in percentage quotas for all major agricultural commodities.[33]

Percentage share of officially procured crops in total outputs

Commodity	1989	1990	1991	1992	1993	1994
Paddy	9.5	10.8	11.8	11.1	11.5	11.1
Pulses	10.6	5.9	5.1	7.0	10.1	11.6
Maize	7.2	6.9	3.1	7.2	7.8	10.2
Cotton	15.9	14.5	36.5	13.2	20.9	31.4
Sugarcane	17.7	10.8	29.2	20.7	21.3	31.5

Source: IMF, *Myanmar: Recent Economic Developments* (Washington D.C: IMF, 1995 and 1997), 69.

The US Embassy reported in 1996 that "much of the growth in the important rice sub-sector has been achieved by state coercion, which appears to have increased since about 1992."[34] Along with the rice sector, there were simultaneous moves to put restraints on the production of beans and pulses.[35]

---

[30] Text of US Department of Agriculture on Burma Rice Procurement Policy, *Dow Jones* (December 1, 1997).
[31] Interview by author, *Lucky* village, *Love* township, *Pegu* division, June 1999.
[32] Interview by author, *Lucky* village, *Love* township, *Pegu* division, June 1999.
[33] Comments from farmers from *Alei* township, *Sagaing* Division.
[34] The US embassy, *Country Commercial Guide: Burma* (Rangoon, July 1996), 12.
[35] Ibid., 16.

This slow but noticeable rise in the proportion of paddy procurement, and the restrictions on the choice of crops farmers were willing to grow failed to ensure consistency and predictability on long-term policy prospects, and confused the majority of paddy farmers. Consequently, the UNDP observed that "due to constant uncertainties with and sometimes abrupt change to policies, farmers' willingness to take risks and make new investments in the agricultural sector have also been limited. This is evidenced through recent decline in acreage under cultivation as well as decrease in farm income."[36]

General Views toward the Partial Liberalization Policy
Partial liberalization did not generate similar levels of growth and productivity in rice sector as did the HYV campaign, and yet there was overwhelming rural support for this market-oriented reform. First of all, improved living conditions explained the popularity of partial liberalization as the policy package opened up new opportunities for extra income for many rural residents.

Secondly, unlike the HYV program, which strictly monitored and supervised paddy farmers, the "market approach" to agriculture operated under a more relaxed atmosphere. Since 1988, the central government has eliminated local authorities' daily supervision and loosened bureaucratic rigidity.

Farmers were no longer required to attend the mass meeting on Peasants' Day. Nor was Peasants' Day publicized or celebrated. Most farmers seemed to like the fact that they no longer had to march up to the city on Peasants' Day.[37] Many farmers, except for those whose farms were adjacent to main roads and highways, could now get away with regular row transplanting (instead of string-row transplanting) without being penalized. Aside from the reduced pressure to over-report their yield, and freedom from close monitoring and supervision, farmers appreciated the flexibility involved in bargaining with the local governing officials, and the emergence of a variety of channels to address their plight. The wife of a village tract chairman in Rangoon division, for instance, commented that farmers can now express and address their concerns directly to the high ranking officials in Rangoon, an access that did not exist under the "socialist" government. One farmer from *Sagaing* Division also noted that "the current government is much more lenient and flexible when it comes to collecting quotas from the farmers. Instead of confiscating our lands and imprisoning us, it now allows us to submit a letter explaining why

[36] UNDP, "Agricultural Sector Development in Burma: A Trend Analysis of Published Statistics", iii. The UNDP also concluded that the real farm income started to decline from 1995/96.
[37] Conversation with farmers from *Alei* township, *Sagaing* division, April 1999.

our crops failed. If our crops failed, we are not required to sell the full amount of quota, and a new quota was negotiable depending on how badly one's crops are damaged." Instead of over-reporting their produce, farmers now under-reported their produce, and shared their concealed grains with local officials without worrying much about the potential punishment from the central government.

Last but not least, despite its failure to provide sufficient material and human support, the partial liberalization program was popular because it extracted less grain from paddy producers. Definitely, the government has gradually increased its procurement quota since the implementation of partial liberalization in 1987, but the percentage of the procured output was considerably less than it was under the HYV period. Occasionally, farmers may miss the availability of cheap chemical fertilizers, and the assistance they enjoyed back in the seventies. Nevertheless, none of them would like to relive the hardships of HYV period, where a high quota system was the norm. Furthermore, the skyrocketing prices on chemical fertilizers have relatively less impact on farmers' lives since chemical fertilizers can be substituted with organic fertilizers, or can be bought on credit from private traders. A farmer's daughter from *Irrawaddy* division, for instance, remarked that "we do not need chemical fertilizers for our fields because they are very fertile. We used chemical fertilizer only because we have been forced by the government."[38] In the same manner, insufficient loans from the government can be complemented by borrowing money from private money lenders.

However, although partial liberalization has been popularly welcomed and accepted by rural populations, the uncertainty and confusion involved in the policy itself did not significantly help to promote the popularity of the military regime. The local governments' treatment of the policy remains the foundation upon which local population developed different perceptions of their local officials as well as the central authorities.

The Varying Levels of Support for Central and Local Authorities through Partial Liberalization
Both the local and national leadership enjoyed rural support at the initial stage of partial liberalization. Some villages in <u>Hope</u> township, *Irrawaddy* division during the period of 1987-91 provide good examples. Such broad-based support, however, was no longer the case from 1992 onward. Since 1992, the government has gradually reimposed control over the agricultural sector. Nevertheless, some

[38] Conversation with a farmer's daughter from *Irrawaddy* division, December 2002.

villages such as *Taung* village in *Auk* township, continued to hold favorable views of both governments because they were less susceptible to changes in agricultural policies and had a relatively uncorrupted local governing system. In *Taung* village, changes in policy had little impact on farmers since the local soil was not favorable for high return cash crops such as beans and pulses; thus farmers did not lose much from the policy that prohibits the cultivation of beans and pulses in paddy-designated areas. In addition, the gradual increases in quota procurement were too small to make substantial impact on these farmers' lives.

On the other hand, the popularity of both leaderships (quadrant 4) was highly contested in the regions that were hit hard by the changes in the policies, and where there was little or no attempt on the part of the local officials to shield their constituents from the effect of policy changes. Some villages from *Hope* township, *Irrawaddy* division from 1992 onward, which prospered from the cultivation of beans and pulses, fit this quadrant. There, farmers' discontent was targeted at the central government, which formulated unpredictable and unstable policies. Their resentment was further compounded by the unwillingness or inability of local authorities to moderate the central directives. The situations described in quadrant four also occurred when farmers believed that local exploitations took place with the tacit acknowledgement of the central governing authorities.

For instance, some farmers believed that the military regional commanders and the local ruling government had been exacting a certain proportion of produce (in addition to MAPT procurement) at the low fixed prices within the range of permission by the central authorities, because they were conducted under the banner of contribution for local administrative funds. When asked whether central authorities were aware of these practices, one farmer from *Tharawwady* township, *Pegu* division, for instance, remarked that "I guess the central authorities are no different from the local authorities."

However, it is possible for farmers to support the local government despite the changes in agricultural policies by the central government. The local governments tended to be popular when they were lenient on the local population, thereby making changes from the capital less noticeable to the local population (quadrant 2: local popular/central unpopular). Such incidence can be observed in 1988-92 in the *Atek* village tract, *Alei* township, *Sagaing* division. Despite the policy shift to reimpose the procurement system in 1989, the township PDC chairman negotiated with the village tract chairman *U Khant* on the amount of produce farmers were willing to sell to the government. Both sides were satisfied. When farmers were aware that the local authorities did attempt to stabilize the local situation against the mood swings of the central political elite, they developed a high regard for the local governing officials at the expense of the national government.

However, rural support for the local governing authorities was weak in villages with a high degree of corruption, especially if the practices of corruption were based on extortion and coercion, rather than on mutually beneficial exchanges between state officials and their local constituents (quadrant 3). Whereas farmers under the "socialist economy" were left with little or no grain after they had sold their output to the authorities, under the partial market-oriented reform they now had surplus agricultural commodities and extra cash. Consequently, the local governing authorities demanded an additional proportion of already procured produce, such as rice, pulses and beans. Some townships that hosted army headquarters and residences were also forced to provide free, or to sell certain amounts of agricultural commodities at government fixed prices to the military.[39] For instance, the US embassy in Burma reported in 1996 that villages from rice surplus regions have routinely been required by local military authorities to sell paddy, in addition to the MAPT quota. It estimated that the military and MAPT may have procured as much as 18 per cent of national paddy output at the state-set price in 1994/95, a percentage considerably higher than that from the IMF report which is based on the Burmese official statistics.

Most corruption, in fact, was hidden from the central authorities as farmers were either intimidated by the local officials or did not have access to the central authorities. Mya Maung, for instance, reports that

> Farmers dare not report this abuse (at the buying depot) to the military commanders who regularly visit village buying depots to inspect the paddy output in various regions. *Farmers are under the threat of the head procurement agent who intimidates them that if* any farmer reports the theft to the military authorities his next sale/delivery will be under cut further, 15% to 20% or 15 to 20 baskets of paddy per 100 per baskets for example.[40]

Thus, rice farmers were more likely to place the sole responsibility on the local authorities for their economic hardship if they were convinced that the national government had no knowledge of what had occurred or was occurring in their villages and townships (quadrant 3; local unpopular/central popular). A well-off farmer from *Irrawaddy*

[39] The US embassy, *Country Commercial Guide: Burma* (Rangoon: July 1996), 15.
[40] Mya Maung, op.cit., 106.

division, for instance, mumbled grudgingly that the central authorities had officially announced that they would no longer procure mungbean, and therefore they may not have been aware that farmers, including himself, had to provide one basket of mungbean per acre to the divisional and township political authorities. He also commented that the state/divisional PDC authorities instructed the township PDC to extract one basket of mungbean per acre from farmers, but the township authorities appropriated one and a half basket of mungbean, and thereby kept half a basket to themselves.[41]

Increases in the prices of fertilizer and other agricultural inputs due to "liberalization" significantly handicapped the rural economy, but farmers put little blame on the national leadership. If farmers ever complained, their complaints were not directed at the national authorities who were unable to supply fertilizers, but at the local agricultural officials who made illicit sales of chemical fertilizers to private traders. Many farmers eventually avoided buying from the Myanma Agriculture Services, which not only sold low-quality and under weighed chemical fertilizers, but also required long and complicated bureaucratic procedures to obtain them. After all, the price differences between better quality and correctly weighed fertilizers acquired from the market, and low quality and incorrectly weighed government distributed fertilizers were minimal.

Situations under quadrant 1 (both governments enjoy popularityquadrant 3 (local unpopular/central popular) and quadrant 4 (both governments unpopular) are common trends in the partial market-oriented reform. Situations under quadrant 1 more commonly occur at the earlier stages of liberalization. Quadrant 3 and 4 are typical in the later stage of partial liberalization, depending on whether farmers perceive the central government responsible for their problems (quadrant 4) or not (quadrant 3).

---

[41] Interview by author, August 1999.

Chart 2

The basis of support or lack of support for local authorities and central governments in partial liberalization

		Central Government	
		Popular	Unpopular
Local government	*Popular*	Areas that had done well from growing cash crops and were least susceptible to changes in policies. (1) e.g. villages in <u>Hope</u> township, *Irrawaddy* division (1988-1992). A village in <u>*Auk*</u> township, Rangoon division (1988-present).	Oscillation of policies from the center moderated by the local governing authorities. (2) e.g. A village in <u>*Alei*</u> township, *Sagaing* division: 1989-1992.
	Unpopular	Local government raised quota and restricted decision over the choice of crops without the knowledge of the central government. (3) e.g. A village in <u>Beauty</u> township, *Irrawaddy* division: 1999 A village in <u>*Alei*</u> township, *Sagaing* division: 1997-1998.	Oscillation of policies had direct drastic impact on farmers' lives because there was no attempt by local government to moderate; widespread local abuses and practices with the tacit approval of the central government. (4) e.g. villages in <u>Hope</u> township, *Irrawaddy* division: 1992-present (1999).

(3) Summer paddies (1992-present)
Until the late 1980s, irrigated land covered only 12 per cent of the
total cultivated areas, and most farmers practiced a single (monsoon)
cropping pattern in the country. By the early 1990's, a shortage of
foreign exchange for fertilizer imports had shifted the government's
emphasis from vertical expansion, through intensive use of chemical
fertilizers, to horizontal expansion (or sown area expansion) through
multiple cropping and land reclamation.[42] Water is crucial for multiple
cropping. To fulfill this need, the military regime constructed and
remodeled small- and large-scale irrigation systems. The government
was able to promote the project cheaply because it was able to utilize
free rural labor for irrigation building, without relying heavily on
foreign exchange.

Subsequently, the summer paddy program was launched in 1992.
Free labor was the key to constructing irrigation, sparing millions of
dollars for otherwise costly projects. The government, for example,
estimated the value of new irrigation works constructed by local
projects in 1993-1995 to be about 100 million kyat. This is compared
to only 126.7 million kyat spent on local irrigation projects for the
entire 30 year period between 1962-1992, and of which the people's
contribution accounted for 49 per cent, up from an average of 38 per
cent between 1962-1993.[43] Between the period of 1990-1996,
seventy four irrigation projects were completed.[44]

Promoted by "uncompensated" or "under compensated" labor,
official statistics revealed that the total irrigated area increased from
2.5 to 4.1 million acres from 1991/92 to 1994/95.[45] Irrigated areas
have nearly doubled since 1989. The first summer program, which
started in 1992-1993, covered 0.82 million acres, and produced a total
of 45 million baskets.[46] By 1995-96, it constituted one quarter (4.9
million metric ton out of 19.9 million metric tons) of the total
national output. This is the impressive growth that IMF referred to as
the consequence of better irrigation and fertilizer input, which allow
two and three crops a year.[47] Led by the improvement in agriculture

---

[42] Whereas the availability of fertilizer was made possible by foreign aid and loans during the HYV periods, international protest against the massacre in 1988, and the dishonoring of the election result by the military junta in 1990 resulted in a trade embargo, sanctions, and stoppage of aid to the government, leaving the military regime cash-strapped and almost bankrupt.
[43] The US Embassy, *Foreign Economic Trend Report: Burma* (Rangoon: 1996), 14.
[44] Ministry of Agriculture and Irrigation, *Information on Myanmar Agriculture: 1996* (Yangon: 1996), 9.
[45] The US Embassy, op.cit., 14.
[46] Ibid., 17.
[47] The IMF, *Myanmar: Recent Economic Development* (Washington D.C: 1997), 10.

due to the expansion of irrigated lands, the Burmese economy averaged six per cent of annual growth from the early 1990's until 1997.

There are many reasons why the summer paddy program is fairly popular in Burma. First, summer paddies utilize idle labor and provide additional income for farmers who had previously grown a single crop annually. Second, there is no official procurement quota for summer paddies; farmers can sell all of their produce to the market. Third, many farmers prefer summer paddies because of their short maturing duration, easier cultivating practices (which use a broadcasting rather than transplanting method), and higher yield. Unlike paddy products that are grown in the rainy season, when harvested crops are more subject to rain-related damage, summer paddies have experienced less harvesting wastage and fewer crop losses. Plentiful sunshine also means higher output per acre, as dry paddies are drought resistant, and heat responsive. Thus, the average yield of summer paddies is higher than that of monsoon paddies.

Although the program was initially greeted with skepticism by nearly all farmers, summer paddies have brought prosperity to well-to-do farmers and have created breathing-space for poor farmers. Needless to say, the summer paddy program has proved so successful and popular in some areas that farmers now want to be part of the summer program, which can utilize only a limited number of cultivated acres due to the restricted water supply, especially in the dry zone. [48]

One major problem associated with the summer paddy initiative, however, was the failure on the part of the policy makers to take into account ecological variations across the country. The US embassy, for instance, observed in 1996 that

> In some regions, multiple-cropping increased farm income with little risk and farmers complied willingly and successfully with the government's new production directives. In some other areas, including regions near the sea in Irrawaddy, Rangoon and Pegu divisions--Burma's rice-surplus region---salinity problems, high flood risks, and seasonal pest problems made multiple cropping inappropriate, it was nevertheless imposed on villages, with sometimes disastrous results, by regional and local military authorities who had production targets to meet.[49]

As this report indicates, the decision to implement the program across the board has not been successful because of the differences in climatic conditions.

---

[48] Accounts based on farmers from *Alei* township, *Sagaing* division, and *Auk* township, Rangoon division.

Another controversy which has emerged from the implementation of the summer paddy program is the use of forced or free (loke-ahh-pay) labor to implement the project. This has been an emotional issue. At its most extreme, forced labor practices by the military in the conflict zone have constituted egregious human rights abuses, including forced porterage and the use of human mine sweepers. This issue received a great deal of attention during the mid 1990s when forced labor was used in constructing tourism facilities and other infrastructure projects, such as road building and clearing military cantonment sites. The use of "loke- ahh- pay" (free labor) in Burma's main rice producing areas, however, is more complex. Specifically, farmers' judgments about labor contribution were predicated on how it affected their lives, whether they were paid or not, and the season in which they were drafted or called upon.

First, farmers who received immediate and direct benefits from their labor developed a more favorable attitude toward the military regime than those who do not receive anything in return for their efforts. A former government employee from Chin State also commented that,

> Farmers were appreciative of the government's initiatives to construct dams, roads, and to reclaim lands, which would otherwise not have been possible without the military exhortation, coercion, and mobilization. But corruption and the mismanagement of public funding were so widespread among people in charge of constructing the projects that farmers began to lose faith in the potential benefits associated with their labor contributions. The quality of the majority of irrigation works remained poor as funds designated for construction projects went into the pockets of project managers, party officials, and military officers. Most small-scale irrigation did not last long, and needed to be constantly repaired and reconstructed within a short period of time after the completion of the project.[50]

A farmer from *Taung* village admitted that he was very angry when he was ordered by the authorities to help construct a small-scale irrigation network adjacent to his village. In retrospect, however, he was very grateful for the leadership of the military regime and the local political and civilian officials who made summer paddies possible. Another farmer from *Praise* township, *Pegu* Division, said that they would not mind volunteering their labor as long as the project made direct positive contributions to their villages. Most of the time, however, they were asked to clean the gardens or till the lands of the local military officials, which made farmers reluctant to respond positively

---

[50] Charlie, interview by author, Washington D.C, May 1998.

to the call of involuntary labor. Another farmer from *Hle Gu* township, Rangoon division, remarked that he would be willing to contribute his labor toward his village (rather than for the township) and toward building roads surrounding his village. He would, however, be unwilling to "clear bushes along the highway," which he considered to be secondary and time-consuming.[51] Likewise, cultivators from *Lucky* village, *Love* township, *Pegu* division, complained that they had to contribute a specific amount of money and labor to the construction of irrigation work. The construction of the new irrigation dam had already claimed some of their lands, and they were not sure of its potential benefit since (1) the surrounding areas, which supposedly benefited from new irrigation work, were already short of water and experienced crop failure and (2) some of their paddy fields would be too far from the new dam to receive water.

Second, rural residents who were paid were less hostile to the authorities in charge of projects than those who did not get paid. Gordon Fairclough, for example, notes that although some Burmese farmers complained about being ordered to work two weeks a month for six months building a road near their village with the minimum payment of 40 kyat a day, others commented that they found the money "a help, especially in the dry season, when there is no work to do in the fields."[52] Another farmer, who was routinely paid for his labor, in fact, said he looked forward to new public projects which provided employment opportunities for him.[53] Others said they were not only paid and fed sufficiently, but were also entertained by famous national dancers, actors, and actresses every evening at the construction site. Consequently, many rural residents had fought over who was to be sent to the construction sites for the available jobs.[54] Contrary to this, farmers from *Alei* township in Upper Burma vividly remembered how they had to walk forty to fifty miles home from the construction site, since they were not even paid for travel expenses, let alone fairly compensated for their labor.

Finally, local residents were relatively more conciliatory toward the concerned authorities if they were conscripted in the off-

[51] Conversation with a farmer from Rangoon division, December, 2002.
[52] G. Fairclough, "That's an Order", in *Far Eastern Economic Review* (August 31, 1995): 27.
[53] Conversation with a farmer from *Alei* township. Another seventy-five year old farmer from *Alei* township, *Sagaing* division, said some of the local residents like himself could afford the financial contribution, but he accompanied the workers to the construction site because he was simply "curious." He was designated as a chief cook of ten farmers at the construction site. He thought it was an interesting experience.
[54] Here, the local officials demanded a specific contribution from each household within a village, and the money collected was spent on the workers who "volunteered" their labor at the project site. Conversation with a farm laborer from *Kyauk-ba-daung* township, Mandalay division.

agricultural season rather than in busy season. Gillis et al., for example, argues that, "(i)n the off-season labor in the rural sectors of developing countries is unemployed or underemployed... Therefore the opportunity cost of using labor on rural public work projects is zero or near zero."[55] Again, to reiterate the quote by Fairclough, some Burmese farmers did not mind being paid minimum or standard wages for their labor, "especially in the dry season, when there is no work to do in the fields."[56] Other Burmese farmers, however, contested government's employment of low-paid or "voluntary" labor in off-agricultural season, because Burmese farmers still have to work on non-farm activities, such as repairing roofs and collecting firewood.[57] These varying opinions nonetheless show that although Burmese farmers have objected to being conscripted in certain circumstances, their attitudes toward this practice has not always been negative.

General Views Toward the Summer Paddies Program
The views of many farmers toward summer paddies are mixed depending on the areas of experimentation. Summer paddy work was widely welcomed in places suitable for dry paddy cultivation, but was dreaded by farmers who were forced to cultivate dry paddies in place of better alternative crops and in the circumstances of unavailable and unreliable water. Here again, the data on summer paddy production and sown acres can not account for the level of popularity enjoyed by the government in different regions, although the rate of success of the program may capture rural sentiments toward the regime.

In the region where summer paddy succeeded, the popularity and acceptance of summer paddy can also be explained by the reemphasis of a traditional broadcasting method, which, unlike the string row transplanting method, is labor- and time- saving, and does not require complex technical knowledge. Farmers responded very positively to this practice because summer paddies dispense with the need for training and close supervision by professional staff. The higher level of government support through the irrigation network and exemption from procurement quota made the summer paddy program attractive in many areas with successful experimentation.

The success of summer paddies had a direct and positive relationship with the popularity of the military junta, as would be predicted by "legitimacy based on economic performance." However, the relationship between the degree of success of the summer paddy program and the level of popularity enjoyed by the military

---

[55] Gillis et al., eds., *Economics of Development*, 4th edition, 444-445.
[56] G. Fairclough, op.cit., 27.
[57] Conversation with a Karen farmer from Rangoon division, December, 2002.

government was still mediated by the state-societal interaction at the local level.

The Degree of Popularity Enjoyed by Central and Local Authorities through Summer Paddies

There was dual support for the local state agencies and the central government in situations that are described in quadrant 1 (chart 3), where there was plenty of water to accommodate the demands of the potential beneficiaries. Because water was sufficient for everyone, farmers did not have to bribe the irrigation officers or local governing authorities in return for access to water. These areas occasionally experienced a "labor draft" by the government, but they were more likely to be required in off-season, to be fairly compensated, and to benefit directly from the project. Such a situation can be observed in *Taung* village, *Auk* township, Rangoon Division.

The local state agencies and departments, however, were subject to resentment and criticism once local corruption became widespread and excessive. A case in point was when junior irrigation officers, or the village chairmen or township ruling authorities secretly sold water to farmers who were outside the summer paddy project. This led to shortages of water for the majority of paddy cultivators who were under the summer paddy program, and eventually led to low output and bad harvest. To make matters worse, the local military officials demanded a proportion of produce from farmers who suffered from crop failures. Farmers were convinced that these practices occurred without the knowledge of the central government because the national policy mandated that farmers must pay only 10 kyat per acre for the use of irrigation water.[58] Furthermore, the central government had earlier announced that it would not procure summer paddy from rice farmers. Thus, addressing their problems directly to a score of military officials at the national level would be the only effective way to resolve their problems (quadrant 3; local unpopular/central popular). In 1998, for instance, villagers from one village in *Sagaing division* threatened to report their crop failure to national government officials after they were asked to provide a certain amount of produce to the local government. They took a video of a crying lady standing by the dry fields and the failed crops, and threatened to take it to the central authorities. Realizing that such moves could uncover the illegal sale of water by local officials which led to shortages of water and failure of

---

[58] Mya Thein and Maung Maung Soe, "Economic reform and agricultural development in Myanmar", 28.

project, the local government immediately withdrew their demands upon farmers.

Sometimes, the mere threat that cultivators would take the case to the capital got an immediate response from the local government, which subsequently acceded to farmers' initial demands. Like other typical Burmese villages, rural residents from these places also had to contribute their labor for large and small scale infrastructural projects. Doing so may help them directly and indirectly reap the benefits of their work. Their major complaint, however, was directed against the local military and civilian officials, whom they accused of embezzling a large fraction of project funds initially set aside for labor costs. Oftentimes, local abuses came in the form of the local authorities enforcing the project in an unsuitable region without reporting the actual situation to the central authorities. In fact, the government-owned daily newspaper, *The New Light of Myanmar*, reported in 10 November 1995 that the SLORC second Secretary Lt. Gen. Tin Oo, in a speech to a September 23rd Interministerial meeting of Government of Myanmar employees held at the Ministry of Agriculture, "had chastised some regional authorities both for imposing on farmers cropping patterns inappropriate to local conditions, and for providing incorrect data on acreage sown and on yield per acre."[59]

Under circumstances described in quadrant 3, the positive image of the top echelon of military personnel emanating from the summer paddy policy is strengthened by its perceived presence as the protector of rural interests. Again, such a trend occurred in villages in *Alei* township, *Sagaing* division, where improved economic conditions from the cultivation of summer paddies coexisted with widespread corruption and abuses by the local officials.

On the other hand, there was a basis of rural acceptance for the local government officials, who not only exempted their local constituents with no access to water from cultivating dry paddies, but also let them grow alternative crops. An example can be seen in villages in *Beauty* township, *Irrawaddy* division, where the summer paddy program had been arranged in such a way that those whose fields were adjacent to streams and rivers, and those who could drill a well and afford to pump underground water can cultivate paddies. This practice allowed farmers some flexibility, since most farmers preferred mungbean because it required less time, investment, and labor. Similarly, in *Peace* township, *Irrawaddy* division, farmers had the option of planting summer paddies on more fertile soil, and mungbeans on salinite gritty soil. It is unclear whether this flexible arrangement is

---

[59] A quote from the US embassy, *Foreign Economic Trend Report: Burma* (Yangon: 1996), 29.

157

the result of the central order or the initiatives taken up by local authorities. Most farmers seemed satisfied with the practices; they neither praised the authorities at both levels nor expressed their dissatisfaction against them (quadrant 1; both governments popular).

Finally, local military officials and professional bureaucrats tended to lack support among paddy cultivators, when they were insensitive and unconcerned about local needs and difficulties, and when they continued to enforce the unpopular and unsuitable program that was handed down by the central authorities (quadrant 4; both governments unpopular). At the same time, there was also a lack of support for central authorities because of their rigid policies. There were occasional labor and financial demands from these rural residents, but they came in the form of unpaid private work for local military officials or public work with no direct or indirect benefit to the rural population. Cultivators were also convinced that some public works were designed by the central government to result in a lack of payments or underpayments.

Consequently, these peasants were resentful and hostile to both the local and national governments. Such a situation took place in villages in *Hope* township, *Irrawaddy* division, where the summer paddies program was forced upon farmers who preferred to grow better alternative crops. Lack of reliable access to water also led many farmers to go bankrupt from cultivating summer paddies, losing their land, houses and property.

Generally speaking, situations in a quadrant three scenario (local unpopular/central popular) and quadrant four scenario (both governments unpopular) were most commonly observed under the summer paddy program. Higher returns and profits from the success of the summer paddy project made competition for water more intense and local corruption probable. Since such activities were usually kept at the local levels, farmers were more likely to be convinced that the central authorities were unaware of the real situation. News and rumors about the purging or demotion of particularly corrupt local officials by the national authorities, and any successful experiences by farmers in appealing their problems to the capital, enhanced the positive image and legitimacy of the central authorities. On the other hand, the central government's strategy of prioritizing rice over other crops led

Chart 3

Relationship between the legitimacy of the local government and that of the national government on summer Paddies

		Central Government	
		Popular	Unpopular
Local Government	*Popular*	Summer paddies implemented in suitable region, and with relatively no local corruption. Flexible arrangement over the choice of crop. (1) e.g. a village in _Auk_ township, Rangoon division. _Beauty_ and _Peace_ townships, Irrawaddy division	Central government assigned the project in areas not suitable for summer paddies, but local government lenient in terms of implementation. (2) unobserved
	Unpopular	Central government assigned the project in suitable region, but local government took bribes in return for the provision of water or the inclusion in the project, e.g._Alei_ township, or local government demanded additional percentage of output, or local government instituted the program in unsuitable regions without reporting the actual situations to the central government, or local government appropriated funds designated for irrigation projects by the central government. (3)	Central government assigned the project in unsuitable areas, and local government rigid in enforcing it. (4) e.g. _Glory_ township and _Hope_ township, *Irrawaddy* division.

to the situation stated in quadrant four, where tremendous pressures were put on the local authorities to implement the projects in inappropriate regions. This type of situation was common in many places, especially after 1992, when the government began to place emphasis on sufficiency and surplus in rice.

(4) Reclamation of land, 1991-present
The objective of this ambitious plan is to take advantage of and to utilize the availability of cultivatable land that lies fallow, a factor which covers almost the same area as the present net sown area. According to official statistics, the potential arable land is about 18.2 million hectares, of which only 8.7 million hectares are currently being utilized for crop production.[60] The government thus encouraged private entrepreneurs to reclaim fallow and virgin lands and to launch paddy-fish farming schemes in deep water. Under paddy-fish farming schemes, the construction of small scale embankments and sluice gates has enabled agricultural producers to drain water out of low-lying areas in the rainy season. In doing so, they can cultivate paddies in the drained fields and simultaneously raise fish in the areas that are flooded after the draining process.[61]

Accordingly, a Central Committee for the Management of Culturable Land, Fallow Land and Wasteland, chaired by the Minister of Agriculture, was formed in 1991 to carry out land expansion plans. Private enterprises may engage in the production of any annual (paddy, mungbeans, pulses, oilseeds) or perennial crops (pineapples, orchards, palaw, mangoes, and rubber), or in livestock, poultry farming, and aquaculture. The contract for land lease is thirty years and is renewable.[62]

The government also provided many incentives to private business people to lure them into its new projects. They included:
(1) Two to eight years of land tax exemption, and at least three years of income tax exemption from the year of the operation until a commercial production or servicing stage is attained.
(2) Free provision of public works required for flood control, drainage, and irrigation, technical assistance in developing the project, and security services to protect project staff and equipment
(3) Supplies of heavy machinery and fuel at subsidized rates
(4) Disbursement of loans by local private banks on a preferential basis
(5) Permission to export half the rice investors' produce and exemption from the rice procurement system.

[60] Kyaw Myint, *Study on the Changes of Rice Production in Myanmar*, 40.
[61] Dephane Aye, 7.
[62] Tin Htut Oo, 7.

(6) Provision of telephone services, including cellular phones and land-based phone lines on a preferential basis.

(7) Exemption from taxes and duties on imported equipment, including water pumps, tractors, bulldozers, and excavators, in unlimited quantities without the need to demonstrate foreign exchange earnings, as other importers must do.

By December 1998, the Ministry of Agriculture announced that seventy-six companies have claimed 1.2 million hectares. Most holdings were around 3,000 to 5,000 acres, though a few were much larger.

Many experts on agriculture and economics, however, warn that the current land expansion policy is uneconomical because all of the projects are heavily subsidized, and do not really reflect the market costs of the operations.[63] The costs of the projects would be even higher if the effects of environmental damage and the local communities' loss of access to the wetlands were added. A farmer's daughter from *Irrawaddy* division, for instance, commented that the construction of dams and irrigation works has caused heavy flooding in their areas. The flood, which has occurred every year in the last three years, destroyed crops and dramatically hurt farmers' economic status.[64]

The World Bank observed that "(t)he threat of creating lasting social conflict between the local groups now denied access to these lands and the business groups being established on large agricultural estates is also considerable."[65] The policy is also considered inequitable because, some argue that "the junta is hoping to use the plan to return to the old land-based oligarchy," since providing businessmen with incentives means giving privileges to the rich urban entrepreneurs at the expense of the poor small farmers.[66]

In fact, the number of landless tenants continues to rise even as the government rushes to open fallow land, which is ultimately reserved for the urban upper class businessmen.[67] Some other farmers lost land on which they have worked for years to private entrepreneurs, because the land was incorrectly considered "fallow and uncultivated" and thus must be properly "reclaimed" by the government. For instance, *Daw Wah* from a Karen village in *Auk* township, Rangoon division, who lost her land to a local military officer, angrily said that "the current policy drives the farmers out of

---

[63] The World Bank, *The World Bank Report on Myanmar* (Washington D.C: 1999), 55.
[64] Conversation with a farmer's daughter from *Irrawaddy* division, December 2002.
[65] The World Bank, 55.
[66] Philippe Agret, "Doubles on junta's agricultural revolution."
[67] Ibid.

their lands toward the town to work for low wages, whereas it attracts the army back to the villages and rural areas!"[68] *Daw Wah,* who has until recently refused to leave her land and property, also said that she now had to ask permission from the owner of her previously-held land to pick mangoes and fruits from the trees she has grown and nurtured for years.

In addition, it is a matter of controversy whether these private companies are making profits and operating efficiently at all.[69] While some scholars comment that it is too soon to evaluate its performance because the land reclamation program is highly capital intensive, as well as being geared more toward perennial growing rather than annual cropping, other experts are more pessimistic. Many observers state, and it is unofficially confirmed, that the private enterprises that are currently engaging in land reclamation processes are better off, not from the returns from operating the agricultural fields, but from the sale of machinery, fertilizer, and other agricultural inputs that they were allowed to import cheaply. The director of a private company in *Irrawaddy* division stated that the government provided them a quota of 100,000 gallons of diesel and gasoline per year at low official rates. They were also given export licenses on a variety of beans and import license on cars, trucks, oil, fertilizers, and agro- machinery. Some firms have even imported non-agricultural related machinery, such as motor vehicles, selling these for huge profits. On the other hand, they were unable to produce their own crops due to their limited experience in agriculture and because of the poor quality of land they had cleared. Consequently, these private businessmen bought rice from the surrounding farmers at higher prices and then exported it as their own produce to be qualified for the import exemptions and other subsidies.

General View on Land reclamation
Land reclamation is the least popular policy in the countryside, since its enforcement can result in the loss of one's assets, including food, income, and shelter. The increasing amount of sown acreage and total crop production could not explain why farmers were so unhappy with the land reclamation program. This seemingly unpopular policy, which

[68] Interview by author, August 1999.
[69] The director of one of the private companies in *Irrawaddy* division which participated in land reclamation (it was assigned to reclaim 5858 acres out of 200,000 acres in Irrawady division) remarked on the huge investment costs borne by the company on clearing the forests. According to him, shrubs and wild plants (particularly referred as *kyee bin* in Burmese) were difficult to clear and uproot. He estimated that there were about 1,200 *kyee* plants per acre, and his company had already spent 180 lakh on uprooting 100,000 *kyee* plants (it costs 10 kyat per plant to remove). The total investment cost, up to October 1999, was 250 lakh. The total revenue from last year, though expected to be 30 lakh, turned out to be only one lakh.

162

has little or no positive contribution towards the welfare of the people in the countryside, does not however, always lead to an equally tainted image of the regime in power.

Level of Support for Central/Local Authorities through Land Reclamation

Most farmers were convinced that the central authorities authorized their subordinates to reclaim only unoccupied land, and that local officials were using various means to take advantage of the new system. Although land reclamation was initiated by the central government, it is possible that the top executive military elite in the capital fails to keep track of the actual implementation processes in various places. One agriculture extension worker in _Auk_ township, Rangoon division, for instance, blamed the local Forestry Department for the resulting land alienation. He criticized the department for informing its ministry in Rangoon that the lands which had in fact been occupied and worked by "illegal" settlers for forty years were unoccupied lands. Another account by a farmer in the same township revealed that the Fire Department staff, which took over land based on recommendations by the Forestry Department, were surprised to find that the lands they were previously told were unoccupied and uncultivated turned out to be just the opposite. Thus the land reclamation policy has given local military authorities, forestry and land record officials different "legitimate" excuses to claim the lands already cleared and periodically worked by farmers and redistribute to local businessmen.

Not very surprisingly, the popularity of the local officials was highly contested in the countryside if they were simply using the existing policy as a means to serve their private interests and those of the local businesses. The loss of confidence in local authorities led to increased reliance on the political elite in the capital when cultivators were convinced that these rampant activities were not approved of, nor recognized by, the central government (quadrant three; local unpopular/central popular). Rural acceptance of the national leadership was further strengthened when farmers took their cases or threatened to take their cases to the capital. This often resulted in either a change of practices on the part of the local governing officials, or the reshuffling of the local authorities by the central government.

An example can be seen in one village in _Alei_ township, *Sagaing* division, where the township chairman of PDC withdrew claims on the fish ponds and other lands (initially aimed to redistribute to his associates and cronies) upon hearing that the highly honorable abbot in the local area had agreed to represent the victims and lodge a complaint to the central authorities. A village agriculture extension manager in Lower Burma once commented to me that farmers must directly address their problems to the central government, which he assumed to be unaware of rampant takeover of land under his area of supervision. Quadrant 3 situations are a recurring theme of the current land policy implementation in Burma.

Rural support for both governments was weak (quadrant 4) if cultivators were convinced that the central government was fully aware of the damage associated with a particular land project, but all the same ordered and permitted these activities while showing no sympathy to the victims. Such a situation occurred more commonly under the projects that had specific purposes and clear directives from the center, such as building a new city, relocating towns, or building an airport, that is, where the source of the people's plight could be clearly traced back to the central authorities.[70]

Quadrant one (both governments popular) and quadrant two (local popular/central unpopular) remain ideal scenarios, which were not observed during the research period. It is quite possible that situations like those described in quadrant one might have occurred in regions that benefit from land reclamation through the opening of employment opportunities to the surrounding areas and that are not subject to forced take-over and land alienation.

A situation similar to this scenario was observed in *Auk* township, Rangoon Division, where local residents competed for better paid jobs provided by a private agricultural company that cultivated perennial crops. However, these residents were simultaneously subject to harsh treatment in the form of their lands being taken over by local authorities. New job opportunities alone do not significantly make the military leaders at both levels more popular. The scenario depicted in quadrant two, which highlights local government officials' leniency in terms of shielding the local populations from the capital's order to relocate them, is almost unheard of in Burma.

---

[70] For instance, during 1989-90, the SLORC relocated approximately 500,000 people from major cities into new settlements to make way for economic projects. See Mya Maung, *The Burma Road to Capitalism* (New York: Praeger, 1998): 41-43.

Chart 4
The relationship between the legitimacy of the central government and that of the local government on land reclamation

		Central Government	
		Popular	Unpopular
Local Government	*Popular*	Private companies provide new employment opportunities to local residents; Local population retained their lands. (1) (Unobserved).	Central government ordered to reclaim land, but local government lenient on residents. (2) (Unobserved).
	Unpopular	Central government formulated policies, but local government misused and misapplied policy. (3) e.g. *Alei* township, *Auk* township.	to be reclaimed without concerns about the livelihood of the local population, and local government strictly followed the policy. (4) e.g. Peace township in *Irrawaddy* division.

A summary chart on the rice farmers' varying level of support for four different agricultural policies

	The HYV	Partial liberalization	Summer paddy	Land reclamation
Overall support	limited	enthusiastic	mixed	limited
Rural disposable income	Not improved	improved	Improved in some places and declined in others	declined
Strict control/supervision	yes	no	no	no
Government support	high	low	high	Low
Level of extraction	high	low	low	high

Legitimacy enjoyed by central and local governments

	Quadrant (1) Both governments popular	Quadrant (2) Local Popular	Quadrant (3) Central Popular	Quadrant (4) Both governments unpopular
HYV	A village in *Auk* township	None	A village in Love township	A village in Natalin township
Partial Liberalization	A village in *Auk* township (1988-present) A village in Hope township (1988-91)	A village in *Alei* township (1988-92)	A village in *Alei* township (1997-98) A village in Beauty township (1999)	A village in Hope township (1992-present)
Summer Paddy	A village in *Auk* township	None	A village in *Alei* township	A village in *Hlegu* township and a village in Hope township
Land reclamation	None	None	A village in *Alei* township and a village in *Auk* township	Villages in Peace township where farmers' lands were taken over to build an airport

Summary

During the military regime's implementation of four different agricultural policies, two recurring patterns emerged. They are farmers' favorable views of central but unfavorable views of local government (quadrant three) and farmers' unfavorable views of both central and local governments (quadrant four). Although quadrant three is predominant in all four policies, the reasons for the absence of rural support for local governments vary from one development program to another. Under the HYV program, the local government was unpopular because of its tendency to cave into pressure for over-reporting performance at the local level. This misled the central government which then demanded additional output from farmers. On the other hand, the summer paddy program and partial liberalization created new opportunities for local corruption. Local officials demanded bribes from farmers in exchange for their inclusion in the program, and extorted additional grain. In a similar manner, the land expansion program gave local state officials a certain flexibility and discretion to make decisions and implement projects, and this led to widespread abuse and exploitation at the local level. Although different programs led to different kinds of local abuses, the results were the same: the local government was perceived to be illegitimate and lacked support among the rural population. The local government unpopularity did not necessarily mean that central government was equally unpopular; rather locally based disaffection often went with an improved image of the central authorities.

Taung village in *Auk* township, Rangoon Division, in which both governments enjoyed popularity under the first three agricultural policies, is an atypical village. It has an unusual combination of an honest village chairman (who also happened to be a model farmer well respected by the local residents) and relatively uncorrupted civilian officials. Unlike the typical agricultural officials (holders of BA degrees) in other townships, who belonged to the urban middle class and were relatively unconcerned about rural welfare, the majority of agricultural extension workers in *Auk* township were not as highly educated. They had been long-term residents of the rural areas under which they were assigned responsibility. Because of these ties to the rural areas, they tended to be protective of local interests. Furthermore, their relationship with the village chairman could be traced back twenty and more years when the HYV program was introduced. Both sides enjoyed a relatively longer period of tenure, (though against their will, at least in the case of the village chairman), an uncommon situation which improved their flow of communication and mutual understanding. Only after the land reclamation policy was enforced did local military officials, who were then given certain privileges and authority over the appropriating process, begin to get involved in the claiming of lands from peasants for their own use or the use of their cronies.

Conclusion

This chapter examines the various ways in which agricultural policies are implemented and how different implementation processes influence the legitimacy of the central and local authorities. It demonstrates the significant and mediating role occasionally played by local authorities in shaping farmers' perceptions of the military government. The research underpinning this chapter shows farmers wanting local government officials to be even-handed, to use their official positions to serve the public rather than their own private interests, and to be responsive to villagers' needs. At first glance, this finding may seem to reinforce James Scott's analysis of the "moral economy of the peasant," which is based on the notion that good government policies and officials will not demand more of villagers than they can afford to provide. That is, a legitimate government is the one that should leave farmers enough food and cash to feed themselves and to perform certain religious and cultural ceremonies.

However, it is difficult to articulate a uniform concept of what farmers regard as the "minimum obligations of a legitimate state" because different rice cultivators hold varying sets of expectations of government. Why did some model farmers during the HYV period support the local and central governments, which basically appropriated almost all of their produce? The moral school of thought has failed to consider other non-material and non-moral issues (such as the opportunity to shake hand with Ne Win and the joy of seeing one's name printed in official journals, newspapers, and books) which can mitigate or exacerbate a legitimacy crisis arising from the violation of the minimum obligation of the state. Why have the better-off Burmese farmers, who have more than enough to eat and spend, developed unfavorable attitudes toward the central and local authorities? The answer was that they were exasperated by the central government's policies which lack predictability and local authorities' abuses and exploitation, although both practices did not really significantly and negatively impinge on their lives. Thus the moralist claim fails to consider farmers' varying expectations of government authorities and the specific contexts within which state-societal interactions take place. Rice farmers prefer local authorities and village chairmen who are responsive to their needs, but their expectations of the degree of leniency of local authorities vary depending on their past and present relationships with state authorities and the specific political and economic environments within which they interact with state authorities. The central governing authorities, on the other hand, enjoyed popularity when they were seen to be implementing appropriate development policies, and when farmers perceived them as the protectors of rural interests against local abuse and mistreatment. Whether farmers hold the national government accountable for the abuses of the local authorities depends on their individual experiences with both local and central authorities, the collective memories of their village, and their knowledge of national politics. These perceptions, though not fantasies, may or may not be based on objective situations. However, they are real to the extent that rice farmers have acted upon the beliefs and attitudes that are based on their specific perceptions of state authorities. It is a subject which I now turn to the next chapter for further elaboration.

Chapter 5

The Roots of Silence: Paddy Farmers and Rural Grievance

Democracy is a situation under which everyone is employed and has enough food and basic necessities.

A farmer from Sagaing township, Upper Burma.

Peace and tranquility in our village depend on the type of headman (village chairman) we have. We are better off if we have a good headman, and worse off if we have a bad headman.

A farmer's son from Pegu division.

Introduction

That peasant protests and rebellions are almost unheard of throughout the entire era of military rule in Burma is an axiom, provoking little or no intellectual curiosity on the part of academicians and policy makers. This is contrasted with the situation under the British colonial government, which saw periodic outbursts of peasant revolts following its occupation of the country, including the famous Saya San's peasant revolution in 1929.[1] Since the military government's takeover in 1962, Burmese cultivators have hardly appeared to voice their demands nor express their problems openly through public protests, let alone take up arms against this oppressive state.

This chapter will examine the question of political quiescence in the countryside. In broad terms I will examine how three crucial factors--- Burmese farmers' fear of the military's retaliation and suppression, their ambivalent attitudes toward authorities, and farmers' utilization of mechanisms to alleviate their situation--- taken together, have reduced the chances for collective violence against the regime in power.

---

[1] See J.A. Mills, "Burmese peasant response to British Provincial Rule 1852-1885", in *Peasants and Politics: Grass Roots Reaction to Change in Asia*, ed. D. B. Miller (New York: St. Martin's Press, 1978), 77-104. Michael Adas, "Bandits, monks, and pretender kings: Patterns of peasant resistance and protest in Colonial Burma, 1826-1941", in *Power and Protest in the Countryside: Rural Unrest in Asia, Europe, and Latin America*, eds. R.P. Weller and S.E. Guggenheim (NC: Ruham, 1982), 75-110. Thant Myint-Oo, *The Making of Modern Burma* (Cambridge: Cambridge University Press, 2001).

The first section of this chapter will analyze the issue of political repression and coercion and how it affects farmers' willingness to risk rebellion. Chapters three and four discussed Burmese farmers' reactions toward specific agricultural policies and particular local and central authorities, and how these attitudes have been subject to change depending on changes in local governance and agricultural policies and practices. Consequently, these dynamic state-societal interactions have produced conflicting perceptions of state authority figures in rural society. The second section of this chapter will examine how these contrasts, which show no homogenous view of authority, play out in every day village life, and how they lessen the chances of peasant rebellion in the countryside.

The last section of this chapter will discuss a number of strategies that Burmese peasants have employed for solving their specific problems, and explains how and why the utilization of these avenues has reduced the likelihood of open revolt against the military government. It will extend chapter four's analysis and demonstrate how Burmese cultivators have acted on their feelings about particular aspects of agricultural policies and specific people in authority by using different methods in order to alleviate their grievances.[2]

Political Repression and Farmers' Reaction
It is misleading to treat the relative stability and tranquility of the countryside and the absence of rural protests and demonstrations against the government as a sign of farmers' overwhelming acceptance of the military regime. In fact, quite a number of farmers joined the 1988/89 pro-democracy protests and voted enthusiastically for the NLD in the 1990 election. In addition, General Ne Win's decision to "partially liberalize" the agricultural sector in 1987 was a response to the actions of angry farmers from *Irrawaddy* (Burma's main rice growing region) division, who stopped trains from *Irrawaddy* delta to Rangoon, and looted rice storage bins in the countryside to show their dissatisfaction against the government's stringent procurement policy. Except for these rare occasions, however, the Burmese cultivators usually maintain low profile lives. Why?

The majority of academicians who stress the government's popularity in the rural areas tend to neglect the *tatmadaw's* (military) monopoly over the use of force, which is occasionally employed to extract resources from

---

[2] I will omit or change the names of people, villages, or specific location of the villages and townships. I will underline these names to indicate that changes have been made.

agricultural producers. In addition to forcefully imposing its claim on a great proportion of farmers' crops, the military government has occasionally drafted rural labor to work for the construction of roads, bridges, and irrigation works. Those who failed to comply with the government's demands have been fined, imprisoned, or forced to contribute their labor for a variety of public works or military projects. In addition to these well-known facts, the Burmese farmers have heard numerous stories about how the regime has killed, imprisoned, and tortured urban workers and students in Rangoon who challenged the authority of the government and villagers who were suspected as sympathizers and supporters of anti-regime activities.[3] They also have witnessed or experienced at first hand the military's confiscations of their lands and the plundering of their resources. They are very much aware of the government's restrictions on various forms of political participation and prohibition of criticism against the regime.

Samuel Huntington and Joan Nelson have persuasively argued that "(t)he attitudes of the political elites towards political participation is, in any society, probably the single most decisive factor influencing the nature of participation of that society.....Elites in power....often seek to restrict or to reduce political participation in an effort to prevent challenges to their authority."[4] James Scott points out that "the main deterrent to revolt is often not the survival alternatives open to the peasantry but rather the risk of rebellion. These risks are largely proportional to the coercive power of the state (and, of course, its willingness, to use that power); the more overwhelming its power, the more likely the only alternative to an uncertain subsistence will be death."[5] Given the military's prevailing practices of coercion and repression, Burmese peasants have been unwilling to take any action that would jeopardize their already precarious situations. Thus the military government's despotic and arbitrary practices have effectively deterred the Burmese cultivators from openly challenging the government's authority. The son of a farmer from *Natalin* township, for instance, remarked that

> They (farmers) did not protest/demonstrate simply they are not
> accustomed to these kinds of political activities. And, they knew it was no
> use to do that to an authoritarian government. They knew how brutal the

[3] Conversation with farmers from Rangoon, *Pegu*, and *Irrawaddy* divisions. December 2002.
[4] Samuel P. Huntington and Joan Nelson, *No Easy Choice: Political Participation in Developing Countries* (Massachusetts: Harvard University Press, 11976), 28, 162.
[5] James Scott, *The Moral Economy of the Peasant*, 195.

government could be: 1962 shootings at Rangoon University, the 1974 U Thant affair and the killings, and anti-communist military campaigns in the late 1960's and 1970's. For instance, in my area, over 500 peasants who were sympathetic to or members of BCP (Burma Communist Party) were captured just before the BCP headquarters in the Pegu Mountain Range fell. At the time, an operation called 'four cuts' was staged by the BSPP/revolutionary (Burma Socialist Program party) government. Those communist-sympathizer peasants were beheaded right away by the Special Light Infantry Division (77) in my area. Peasants were forced to witness the executions. Therefore my point is "terror and fear" was already instilled in the minds of peasants. *When I talked to them to join us in 1988, their response [was that] they would be killed for sure because we did not have any weapon to fight back.*[6]

Many farmers with whom I have talked avoided sensitive political topics or lowered the tone of their voice if they wanted to make comments about particular aspects of the government or authorities. James Scott thus accurately reflects upon peasants' reluctance to test the limits of the authoritarian state by saying "the tangible and painful memories of repression must have a chilling effect on peasants who contemplate even minor acts of resistance. It may well be that the experience of defeat for one generation of peasants precludes another rebellion until a new generation has replaced it." [7]

Burmese farmers' fear of retaliation from the repressive state is also reinforced by their lack of education and insecure economic conditions, which have prevented them from taking a more aggressive approach to political participation. A combination of these factors may have led peasants to find solution in their "karma." According to Buddhist thought on "karma," one's present situation is already determined by the actions of one's previous life, and this karma is predestined and unalterable. The only situation one is capable of controlling is the condition of one's next life. Scholars argue that these fatalistic views are held by the majority of poor peasants, who tend to attribute their current hardships to the results of their previous actions.[8] This, however, by no means implies that

---

[6] Ye Myint, personal correspondence with author, November 4, 1997. Emphasis added.

[7] James Scott, 226.

[8] For example, Dr Ba Han wrote that the Burmese peasant "cannot elude the present consequences of his past actions (karma). What is to be must therefore be. Why should he give way to carking care? If his karma is good, it cannot be countered by intelligence. (*Kan kaung yin nyan yaung ma lwan naing*). On the other hand, should his karma be bad, even a house that is built with pillars or iron will crumble to pieces (*kan ma khaing than daing ain sauk thaw lei pyo*). The Burmese is an impertinent optimist. His attitude may be viewed as fatalistic. But it makes him cheerful and enables him to endure calmly the poignant sorrows of life." Dr Ba Han, "Aspects of Burmese rural life of old*", Journal of Burma Research Studies* (June 1968): 9.

Burmese cultivators did not blame the repressive policies of the government for their economic backwardness. In other words, a fatalistic attitude is the result, rather than the cause, of Burmese' farmers' feelings of powerlessness and insecurity, which has emerged from their awareness of the government's readiness to use force against them.

Mixed and Ambivalent Attitudes Toward the Authorities in Power
A close observation of Burmese farmers' values, beliefs, and practices reveals that their position toward the regime in power is not as clear-cut as would point to complete rejection or acceptance of the ruling elite. These ambivalent attitudes, which are reflected in their everyday life experiences, also mitigate the possibility of open revolt against the government.

Generally speaking, rice farmers are suspicious of any government-sponsored organization, including one that is named the Union of Solidarity and Development Association (USDA). The USDA is comparable to *Golkar* in Indonesia,[9] and it was initially formed in 1993 "as a 'welfare' organization to do community projects" but has since been "explicitly recognized as the political wing of the junta."[10] It has recruited members through a combination of coercion and incentives (such as access to computer and language training). Official reports estimate that membership rose to 10 million by September 1998, a fifth of the total population of Burma. The USDA's presence has increasingly been felt in the rural areas, especially through its leading role in high profile social, religious, cultural and political activities. [11]

The dress code for the members is a white blouse or shirt, a green *longyi* (sarong wrapped around one's waist), and a pendant with a lion picture (a symbol of USDA) inscribed on it. Dressed up in their uniform,

---

[9] According to William Liddle, *Golkar*, the state political party under Soeharto's regime in Indonesia, was created by army politicians in 1964 "to counter the rapidly growing strength of the Communist party." It was then transformed in the late 1960s "from a loose collection of military-supervised interest group into a state party." While military officers were given the key positions in *Golkar* party, most civilian officials were required to sign an oath of loyalty to *Golkar*. *Golkar* also incorporated various organizations under its wing to mobilize as well as sanction their behavior. William Liddle, "Indonesia", in *Political Science* (Columbus, Ohio: McGraw-Hill, 1997), 209.

[10] The Economic Intelligence Unit, *Country Report: Myanmar* (Washington DC: 4th quarter, 1998), 12.

[11] For instance, the USDA, in cooperation with the township and village political authorities, provided lectures and training courses on Buddhist culture and custom, midwifery training, fire drill training, management training for its members, and took a leading role in the illiteracy elimination program. The dedicated members of the USDA also volunteered to teach at the residence of illiterate people, who were too shy and intimidated to attend regular courses.

the members are always at the forefront of important social, political, and cultural occasions, and it is not surprising that association with the organization has boosted the ego of rich, arrogant, and spoiled youngsters who enjoy attention and the spotlight.[12]   Undoubtedly the USDA was formed to provide credibility for the military regime's ethos and ideology by mobilizing and controlling the country's population through a variety of carrot and stick mechanisms. *Atek* residents in *Sagiang* division, Upper Burma, were very much aware of the objectives of the USDA, and remained skeptical and critical of the organization, which they referred to as the pro-junta organization.

Interestingly, however, peasants' relationships with the active members of the USDA by no means reflect general attitudes about the organization. They have a high respect for *Ma Ni*, who is the leading organizer of the USDA in *Alei* township, *Sagaing* division. She is in her mid-thirties, single, and is a fourth grade teacher from *Ywa Ngwe* village, half an hour bike ride from her residence in *Taw Latt* village. She is outgoing, and yet caring and sensitive to the needs of others, and always occupies herself with social and humanitarian works. She talks incessantly, and her energy and enthusiasm are unmatched by her short, fragile, emaciated body. She engages in many extra-curricular activities, usually leaving her house at six o'clock in the morning and returning home at seven in the evening. She seemed to strongly believe that her organization is a "social" and "cultural" organization, and emphatically stated that there was no room for opportunists who would like to advance their private interests through her organization. She told me that the USDA did background checks on prospective members to make sure they hold a sincere interest in serving societal needs rather than using the organization as a venue for self-advancement.[13]

Ma Ni joined the organization upon its inception in 1993.[14] She was then promoted from *ayan* or part time member to full time committee

---

[12] This is the perception based on one agricultural worker in *Alei* township in Upper Burma. She mentioned seeing, on many occasions, snobbish and spoiled children of well-off families in a township in Mandalay division, actively and proudly participated in the social and religious ceremonies organized by the USDA.

[13] One agricultural worker from Mandalay division disputed this fact. She said that the organization operated almost like multi-tiered marketing organization, rewarding its members with tangible and intangible benefits every time they recruit five new members. For instance, the existing members who recruited up to 15 new members were taken to visit various famous pagodas out of town. In fact, a military officer who came to the village to mobilize farmers explicitly stated that the USDA has and would continue to contribute money, 1000 kyat per household, in the case of its members' and their family members' death.

[14] A detailed description of the USDA is provided in Gustaaf Houtman's book on *Mental Culture in Burmese Crisis Politics*, 116-119.

member with one and a half months of training in *Mawbi*, where the USDA headquarters is located. Though suspicious of the USDA, the majority of residents in the village thought very highly of *Ma Ni*, and did not immediately identify and associate her with her organization. They praised her devotion to her communities, extraordinary accomplishments, and her friendliness and modesty.[15]

On the other hand, though they often show tacit reverence and respect for the opposition leader Daw Aung San Suu Kyi and her party NLD (the National League for Democracy), farmers disliked their local NLD opposition leader, *U Pu*, whom they regarded as arrogant, controlling, condescending and patronizing. *U Pu* is said to be an intelligent person, but he lacks social skills or a likeable personality, which placed him at odds with the community residents. Unlike *Ma Ni*, who reaches out to the community and devotes her time and energy to improving the quality of the neighborhood, he is criticized by villagers for wanting to have a major voice in village decision making. Villagers disliked his tendency to preach to them about the "appropriate" way of doing things. The villagers also said he was once beaten severely with a cane by the village abbot because he criticized the monk for degrading the environment by cutting the trees and clearing the bushes. The farmers were in favor of the NLD opposition party, but they could not seem to stomach its local party representative; so while *Ma Ni*, the representative of the pro-military party, is loved and adored for her unassuming and down-to-earth mannerism, *U Pu*, the leader of the local opposition branch, is shunned for his domineering and patronizing attitudes.

The farmers in *Atek* village in *Alei* township, Upper Burma, not only have a tendency to see a person differently from the organization he or she personifies. They also recognize and appreciate different sides of a person. Undoubtedly, they have heard of the massive atrocities committed by *Bogyoke* Myint Aung, the former Minister of Agriculture and Irrigation, during his tenure as an *Irrawaddy* Divisional Commander, as well as his corrupt practices, his impetuous and irrational sacking of personnel and the many demotions of agricultural personnel while he was the Minister of Agriculture. But they continue to praise him for implementing new irrigation facilities, introducing summer paddies, and for providing remedies and relief against local abuses and exploitation. While never rejecting Myint Aung's aggression, capriciousness, and irrationality, these attributes did not represent their own experience and perception of the

---

[15] Most active members of the USDA in *Alei* township are school teachers, who are highly respected in their communities.

General. In the minds of many farmers, the anomalous caring and sensitive aspect of General Myint Aung is real.

The peasants' varying dispositions towards the authorities in power and those in opposition, towards the state officials at the center and those at the local levels, and their tendency to dissect different aspects of persons who wield influence and make an impact on their lives, are also manifested in a number of rumors that were circulated within the village. One story reveals that the former Minister of Agriculture, his name unknown to farmers, went to the IRRI (International Rice Research Institute) in the Philippines for a tour, and was immediately impressed by the high yielding, short life, drought resistant, and heat-responsive paddies that were produced in the lab. Wanting to disseminate the miracle seeds to Burma, he secretly stole the seeds and hid them underneath his jacket, and flew back home. After he boarded the plane, he began to think about the appropriate name for the seeds he had stolen. Looking out the window of the plane, he saw the number 747 written on the wing of the Boeing craft, and from then on the new summer hybrid that has become so popular in *Alei* township in Upper Burma is named IR 747. The story portrays and ridicules one of the common traits of the government officials, one that is associated with dishonesty, deceitfulness, and stealth. Yet, the fact that IR 747 has benefited *Alei* farmers from Upper Burma highlights the positive aspect of the regime, which has improved the lives of many farmers. To the peasants, there are almost always two sides to the regime.

The farmers in *Atek* village in Upper Burma also saw Aung San Suu Kyi, the leader of the opposition party, in many unique ways. To many of them Suu Kyi is a mystical and mythical entity, whose power and qualities remain untested yet unchallenged. One rumor, for instance, claims that Daw Aung San Suu Kyi and the Thai princess were close friends. The Thai princess, who is claimed by the villagers to be the owner of the *Chei* lottery, has given Suu Kyi the formula for calculating the right/winning numbers for *Chei*, but she has asked Suu Kyi to never expose it to the Burmese public. I will briefly describe the context within which Suu Kyi has been given this high accord by demonstrating how *Chei* has come to dominate farmers' lives.

Many rural residents in Burma religiously purchase *Chei*, a Thai lottery, which is illegal in Burma. *Chei* is popular because the player in Burma bets only three serial numbers, whereas the player in Thailand has to come up with six serially correct numbers.[16] *Chei* tickets are sold twice a month, and the winning three numbers for the first round are usually announced during the second week of the month, and those for the second round are announced at the end of the month. This was introduced thirty or so years ago in Burma, and was very popular in Rangoon for the initial 10-15 years. The local and central authorities have suppressed *Chei*-related businesses in Rangoon but the enforcement has been tenuous in the remote areas. The Burmese cultivators preferred the Thai lottery to the Burmese lottery because the Thai is cheaper. The minimum amount one can spend on *Chei* is ten kyat (1999), whereas the minimum amount one must spend on the Burmese lottery is sixty kyat. Second, the player has a higher chance of winning *Chei* despite its smaller entry fees. Third, while the winning numbers for the Burmese lottery are announced only once a month, those for *Chei* are announced twice a month. The shorter waiting period for *Chei* results reduces anxiety and agony, and quickly heals the pain and desperation from the previous loss by creating new hope for the upcoming round. Nevertheless, since *Chei* is illegal and most local representatives operate clandestinely, there is no legal guarantee for individuals who win the lottery. The brokers usually ran away if there were too many winners for a particular round.

Although some villagers pull cash together to minimize their risk, the majority of rural residents, particularly rice farmers, continue to spend excessive amounts of money on *Chei*. Some even take a bold step by betting on the potential winning numbers and buying off all the numbers that they think will make it to a specific round. *Chei* has infected all aspects of life in <u>*Atek*</u> village in Upper Burma, and it has become a hot topic of conversation among ordinary folks, and even mentally disturbed people and small kids. Many farmers spend their leisure time calculating and estimating the potential winning numbers. A farmer from <u>*Atek*</u> village, for instance, told me that he used up all the papers in his house on calculating the right numbers for *Chei,* and now had to use the cover bags of chemical fertilizer for this purpose. Much of the conversation within the village revolved around *Chei*, i.e. who won how much and who became rich or poor because of *Chei*, who were not being compensated by the selling centers, what are the potential winning numbers, and who lost what kind of property because of heavy spending on *Chei*. On one

---

[16] For detailed information about how *Chei* is played, see Ardeth Maung Thawnghmung, Paddy Farmers and the State: Agricultural Policies and Political Legitimacy in Rural Myanmar (Ph.D. diss., University of Wisconsin-Madison, 2001).

occasion, a small child who imitated a *Chei* broker said to his playmate that his business went bankrupt because "there are too many winners."

The obsession for *Chei* was profound to the extent that some players immediately rushed to the *Chei* brokers and bought more tickets whenever they overheard other people talking about the possible winning numbers. After I bought a *Chei* ticket, which was basically my wedding date, the next thing I knew was that all the villagers were out to buy the same numbers I bought because "*sayama* (teacher) could be right." Even the village monk, who stopped by my friend's house and heard about my unusual act (I always had refused to buy *Chei*), had decided to buy the same numbers I bought. Like lay people, the Buddhist monks are addicted to *Chei*, and ordinary Buddhist farmers remain indifferent about the monks' obsession for *Chei*. Burmese farmers in Upper Burma, in fact, commented that "*ponegyi* (monks) will be able to donate more money to build and repair the monastery, pagodas, roads, and bridges if they win the lottery." And they did! After winning a fortune from *Chei*, a *ponegyi* from one village in <u>*Atek*</u> township spent a great deal of money on building a new monastery and giving *alu* (a religious feast undertaken to earn merits for the next life) to villagers from around his village. Burmese farmers were even envious of the monks who had more leisure time to spend on calculating the right numbers for *Chei*.

Although a farmer usually buys *Chei* on a piecemeal basis, the annual accumulated expenses are considerable and their combined impact on the individual or village economy is by no means negligible. For instance, while the better off farmers, on average, spent about 2000-4000 kyat (1999) per round, the poorer ones spent about 50-300 kyat per round.[17] The extent to which the proportion of income is spent on *Chei* is the extent to which an alternative consumption or investment choice is rejected, and it is here that the economic effect of *Chei* expenditures can be overwhelming. For instance, if we multiply two thousand kyat, which is the average expenditure per round of a better off farmer, with 24 rounds in a year, we will get a minimum of 48,000 kyat (1999), the total annual spending on *Chei*. This huge sum of money, in fact, is enough to buy 13-15 bags of chemical fertilizer or half an acre of paddy land (1999). Mired in *Chei* habits, some poor farmers never rise from poverty, and a few better off farmers have even lost their land and property.

In most villages, winning *Chei* is almost like a miracle, since most farmers never have won despite repeated attempts and endless

---

[17] Two thousand kyat was equivalent to a monthly salary of a medium ranking government employee.

178

applications of a variety of formulas for the possible winning numbers. Thus, by placing Suu Kyi in a position of an individual who has access to the appropriate code to *Chei*, the story implies that Suu Kyi possesses unusual magical and mystical power, something denied to most Burmese people. Another rumor also reveals that Suu Kyi is surrounded by a coterie of top-notch world leaders (that she went to school with Bill Clinton, Rajiv Gandhi, and the Thai princess), which again reinforces her symbolic role as an authority with high command and influence, who knows and interacts with world-renowned celebrities.

The following account provides Burmese farmers' reactions toward a stranger outside their community, which are influenced not only by their general knowledge about the military regime but also by their everyday life experiences. Again, the central government is perceived in both ways; as a "monster" that arbitrarily squanders and exploits material resources and human lives and brutally punishes and suppresses the antagonizing forces; but it is also seen as a "redeemer," with the power and authority to quell evil forces that are abusing and mistreating the farmers, and the capacity to elevate their economic status and to relieve or even eliminate their plight.

Perceptions of Outsiders

Having lived under repression, despotic practices, and watchful eyes of government intelligence, farmers in *Alei* township in Upper Burma fear the military government. After all, they are very much aware that the central government claims itself to be the rightful owner of all lands, produce, and natural resources. They are also convinced that the regime has the desire and capacity to take away some or all of their possessions if it discovers them, and to incarcerate those who use politically incorrect words or organize opposition against the regime.

I was immediately branded a government spy upon my arrival at a village in *Alei* township. Such a speculation took me by surprise, because I was expecting the opposite comment (i.e. the spy of the NLD party) due to my long stay in the United States. My visit coincided with a period when *Myawaddi* and *Myanmar* television, the only two official television channels in Burma, aired a couple of Chinese thriller movies, including stories about female secret intelligence agents who excelled in martial arts, wiretapping, shooting, and killing. I was asked a couple times whether I carried a gun along with me. One farmer asked me whether I wore a wiretap "just like the one in the movie." Others assumed that there must be lots of security-related machines in my bag since I carried it along

179

with me all the time.[18] Many villagers were mesmerized by the technical complexity of my camera and tape recorder, but they shunned them as much as possible.

Gradually I got used to being called, behind my back of course, the eyes of the government, but I was amazed, impressed, and horrified by the varieties of reasoning from which the farmers derived their conclusion about who I was and what I was. One cogent argument was that "she must definitely be working for a government because it is totally impossible for her to come and learn our backward agricultural technologies. She comes from an industrialized and wealthy country, the country we have to ask for advice on agricultural improvement. How could she be learning new things from us?" Another person argued that "she would not need government guidance and assistance had she stayed in the country and never left for abroad. She must have settled a deal with the military regime since she is coming from abroad." The same person also speculated that I must definitely be a government spy, since I was "asking specifically about the yields and holdings of each farmer."

In fact, the idea that any stranger, not to mention a researcher who is interested in agriculture, could have been a government spy did not emerge out of thin air. The villagers in *Atek* village, *Alei* township, vividly remembered two intelligence officers, on two separate occasions, who stayed in the village for six to seven months to investigate two different murder cases. One disguised himself as a manual laborer, working at the irrigation site where the murder occurred. He wore dirty clothes, mingled and made friends with other laborers, asked them questions, and left the scene once he believed he had accumulated enough information, and knew who the murderer was. He came back a few days after he left, now in a military officer's uniform, and arrested the alleged murderer. I am not sure whether this account is based on a true story or is a rumor. The rumor that circulated around the village was that I would one day return as an intelligence officer and arrest those who have been lying about their actual yield, total production, and land holdings.

Though they stigmatized me as somebody working for the government, most villagers, however, did not shun me altogether. They tried to take advantage of my presence whenever the occasion served their interests. For instance, when the tank ran out of water, and there was no water left for the maturing paddies, a number of farmers asked me to take

[18] In fact, I was overprotective of my bag, and more specifically of my journal. I always kept my journal in my bag and carried it along with me for fear of losing or damaging it. This obviously created misunderstandings among the people I encountered.

a picture of the empty irrigation tank. They assumed that I was the government's intelligence, and that I would definitely report this to my superiors. Some openly asked me to address their problems (a shortage of water due to stealing and selling of water by the concerned authorities and responsible personnel) to the central government on behalf of the farmers. Another farmer approached me and complained about the failure of double paddy cropping in monsoon, and said he told me all these things because I was the only person who "has access to the higher authorities." Apparently farmers wanted me to uncover, record, report, and publicize their sufferings at the hands of the local authorities, but to condone, overlook, minimize, and help conceal activities that were considered "illegal" by the central government. Issues they did not want me to know about included their actual yield, land holdings, and property, the bribing of authorities to obtain water and to be part of the summer paddy program, and fighting over the share of water.

Unlike the rural residents of *Alei* township in Upper Burma, those from *Auk* township in Lower Burma demonstrated less intimidation and suspicion toward me. In fact farmers from *Taung* village in *Auk* township, Lower Burma, seemed to entertain their interaction with a researcher and to enjoy interviews. Specifically, the village chairman's wife in *Taung* seemed to have a better and clearer image of me more than most ordinary farmers I encountered. When I asked one farmer whether he would like to make any comment about his experience as a farmer, he started complaining about how he had lost hold of his saving of eighty kyat through the MARDB (Myanma Agriculture and Rural Development Bank). The chairman's wife immediately interrupted to say that it was not my *gwin*, or area of authority, since I was a mere researcher, and that I would not be able to have much influence on authorities who formulate policies. She gave advice to the farmer that that the Deputy Minister of Agriculture (who had a rice field and plantation in the area) was the more appropriate person to complain to.

Why rice farmers from the *Taung* village were less suspicious and tended to have a more understanding of my role as a researcher may have to do with the "unique" history and location of their village. The village is not only adjacent to the capital city but also has continuing direct interactions with high ranking military and agricultural officials from Rangoon. A number of researchers and scholars also occasionally visit and study *Taung* farmers. Because of its extraordinary role as the first model rice village in Burma, *Taung* village is not typical of rice villages in Burma. On the other hand, most researchers rarely venture into villages in upper Burma because of their distance from the capital. Therefore, it is the rule rather than the exception there to find rice farmers imbued with fear and suspicion toward any strangers who claim to study their ways of life and place them under microscopic scrutiny.

The farmers' varying perceptions of the regime in power, of state and party officials, and the leaders and members of the opposition party make it extremely difficult to make judgments about the overall level of legitimacy enjoyed by the military regime in Burma. Will Burmese farmers support the military regime they have long viewed negatively because they are beguiled and persuaded by its particular local representative? Will the image of the opposition party, the NLD, be tarnished and spoiled by its unpopular local representatives? Will the negative aspects of the dictatorship be outweighed by the positives? This observation is well recognized and acknowledged by Richard Turits, who studied peasants' sentiments and attitudes toward dictator Trujillo's regime in the Dominican Republic. He writes that "peasants' attitudes about regimes were generally far from simple or one-sided, embracing contradictions and balance and eschewing the type of black or white discourse of many written histories."[19] Sally Moore concurs that rural cultivators in Tanzania conceived the state to have beneficent and protective potentialities as well as invasive, punitive, and undesirable possibilities. Whether the positive or negative aspects dominate the lives of agricultural producers depends on "immediate circumstances rather than on any general stance of political support or opposition."[20]

Given the importance accorded to the local governing structure, it is very likely that farmers will be complacent as long as they have responsive and sensitive local officials. Luisa Pare, for instance, observes that in municipal elections in Mexico, rural voters tended to support people they knew, whom they felt would represent their interests, and paid very little attention to political parties and ideologies. What this means is that they would sometimes vote for PRI candidates even if they disagreed with the overall policy of the PRI party. Thus, "voting for PRI candidates in local elections may not be seen as contradicting a rejection of the overall policy of the party."[21] In this aspect, _Ma Ni_, the representative of the pro-junta organization, may be able to secure support from her village,

---

[19] Richard Turits, "The Foundations of Despotism: Peasants, Property, and the Trujillo Regime (1930-1961)" (Ph.D. diss., University of Chicago, August 1997), 677, 703.
[20] Sally Moore, "Legitimation as a process", in *State Formation and Political Legitimacy*, eds. Ronald Cohen and Judith Toland (New Brunswick: Transaction Books: 1988), 158.
[21] Luisa Pare, "The Challenges of rural democratization in Mexico", in *The Challenge of Rural Democratization: Perspectives from Latin America and the Philippines*, ed. Jonathan Fox (Portland: Frank Cass, 1990), 90.

if she is able to provide not only certain material benefits to her villagers, but also safeguards against local corruption and abuses as well as arbitrary demands from the central authorities. Of course, such an example will make only a small dent against the negative impression of the regime and its local personnel, especially in the areas that have long experienced the arbitrary abuses and exploitation of the military.

Responses Towards the State's Actions: Exit, Compliance, Passive Resistance, Individual Contacts, and Voice

Burmese cultivators carry out a variety of activities to evade the state's excessive claims and at the same time avoid severe punishment by the state. Michael Adas postulates that pre-colonial peasants used "avoidance protest" to attenuate their hardships and express their discontent through flight, sectarian withdrawal, or other activities that minimize challenges to, or clashes with, those whom they view as their oppressors.[22] Villagers' resort to "avoidance protest" rather than "confrontation" has been helped by a number of favorable conditions. The first condition is the political and organizational structure of monarchical rule, whose effective control has been severely restricted by rival power centers among the elite. The second factor is the lack of organized bureaucratic and military organizations, and a system of communication which has failed to penetrate to the village level. Third, substantial amounts of unclaimed cultivatable land and large tracts of forest wilderness provide refuge to those fleeing from the control and exploitation of their patrons. Adas notes that the combination of these factors provided numerous opportunities for peasants in pre-colonial Java and Burma to defend themselves from excessive exactions by their overlords. [23]

Peasants can thus avoid direct confrontation with the state and the abuses of local authorities by either colluding with the village headmen to minimize and evade their tax payments, to conceal their property, by migrating or shifting patrons, or by joining cult movements. According to Adas, the availability of these strategies helps lessen the chances of open revolt: "groups or individuals resorted to acts of evasion, rather than to spontaneous outbursts of violence or organization for confrontation, as means of expressing their discontent."[24]

These peasants however were deprived of the avenues that they once utilized to minimize direct confrontation with the state after the colonial

---

[22] Michael Adas, "From avoidance to confrontation: Peasant protest in pre-colonial and colonial Southeast Asia", *Comparative Studies in Society and History* 23 (1981): 217-247.
[23] Michael Adas, 223.
[24] Michael Adas, 228.

power took over the daily operation of the state. The more efficiently organized bureaucracy and military, an improved communication and transportation system, and a higher-population-to-land ratio "greatly reduced opportunities for tax evasion or bribery of revenue officials."[25]

According to Adas, the elimination of opportunities for passive avoidance led to "direct confrontation, and frequently to violent clashes with the colonial authorities." [26] In other words, it was the availability of opportunities that minimized direct confrontation with authorities that explained the lack of collective violence against the authority in pre-colonial societies.

A similar logic can be applied in military- ruled Burma, where contemporary Burmese farmers have used a variety of strategies under diverse circumstances to address their grievances. Definitely, Burmese farmers under the military regime have less available channels and capacities to dilute the demands of the state compared to their counterparts in pre-colonial periods. They nonetheless find means and ways to gain lenient treatment within the constrained atmosphere. How Burmese peasants respond to what they regard as "improper, unjustifiable, and unacceptable" actions of the state depends on the content of these demands, the availability of alternative strategies, and the resulting calculation of the costs and benefits involved in adopting each strategy.

The goal and objective of any types of farmers' reactions against the authorities may vary from persuading or pressuring existing authorities to act (or refrain from acting) in certain ways, to seeking to replace current authorities with others whom Burmese cultivators expect to be more responsive to their preferences and needs. If these needs are not met, they may seek to change aspects of the political system itself, or to alter fundamentally the structure of the entire system to make a government more responsive to their desire. However, most discontented Burmese farmers want to confine their demands to persuading or pressuring existing authorities to act or to refrain from acting in certain ways. They ask for a reduction in procurement quota, withdrawal from a particular program that has negatively impinged upon their lives, exemption from quota demands in case of bad weather and crop failures, and immediate redress from forced relocation, land alienation and human rights violations.

Demands that are above and beyond changing the existing policies or practices are usually shunned by poor rice farmers who often perceive

[25] Michael Adas, 241.
[26] Ibid., 245.

them as either futile or irrelevant to their primary concerns. Joel Migdal, for instance, writes that "peasants' dissatisfaction is with very specific aspects of their immediate environment, and they usually do not have a vision of the overthrow of the entire system with which they are still relatively unfamiliar."[27] He emphasizes that "even among the most revolutionary of peasants, there was no vision of social and political revolution but rather the desire for personal upward mobility and for the landlords' fields. At its most political level, the desire was to achieve relief by eliminating local despots."[28]

Huntington and Nelson also state that "(t)he poor usually take little part in politics because participation often seems irrelevant to their primary concerns, futile, or both. The most pressing problems for many of the poor are jobs, food, and medical aid--for today, tomorrow, or next week." [29] Thus Burmese rice farmers are less likely to take any overt political action against the authorities as long as their most urgent needs are met and their daily routines are not severely disrupted by the government or other forces. One Karen farmer from Rangoon division, for instance, commented that "I will still have to farm if there is a democratic government, or a military government, or a communist government. Democracy is not my priority as long as I can live comfortably. I do not really care what type of government we have as long as the country remains peaceful and consumer prices are low and stable."[30] Seven farmers with whom I have talked in December 2002 consistently pointed out low government procurement prices, high prices on consumer products and agricultural inputs, and abuses and exploitation at the buying deport as their pressing problems.[31] Some of them said they lost one basket of paddy for every twenty five baskets sold to the local government buying depot, others said they lost as many as fifteen to twenty baskets of paddy for every one hundred baskets sold. Another farmer described the situation at the buying depot as follow: "when you go to the bazaar, the seller, not the customer, holds the scale. But when you go to the buying depot, the buyer, not the seller, holds the scale. We, the seller, are

---

[27] Joel Migdal, *Peasants, Politics, and Revolution: Pressures toward Political and Social Change in the Third World* (New Jersey: Princeton University Press, 1979), 262.

[28] Joel Migdal, *Peasants, Politics, and Revolution*, 251.

[29] Huntington and Nelson, *No Easy Choice: Political Participation in Developing Countries*, 117.

[30] Conversation with a Karen farmer from Rangoon division. December, 2002.

[31] Conversation with farmers from Rangoon, *Pegu* and *Irrawaddy* divisions. December 2002.

supposed to handle the scale, but it was the buyer, or the local buying agent who was in charge of."[32]

Burmese peasants therefore have attempted to deal with their personal and immediate issues at the village or township level, from which they see most constraints and demands on their individual behavior coming and where they believe the potential for problem solving lies. Many of their frustrations and anger therefore are directed at arbitrary, capricious and corrupt local authorities. A farmer's son who was attending Christian college in Rangoon, for instance, remarked in 1999 that "peace and tranquility in our village depend on the type of headman (village chairman) we have. We are better off if we have a good headman, and worse off if we have a bad headman." A good village chairman, according to seven farmers interviewed in 2002, is someone who is "righteous," who "stands up" for the peasants, who represents farmers' interests, who demands lenient treatment at the buying depots, and who is not afraid of authorities outside the village.

Thus, the most far-reaching and radical effort that has thus far been exerted by farmers is the removal of particular local government officials, who are held directly responsible for farmers' plights and sufferings. The majority of farmers' protests therefore are localized and aimed at improving their' worsening situations.

To address their concerns, which are confined to their personal, familial, and communal levels, Burmese cultivators have adopted "a host of adaptive or survival strategies". These can be broadly categorized as compliance, exit, passive resistance, individual contact, and voice.[33] "Compliance" means complying with authorities' demands without resisting and "exit" implies avoiding the demands of the government by simply migrating to other areas. Farmers also engage in "passive resistance" when they challenge the claims of the authorities without openly confronting them. This involves non-confrontational strategies such as under-reporting their holdings and crop yield and stealing water. They also use a strategy of "individual contact" to approach authorities to negotiate and compromise. "Voice" is used when farmers openly and collectively confront the authorities through argument or through protest.

---

[32] Conversation with a farmer from *Pegu* division, December 2002.

[33] The terms "exit" and "voice" are borrowed from Albert Hirschman's work on *Exit, Voice and Loyalty: Reponses to Decline in Firms, Organizations, and States*. The term "individual contact" is borrowed from Huntington and Nelson's work on *No Easy Choice*. The term "passive resistance" is borrowed from James Scott's work on *Weapons of the Weak*.

Compliance and Exit

Burmese farmers' initial and natural response to the government's irrational policies is to simply comply with the state's demands, if such demands are moderate and endurable, or if it is too costly to blatantly resist. Migdal, for instance, states that "peasants' action in politics may remain merely that of individual accommodation or passive resistance." [34] They may turn to their families, friends, monks, money lenders, shopkeepers, or merchants or anyone who is in a better financial position to help. Most Burmese farmers, for instance, borrow money from merchants or money-lenders at very high interest rates to buy paddy on the market and fulfill their procurement quota. Some sell or pawn their lands to comply with state demands. My family has friends and relatives in rural areas who often come and ask to borrow money from us during the cultivation season when agricultural producers most need the capital. My mother has occasionally complained about how her relatives and friends in the countryside never seem to have enough money to repay her.

Burmese farmers may also "intensify" their family labor to either increase small increments in yield or to embark on small businesses or economic activities that are available within their local areas. In *Atek* township in Upper Burma, for instance, farmers' wives and daughters hire themselves out as transplanters and harvesters during peak season. They also make additional income by weaving and selling baskets in the market during the slack agricultural season. The older children usually take care of their youngsters, freeing up time for their parents to engage in agricultural and other economic activities. Young boys help out in the field by the time they reach ten or eleven.

Peasants may also obtain help from their communities as well as from outside groups such as religious organizations or opposition groups. [35] However, there has been a weak foundation for local community assistance organization in Burma's rural areas. Manning Nash, for example, described an irrigated rice growing village in Upper Burma in the 1960s as lacking organizational bases to provide meaningful economic opportunity: "(F)or wells and other obvious communal improvements there is no organizational structure or cultural idiom to make self and other interests complementary." [36]

Very few local community organizations have existed in Burma to function as social welfare groups or rotating credit associations to provide

---

[34] Joel Migdal, *Peasants, Politics, and Revolution*, 207.
[35] James Scott, *The Moral Economy of the Peasant*, 201.
[36] Manning Nash, *The Golden Road to Modernity*, 241.

various forms of mutual assistance to farmers. Most farmers' mutual assistance activities do not usually extend beyond helping each other in transplanting and harvesting season. However, village welfare can be promoted to the extent that Buddhist religious values provide the rationale for distributing wealth within the community, and the Buddhist monastery or Christian church serves as the refuge for those in severe economic crises.

In *Atek* township, Buddhist merit-making rituals are performed through the daily offering of alms to monks, donating money and gifts to the monks and monasteries, giving "*alu*" (feeding and offering gifts to monks and laymen) on special social occasions and religious days, and contributing money for pagoda-building. Some farmers carry out these religious functions with the desire to accumulate merits for the next life as well as with ulterior motives of enhancing their social standing within the community. For respect accorded to individuals is based on the generosity of their contributions toward religious activities rather than the actual amount of wealth one might have. Nothing is more spiritually and psychologically fulfilling than having one's name inscribed upon the wall of a monastery or listening to the loud announcement of how much one has donated to a particular religious cause. These cultural expectations and practices propel the wealthy to spend more on religious ends. Manning Nash observed in the 1960s that "the more it (wealth) is accumulated, the more it is lavished, at the village level, on sacrificial giving for *kutho* (merit) and the display and pomp associated with Buddhist ceremonial. The wealthier a person becomes, the more, absolutely and relatively, he spends for religious ends."[37]

The villagers from *Atek* village, for instance, still praised the lavish religious feasts given by *U Tha Htay*, an absentee landlord and a rich merchant in *Alei* township, who allegedly spent approximately 3,000,000 kyat (US $ 9,000 at the market exchange rate in 1999) on *alu* and invited one and all from the town and from surrounding villages. The Burmese also give "*alu*" through a *shinbyu* (the initiation and ordination ceremonies for youths entering monkhood), wedding ceremonies, special occasions such as births, deaths, or national holidays, and the annual *kathein* (robe-giving) ceremony. It is through these various kinds of *alu* that the cultural expectation of the voluntary contribution of the invited guests is reinforced. In upper Burma in particular, it is expected that an

[37] Manning Nash, *The Golden Road to Modernity*, 160.

invited guest bring a gift or money to *alu*.[38] Again, since social status in Burma is partly a function of merit, an individual must contribute in accordance with his/her social standing in the society as well as his/her relationship with the hosts. He/she is expected to send a gift or cash if he/she could not attend the ceremony. <u>*Bo Mei Shay*</u>, my host father, complained that he had been invited to a number of secular and religious ceremonies which had put a considerable strain on his budget. When I suggested that he should go to these places without bringing gifts, he replied that "it does not look good if I do not bring or send any gift once I am invited." He also said that the host usually kept a record of who gave what and how much, and a person's prestige and reputation could go down the drain if he did not live up to social expectations. Through *alu*, all village members can identify generous persons from the miserly ones. Nash observed a similar pattern of practice forty or more years ago

> The practice of keeping account books with the name of the contributor and the amount given is said to have originated about 30 years ago, but it is universal now in Burma. The record books are supposed to insure reciprocity in giving, to make certain that exactly the same amount is returned when the recipient becomes a contributor. To give less is to place oneself in an inferior position; to give more is to make claims on superiority; so reciprocity, the general social norm of Burmese village interaction, is supposedly maintained by the keeping of written account books.[39]

Although better-off as well as poorer peasants are expected to make contributions the host's *alu*, this practice has a leveling effect on the distribution of wealth within the village community since the prevailing norms prescribe that an individual apportion religious and social spending based on his/her socioeconomic status.

Christian farmers use a different approach to communal sharing. They donate a small amount of money to the church on every Sunday, which is then used for mission purposes as well as for helping out the needy. At a Karen church in *Mawbee* township, Rangoon division, each church member would bring a handful of rice to the church every week, and distribute or sell this at subsidized prices to the poor and the needy. Since 1988, however, there have been increased assistance and welfare

---

[38] Contribution toward someone's *alu* is very rare in Lower Burma. One visiting monk from Rangoon, for instance, remarked that "the *alu* givers in upper Burma simply sell meals because they let their guests help them out with the costs. In Rangoon, the hosts take care of all the expenses, and remained the sole sponsor of the ceremony."

[39] Manning Nash, *The Golden Road to Modernity*, 305.

programs, both in volume and intensity, from governmental (such as the UN) and nongovernmental organizations in rural areas. The United Nations Development Program has until recently introduced a variety of community capacity-building programs in the forms of the Farmers' Income Generating Group or a Women's Income Generating Group in the very poor regions in Shan state, *Rakhine* state, Chin state, *Irrawaddy* division, and *Magwe* division. These activities help alleviate the pressing problems that are encountered daily by poor peasants and landless laborers.

If farmers are not willing to comply with the state's orders they may also choose to "exit" or migrate to the city to avoid the state's claims. In Burma, the majority of the rural populations that have flocked to the city are more likely to be young and ambitious, migrating with the purpose of improving their current situation. Some farmers who live near Rangoon area have benefited from the remittances sent by their children who work for private companies and NGOs in Rangoon. However, the fact that there is relatively little change in the composition of the rural and urban labor forces indicate that only a small exodus to the city has taken place during the military regime in Burma. For instance, whereas the agricultural sector employed 66.4 percent of the population in 1931, it employed 62.5 percent of the population in 1987/88.[40] (This is a marked contrast with the urbanization that has characterized the poor nations of the world over the past few decades.) It is the case, however, that some farmers' children, like their city counterparts, have left the countryside to work in the neighboring countries in search of better employment opportunities. The numbers have increased after the relaxation of immigration policy in the early 1990s. In Thailand alone, it is estimated that there are about 300,000-500,000 illegal Burmese workers.[41] Migration or temporary employment in the cities and neighboring countries does not always produce happy-ending stories. The human rights sub-committee of the Australian Parliament reports that in Burma's countryside there has been a growth in the trade in women, girls and young men from Burma into Thailand, and the number of women from Burma involved in prostitution was estimated between 20,000 and 40,000 in that country in any given period of time. These women, most of them from rural areas and ranging from age 12 to 23, are not only subject to debt bondage, harsh treatment,

---

[40] Tin Maung Maung Than, "The Political Economy of Myanmar's Development Failure: 1948-88", paper presented at Burma Studies Conference, Center for Burma Studies, Northern Illinois University, Dekalb, Illinois, October 2-4, 1998, 3.
[41] Asian Watch, *A modern Form of Slavery: Trafficking of Burmese women and Girls into Brothels in Thailand* (New York: Human Rights Watch, 1993), 17.

abuses and exploitation, but also are most likely to become victims of AIDS. [42]

Passive Resistance

If the options for compliance and exit are exhausted, the next step is to rely on individual self-help mechanisms, since collective action is harder and more risky to organize. Individual farmers use various forms of self help, including foot-dragging, false compliance, lying and feigned ignorance. The story of Maung Pyone, or Mr. Smile, as illustrated by Professor Mya Maung, sheds light on the use of self-help mechanisms by ordinary farmers during the socialist periods. [43]

Like many other Burmese farmers, Maung Pyone managed to find ways to undermine compulsory sale to the BSPP (the Burma Socialist Program Party of 1974-1988) by mixing the paddy he had to deliver with sand, pebbles, and other condiments, or selling his "*wunza*" (personal consumption) paddy to ready buyers, or bribing corrupt officials. He also tried to trick the government buyer by selling his paddy at the specific time of the day during the harvesting season when the contracts of advanced purchase are due. For example, since harvesting occurs during the winter months and a harvested paddy weighs more when wet with dew at night or in the early morning hours, Maung Pyone would take his paddy to the purchasing center in the early morning hours instead of late in the day when a basket of drier paddy requires more grains.

A similar episode can be discerned in Gustaaf Houtman's work on *Mental Culture in Burmese Crisis Politics*. Houtman writes that " (I) once traveled with a peasant on his bullock-cart in which he explained how the rice he was carrying he had soaked in water to increase its bulk before he 'donated' it to the authorities, so that he might more quickly fulfill his 'uneconomic' obligations."[44] Burmese cultivators also use lies to maximize their claim and minimize the state's exaction. A case in point is individual reports on holdings and possessions which fluctuate depending on the type of government agency one is dealing with. In other words, peasants tend to report their actual holdings or over-report them when they apply for loans and fertilizers, and under-report them when they have to sell their quotas or pay various kinds of taxes.

On the day the government distributed loans for summer paddy cultivation, which took place in the middle of the growing season, *Bo Mei*

---

[42] The Parliament of the Common Wealth of Australia, *Human rights, and Progress toward Democracy in Burma* (Canberra: The Australian Government Publishing Service, 1995), 48.49.

[43] Mya Maung, *The Burma Road to Poverty* (New York: Praeger, 1991), 126.

[44] Gustaaf Houtman, *Mental Culture in Burmese Crisis Politics*, 113.

Shay, my host father, came home with 12,000 kyat, which he obtained as a loan (2,000 kyat per acre for summer paddy) for his six acre summer paddy farm. With borrowed money in hand, he also bought a bag full of *samusa* (fried potatoes wrapped in flour), which he gleefully shared with his family members. Some other farmers bought stirred fried noodle (a luxurious food by Burmese standards) immediately upon obtaining the loan. The size of *Bo Mei Shay*'s land, however, got smaller when he was asked to contribute money for underground water operations, which required every summer paddy farmer to pay 500 kyat per acre. The village chairman mistakenly told *Bo Mei Shay* that he would have to contribute a total of 2,000 kyat for his four acre summer paddy farm. *Bo Mei Shay* remained silent, and did not the inform chairman that he cultivated six acres under the summer paddy program. *Bo Mei Shay's* land holdings thus expand and contract depending on the specific issues or authorities with which he deals.

Many observers of Third World countries have emphasized the prevalence of these covert activities, which are undertaken to avoid the excessive demands of the state. For example, in his classic *Weapons of the Weak: Everyday Forms of Peasant Resistance*, James Scott demonstrates how peasants resorted to foot dragging, dissembling, false compliance, pilfering, feigned ignorance, slander, arson, and sabotage to mitigate or deny claims made by the superordinate classes or to advance claims vis-a-vis those classes. Although everyday resistance is informal, often covert, and may never confront the formal definitions of hierarchy and power, it may in the end "make an utter shambles of the policies dreamed up by their would-be superior in the capital."[45]

Joel Migdal thus contends that "even where states were presumed to have been pervasive, domineering, and efficacious in the developing world, such as Maoist China and Brazil under military rule, the reach of the state turns out on close inspection to have been limited."[46] Although it appears, on the surface, that peasants could be coerced to accommodate the wishes of the state, they can undo or evade threatening state policies within their constrained political and economic environments.

A number of scholarly writings provide evidence on the powerful impact of farmers' piecemeal employment of "weapons of the weak" on the Burmese macro-economy. Hill and Jayasuriya, for example, write that "the government has considerable power to compel the growing of recommended crops and implementation of recommended cultivation

---

[45] James Scott, *Weapons of the Weak*, 36.
[46] Joel Migdal, 3.

practices, though farmers have often found ways to circumvent these when they have conflicted with perceived private profitability."[47] Mya Than's study of *Mayin* village in lower Burma also found farmers who cultivated sweet potatoes after their failed experimentation with government-recommended crops, such as sunflower, groundnut and sesamum.[48] These farmers found it more profitable to grow sweet potatoes, which was neither capital- nor labor-intensive, and thus secretly planted the crops in the presence of the government's prohibition against sweet potato production. Khin Maung Kyi also concurred that "tales of farmers who tried to beat the system and escape from the physical production quota abound."[49]

Not surprisingly, Mya Than and Nobuyoshi Nishizawa find that under the BSPP (Burma Socialist Program Party: 74-87) leadership, there was an inverse relationship between the amount of government-procured paddy on the one hand and the gap between the official procurement price and the parallel market price on the other hand. This means that the wider the gap between these two prices, the smaller the amount of paddy the government was able to procure.[50] In other words, if weather conditions, the amount of rice production, or the growth of population are held constant, the government will have more difficulty in procuring rice from the peasants when the free market prices are significantly higher than government procurement prices. This apparently demonstrates the peasants' response to market mechanisms and the existence of other channels that were used by peasants to evade the stringent requirements of the government. "Tricking" the authorities also involved dividing the land title among one's family members by a farmer who owns more than 40 acres of lands to skirt the law prohibiting farmers from owning more than 20-30 acres of land.[51]

Individual Contacting
If passive resistance does not work or lacks feasibility, farmers may use the strategy of "particularized contacting" or contacting the local officials

[47] Hal Hill and Sisira Jayasuriya, *An Inward-Looking Economy in Transition* (Singapore: Institute of Southeast Asian Studies, 1986), 40.
[48] Mya Than, "Little change in rural Burma: A case study of a Burmese village (1960-80)", *Sojourn* 2 (1) (1982): 67.
[49] Kyi, "Modernization of Burmese Agriculture", 122.
[50] Mya Than and Nobuyoshi Nishizawa, "Agricultural policy reforms and agricultural development", in *Myanmar Dilemmas and Options*, eds. Mya Than and Joseph Tan (Singapore: Institute of Southeast Asian Studies, 1990), 102.
[51] Until the land reclamation policy, it is not legal to hold more than thirty acres of farm land.

in power if he/she cannot act alone to dilute the demands of the state.[52] Particularized contacting takes place when individual farmers contact local officers to argue, persuade, bargain, or offer bribes for more lenient treatment. A good example of this is the growth of the black market for agricultural products during the socialist era. Ye Myint recalls the collusions among farmers, black market traders and local police men by saying "local authorities rarely blew the whistle when farmers took their surplus to the market....Besides getting small payments or "tea money" from the traders, they set up check-points along the bullock cart trials, but each check-point for smugglers means just one more payment to the police. So, when commodities were resold in the cities, the prices were raised to cover up all the costs."[53] Thus, James Guyot writes that the volume of smuggled rice before the liberalization periods, was estimated at 80,000 to one million tons per year (with 200,000 tons given as the most plausible figure), compared to the 0.7 million tons at the highest peak of official exports in 1983/84.[54] In this respect, what appears to be a repressive and penetrative state turns out to be nearly powerless when it comes to enforcing its proclaimed policies.

In the same manner, the post-socialist periods also demonstrate a variety of 'contacting.' It is not uncommon for farmers to pay a particular government agency a certain amount of money or produce to help conceal their land holdings and total production. Farmers bribe local authorities to appropriate certain benefits (e.g. to obtain water, fertilizers, pesticides, agricultural implements or agricultural loans through unofficial channels) or to exempt them from a particular enforcement (e.g. reduction in financial and labor contributions).

Voice
Again, if individual farmers alone cannot act to persuade the officials responsible for their welfare, and if the option of individual contacting is unavailable or costly, farmers may utilize a collective approach to pressure the authorities. However, individual contacting is still preferred to collective action since a collective approach requires the involvement of others who entail difficulties and risks. Huntington and Nelson argue that "of all forms of political participation, individual contacting presents

---

[52] This term is borrowed from Huntington and Nelson's work on *No Easy Choice*.
[53] Ye Myint, personal correspondence with author, November 4, 1997. Under the Burma Socialist Program Party (1974-87) periods, it was illegal to sell rice at the black market even after farmers fulfilled their obligation to the state. The partial liberalization, however, has allowed farmers to sell their produce at the free market after fulfilling their quota requirements.
[54] James Guyot, "Burma in 1988", *Southeast Asian Affairs* (1989): 116.

the most clear, direct, and (usually) immediate link between action and results. The results of other forms of participation are often uncertain, deferred in time and diffused in incidence. Even though contacting may require substantial initiative and persistence, one would expect low-income people to engage in it more than in other forms of participation."[55]

While bribing the authorities is usually associated with individual contacting, and perceived to be a private issue, arguing, persuading and negotiating with the authorities are usually done on a collective basis.[56] A group of farmers with common problems may try to use verbal argument against the concerned authorities to moderate their claims against them. A farmer from Rangoon division, for instance, told me that "we were initially forced to grow summer paddy in our areas. But summer paddy was a failure. We complained to the township agricultural office, and we are now allowed to grow mungbean and sell a small portion of it to the government only if we have good harvest."[57]

A bout between farmers and township authorities from the *Irrawaddy* division on 2 May, 1998 is another good example of how the peasants used collective persuasion to convince the authorities to withdraw unfair practices.[58] The report did not, however, mention how the conflict was resolved nor in whose favor. Nonetheless, it states that farmers from *Irrawaddy* had a dispute with the SLORC over the issue of procurement for summer rice. According to the report, summer paddy yield and production in 1997 were low because of the damage caused by a flood. The authorities, nonetheless, demanded that farmers sell 20 baskets/acre at an official rate of 300 kyat/acre while the free market rate was 450 kyat per acre. Many farmers who had already lost summer crops could not fulfill their quota requirement. After they were threatened by the local SLORC officials, farmers in *Wah Khe Ma* district "resisted" the local authorities' decision to collect quota rice.[59]

---

[55] Huntington and Nelson, 132.

[56] Huntington and Nelson note that the following conditions must be met for collective action to occur, (1) there must be a recognized common problem that is felt to be of high priority, (2) the problem must be viewed as appropriate or plausible for prompt and specific government action or assistance, (3) there must be some assurance that the benefits will be shared equally, or at least no one individual or clique will reap most of the rewards (4)independent participation by the poor requires leaders with some idea of how to exert influence, and (5) collective political action must be viewed as equally or more cost effective than alternative means. Ibid., 135-136.

[57] Conversation with a farmer from Rangoon division, December 2002.

[58] Report by Hsaw Wah Deh, Independent Human Rights Monitoring Group, Washington D.C: Federation of Trade Unions-Burma, 2 May, 1998.

[59] Ibid.,

The presence of a clearly identifiable common enemy and a sense of misery, combined with a sense of outrage and injustice propelled farmers to take a collective approach, which is otherwise associated with lower benefits and higher costs.[60] I myself witnessed fierce bickering between a junior irrigation officer and a group of angry farmers over the issue of the distribution of water at the agricultural extension camp in *Alei* township in Upper Burma. This is not to mention farmers' constant harassment of agriculture extension agents for their failure to provide sufficient support and to implement pragmatic goals, which I had seen on a daily basis during my research.

If such an approach of collective negotiation and persuasion fails, a group of disgruntled farmers may then attempt to petition their grievances by simply threatening the local officials to take the case to the capital, or by actually petitioning their case to the national government. Some farmers approached visiting agricultural ministers or central PDC authorities to complain about local corruption and abuses. There are many stories about farmers' approaching the late Lt. General Myint Aung during his tour in the countryside to express their discontent about local authorities' corrupt practices. Myint Aung would summon these accused officials, slap them in the face and fire them on the spot. Sometimes, farmers approach those who have connection with the highest ranking authorities (such as monks) in the capital to help them petition their grievances. This was usually enough to pressure local authorities to give in, especially if local officials' practices were not permitted by the central authorities. "Voice" is not necessarily confined to the actions taken by a group of farmers. One farmer from Rangoon division, who had long resented abuses at the local buying depot, for instance, got drunk one day and "threatened" the local officials at the buying depot. According to eye witnesses, "no more exploitation at the buying depot took place" in his area since then.[61]

Another alternative method is to publicize their sufferings and plights by secretly providing information to the opposition party or to the human rights NGOs and foreign journalists and observers clandestinely operating in Burma. The fact that the opposition party is operating through the local branches in the provincial areas also provides farmers with another avenue to publicize their sufferings. Occasionally, the NLD and other nonprofit human rights organizations publish abuses committed by

---

[60] Huntington and Nelson also argue that collective political actions require (1) clearly identifiable common enemy, and (2) a sense of misery as well as a sense of outrage and injustices.

[61] Conversation with a farmer from Rangoon division, December 2002.

the local governing authorities. It should be noted, however, that the option of reporting to the opposition party or NGOs was not available during Ne Win's regime, under which only the BSPP was allowed to function and foreign visitors were strictly prohibited and monitored.

The following are examples of the complaints submitted by the NLD under Statement 176 (12/99), and Statement 177 (12/99) to the central government authorities.[62] The first complaint, which was submitted from *Shwebo* district, Sagaing division, addressed a number of issues. They ranged from the district PDC official's prohibition of the operation of rice mills, low procurement prices, and high proportion of procurement quota, to local abuses and exploitation. The second complaint came from *Prome* township, *Pegu* division. It targeted the military and regional authorities who allegedly took over local populations' lands and forced rural residents to sell their sugar cane to the military at low fixed prices and to stop processing sugar cane into *Kyan-ta-gar* (candies) which fetched higher prices than sugar cane.

National League for Democracy
No: (97/B), West Shwegonedine Road
Bahan Township, Rangoon
NLD: Regime Closes Rice Mills, Demands Payment to Reopen
statement 176 (12/99)

1. For the purchase and for obtaining the entire paddy crop in the De-pai-Yin township, the Secretary of the SPDC (Shwebo district, Sagiang division) issued oral instructions for the closure of all rice mills operating in the region on 14 November 1999. Our information is that all the mills even those operating in the small villages had to close down immediately.
2. The cost of one basket of paddy had dropped from kyats 2400 to 2000 because of the large supply which delighted the people but when the mills had to suspend operations the price of one pyi soared to kyats 120/-
3. On the 20 November, 1999 the township and village authorities said that the mills could reopen on payment of kyats 5000 to 7000 depending on the size of the mills. Though all the money had been collected by the 25th November, permission to mill has not been given to date.
4. Also, since the 19th November, a Security Outpost has been installed outside the telephone office in Saing-pyin village where payment is demanded from all big and small vehicles transporting rice. Right through

---

[62] The activities to obtain complaints from farmers are done clandestinely. Oftentimes, the NLD local leaders would visit villages and collect information farmers on a low profile level, or farmers secretly approach the NLD office in their local areas to make complaints about authorities.

from Monywa, Butalin, De-pai-yin, Ye-U, Kan-ba-loo, road blocks are set up and money is demanded in a variety of ways.

5. Though "open market" is the declared policy, the farmers are aggrieved because they are compelled to sell their paddy at fixed prices. Currently the rate is 15 baskets per acre. For less productive regions it is 12 baskets per acre. The selling price of one basket is 350 kyats while outside the price is double. In addition there is a compulsory quota of one basket per acre each for the township SPDC, USDA and the bureaucrats of trade and agriculture. Wet grain is given as another excuse for demanding extra quantities. Because of the dishonest practices of the officials who weigh and count, the poor and simple farmer has to take along 25 baskets extra for every 100 baskets.

6. The cultivators and farmers are suffering so much because of the use of force by dishonest authorities. We request the matter be inquired into and suffering of the farmers be alleviated. We seriously denounce these illegal and unjust activities.

Central Executive Committee
National League for Democracy
Rangoon
21 December 1999.
NLD: Villagers Land Given By Regime to Private Company
Statement 177 (12/99) (translation)

1. The Myanma-Asia company with the cooperation of the military and the regional authorities have started a cooking sugar-cane plantation in the village tracts of Wa-sone and Kan-gyi-gone village groups in Hte-Kan-Taik region, Prome township, Pegu Division.

2. Lands that cannot be cultivated and lands that have been cultivated are ruthlessly cut down and cleared, then ploughed with machines leaving no grazing ground for the cattle. This has left the villagers with no land for cultivation and the lands where they had grown some crops were forcefully cleared and ploughed. Survival has become extremely difficult. Even animals are starving. A very pathetic state of affairs.

3. The remaining cultivators of the region have been forbidden to sell their sugar-cane crops to any other person apart from the individual authorized by them who is none other than the Superintendent of Police in charge of the Prome district. No individuals are allowed to process the cane sugar into Kyan-tha-ga (Candies). Members of the police force have been threatening to take action if any rising smoke is seen.

4. One ton of sugar-cane fetches kyats 2500. Cost of labor and transportation has to be born by the cultivator, which nets him kyats 2000 only. One ton of kyan-tha-ga fetches kyats 10,000. By forbidding the cultivators to process his own crop into Kyan-ta-ga he is considerably disadvantaged.

5. This state of affairs leaves the cultivator a collie at the mercy of the entrepreneur. Therefore we seriously condemn the authorities that are creating opportunities to bring about such unenviable conditions for the poor cultivators.

Similar incidents of abuse and exploitation by the local authorities made their way into the reports of human rights organizations and unofficial news agencies. On February 22, 2000 the Shan Herald Agency reported that villagers from Tachilek township were forced by "the junta officials, known as the SPDC, to sell rice at government prices in accordance with the amount fixed beforehand...According to the directive that was issued recently, the villagers have to deliver their goods by 20 February or face drastic action from those concerned." The Human Rights-Trade Union Rights Section of the Federation of Trade Unions-Burma also stated that in Kyaukkyi, Pegu division, dry season rice was grown only by the Light Infantry Battalion (LIB) NO. 351, which had more than 400 acres. Villagers from Aung Soe Moe were relocated from the hill region to contribute their free labor for the LIB. 351. The local farmers around Kyaukkyi could not grow rice in summer because the small dam was completely controlled by LIB. 351.[63]

Interestingly, a Karen farmer remarked that, being a minority ethnic member, "we were very cautious in criticizing the government. The Burmese farmers, however, were more outspoken and critical of the government. We appreciated the military's building of roads and bridges, but the Burmese farmers in our areas were less appreciative; they mocked 'if you could not even build or decorate your house, who will build and decorate it for you?'"[64]

Burmese farmers will ultimately resort to violent outburst or the most extreme form of voice if such a strategy is considered superior to, or equally costly as, an alternative means of achieving the same goal, or if perhaps other options are not feasible. A case in point is farmers' violent reaction against the state's stringent procurement policy in 1986. Bertil Linter's vivid account of the angry farmers' violent reactions against the authorities reveals that "In 1986/87, farmers in the *Irrawaddy* delta, Burma's granary, were literally planting their rice at gunpoint—and in *Daik-U* north of Rangoon, four government officials were lynched by angry mobs. In *Kyauktan* southeast of the capital, enraged farmers stormed and burnt down a rice mill which belonged to the father of a

---

[63] The NLD report, 2 May, 1998.
[64] Conversation with a farmer from *Pegu* division, December 2002.

member of the ruling state council."[65] Although it is unclear whether the protest was targeted against the central or local authorities, the violent nature of the protests may have prompted the central authorities to reconsider their existing policies, and to introduce a more relaxed approach to agricultural promotion, which evolved into the partial liberalization policy in 1987.

Although protests and strikes were strictly prohibited and rarely occurred (with the exception of sporadic outbursts in urban areas) during the socialist period, they have gradually increased in intensity and frequency since 1988. This is partly due to the relaxation of control over the rural populace, and it is partly inspired by the actions of students and Buddhist monks in major cities who have increasingly staged protests and demonstrations against the central and local authorities to express their discontent.

In some rural areas, farmers have begun to use protest and picketing, though not as frequently as their city counterparts, as a means to direct their appeals toward the government. A peaceful demonstration staged by three hundred indignant farmers from *Irrawaddy* division on February 5, 2000 demonstrated the employment of a tactic that was not considered an option during Ne Win's government. Farmers hardly protest against the procurement system per se, which requires a portion of crops to be sold to the government at lower prices. The government has named this procurement practice in Burmese *Tarwon Kyay Sabar*, meaning "fulfilling one's responsibility by selling parts of one's paddy grain to the state." The purpose is to instill in farmers' minds that their cooperation and compliance have noble purposes of fulfilling the national obligation as dutiful citizens. The majority of farmers I talked to in 2002, in fact, mentioned that they did not oppose the government procurement policy, because "we must think about *won tan* (government employees) who need subsidized food." What they were weary of was the low procurement price for paddy which was set at 320 kyat per basket, while the market price was 1,300 kyat per basket. They did not advocate the elimination of the procurement system, but would like the procurement price to be raised to "at least half the market price."

Furthermore, authorities are expected to accommodate the needs of farmers in times of bad weather, crop failures, and family deaths. For instance, in April 2000, farmers from *Kyaunggon, Irrawaddy* division, launched a peaceful demonstration in front of the township Peace and Development Council to demand fair treatment on the part of the local

---

[65] Bertil Linter, *Outrage: Burma's Struggle for Democracy* (Bangkok: White Lotus, 1990), 67.

authorities.[66] They were enraged because the authorities did not exempt them from the quota system as they suffered crop failure from heavy rains during the monsoon season. Instead, their paddies were immediately seized by the township authorities for failure to sell the quota to the government procurement agency. In this case, it did not seem like farmers had the economic leverage (money or grains) to offer the local authorities in return for lenient treatment. Argument and persuasion did not work, since the township had already forcefully seized their produce. The feeling of "misery" was now compounded by the feeling of "injustice and outrage," serving as a catalyst to resort to collective political action.

Another recent report by Shan Herald Agency on February 24, 2001 illustrates farmers' demonstrations against the local authorities that refused to give lenient treatment on rice procurement policy. The report, however, reveals that the protest failed to obtain its objective due to adamant refusal of the regional authority to acknowledge the peasants' problems.

Reporter: Khamleng
Sources from Shan state reported to S.H.A.N that farmers in southern township had demonstrated against Rangoon's rice purchase policy during mid January.

Farmers in Hsihseng township, 34 miles south of Taunggyi, rose up to protest on 15 January and an unknown number were arrested, they said. 3 days later, Lt-col Win Maung, Secretary, Southern Shan State Peace and Development Council, arrived in the township to meet the farmers. He reportedly informed the farmers that every rice cultivator must sell 8 baskets of rice per acre at K. 350 per basket price. (In Irrawady Division and Pegu Division, it is 30 baskets respectively, he said.) "You don't own the land. You are only using the land owned by the state with its permission. Those who fail to sell in accordance with their quota are liable to go to jail under Section 406 and Section 420." He admitted that farmers were actually paid only k 300 per basket instead of K. 350 because the official purchasing teams were not given traveling allowance by the State. The meeting, attended by 1,100 farmers, ended with counter proposals from the people going unheeded, said the sources. The market price of unhulled rice is K. 800-900 at present, considered cheap compared to the past years. The farmers' main complaint is shortage of water. Moreover, they said they also had to feed the local cease fire group, Shan State Nationalities People's Liberation Organization of Taklay, better known as the Red Pa-O.

---

[66]Human Rights Solidarity, 10 (4) (April 2000). A variety of sources of news reported that the township ruling authorities promised to hold talks with representatives of the farmers, and the farmers eventually dispersed and nominated their representatives for the talk. No updated news has yet been released.

Regardless of their suffering, farmers rarely make extreme demands for removal of the regime and replacement of the government. This extreme form of protest may occur only when farmers are organized by urban leaders and students and when they are convinced of the likelihood of winning the struggle. Bertil Lintner's account of the nationwide pro-democracy movement in 1988 occasionally discerns farmers' involvement in the mass demonstrations against the military regime. We can see the demonstration against the police station in *Sagaing* on 9th August which "was joined by a large number of peasants from surrounding villages. By the time they reached the police station, the crowd had swelled to about 10,000."[67] Likewise, in "Taunggyi, Shan State, policemen, doctors, local merchants, government employees and *farmers with bullock carts joined* the demonstrations."[68] "Strike centres were established in more than 200 of Burma's 314 townships. Rice farmers from the countryside around nearly every town arrived in lorries, bullock carts and on foot to participate; *it was an entire population, rural as well as urban, who in unison demanded an end to the military-dominated one-party rule.*"[69] In Man-aung on Cheduba Island in Arakan State, "*local farmers* and fishermen carried two coffins, which were decorated with demonetized 75-kyat banknotes and labeled Ne Win and Sein Lwin, to a mock funeral pyre by a riverside."[70] Of course, this type of violent protest against the regime could and would not have taken place on farmers' own initiatives.

Conclusion
Burmese farmers have generally shunned overt protests to express their grievances and have utilized a variety of strategies to evade irrational state demands and simultaneously avoid its brutal suppression. The goal of paddy farmers' resistance against the state is directed toward changing particular policies and practices that negatively impinge on their lives, and it is seldom aimed at changing the personnel or the government responsible for peasants' economic stress and disaster. The order of preference for various mechanisms of responses (compliance, exit, passive resistance, individual contacting, voice), however, varies depending on political and economic conditions specific to particular localities. The Burmese cultivators may also simultaneously employ a combination of two or three strategies, but they are more likely to use passive resistance and individual contacting, which present the clearest, most direct, and

[67] Ibid., 98.
[68] Bertil Lintner, 114.
[69] Ibid., emphasis added.
[70] Bertil Lintner, 114-115. Emphasis added.

swiftest link between action and results. The resort to "voice" through peaceful protests, not to mention violent actions or rebellions, is usually rare, since the results of exercising "voice" are often uncertain, risky, and dangerous. Nonetheless, farmers from rice-surplus regions, such as the *Irrawaddy* division, have increasingly utilized this strategy in the post-1988 period. The relative relaxation of the government's grip on the agricultural sector in the post-1988 period has also opened a number of political spaces carved out by the operation of NGOs and opposition parties through which peasants can address their grievances.

Given the repressive nature of the state and its apparent lack of interest in rural welfare, the Burmese cultivators usually focus on exerting pressure on the state to modify and lessen its claims, rather than on demanding special privileges or support programs. In other words, it is misleading to assume that farmers are better off because they have access to a variety of strategies to temper the state's goals and objectives. Farmers may effectively employ compliance, exit, passive resistance, individual contacting, and voice to alleviate grievances, but the utilization of these strategies does not necessarily significantly alter and improve their lives.

A detailed examination of the question of political quiescence in Burma's countryside reinforces the main arguments of this book in two accounts. The first issue addresses the ways in which farmers have acted on their feelings and sentiments to alleviate their grievances. Burmese farmers selectively use different strategies to target particular aspects of authorities' initiatives and agricultural policies. These actions generally reflect Burmese farmers' perceptions of government authorities at different levels. They negotiate with local authorities to underreport their holdings and yields, and to exempt them from unpopular agricultural programs in order to circumvent the stringent policies of the central government. They attempt to lodge complaints to the capital or approach high ranking central authorities to counter local officials' abuses and exploitation. When Burmese farmers take their impure and mixed paddy to the government buying center, they are trying to deceive both the central and local authorities, who make unrealistic and rigid demands upon the peasantry.

According to Scott, peasants' engagement in clandestine activities to improve their terms of exchange with the landlords (or state) demonstrates the widespread feelings among the peasantry of the landlords' unjust and illegitimate extortion, and implies that the landlords' (or state's) claim to surplus has been a matter of force and power rather than voluntary compliance.[71] However, the fact that poor farmers as well as the more affluent farmers have employed a variety of schemes to circumvent the state seriously questions the practice of passive resistance as a practical response to "illegitimate" government. In fact, my research found that farmers with higher socioeconomic status are in a more advantageous position to use their resources to advance their interests vis-à-vis the state through "passive resistance" and "individual contacting". In other words, such practices are likely to continue even if the state reduces its use of coercive mechanisms. It is therefore necessary to distinguish action and behavior that emerge in response to what the farmers consider the illegitimate claim of the state authorities, and those that attempt to maximize one's gains and enhance one's position. However, Scott contends that "it is precisely the fusion of self-interest and resistance that is the vital force animating the resistance of peasants and proletarians…When a peasant hides part of his crop to avoid paying taxes, he is both filling his stomach and depriving the state of grain."[72]

Yet the resort to passive resistance does not always imply that the regime in power is illegitimate, although it may to some extent imply that the state's practices are unfair and improper. Hypothetically, farmers may not pour water or put pebbles into the grain that will be sold in the market. However, this assumption is debatable because most customers, including my family, have been repeatedly cheated by the meat sellers in Burma's *bazaar*, for example, who inject water into the meat to increase its weight. Is this a gesture of meat sellers to show their dissatisfaction against the customers? Or is this an action of pure interest-maximizing behavior? Why do multinational corporations and small businesses in industrialized countries falsify reports on income or use a variety of schemes to evade government taxes? Is that because they believe that the state's redistributive policy is repressive and unfair? Or is it because they want to maximize their profits?

Because of the difficulties involved in distinguishing behaviors aiming to "symbolically" reject the legitimacy of the state from those that simply attempt to maximize one's gains, the practice of "passive resistance" should be treated as an effort by farmers to moderate or evade the authorities' claims, rather than as a tacit rejection of the "illegitimate" state as such. However, some behavior and actions (especially "voice") more accurately reflect farmers' feelings and sentiments about authorities than others. For instance, farmers openly challenge the legitimacy of the

---

[71] James Scott, *The Moral Economy of the Peasant*, 231.
[72] James Scott, *Weapons of the Weak*, 295.

local authorities when they engage in collective protest or threaten to take their complaints to the central authorities. On the other hand, it is more difficult to prove whether the practices of selling soaked and impure grain to the government, over-reporting or underreporting land holdings, or stealing water amount to tacit denial of the authorities' legitimacy.

The second implication that can be drawn from this chapter is the existence of ambivalent feelings toward authorities within rural society. Burmese farmers' attitudes towards the local representatives of the pro- and anti-regime parties reveal that paddy farmers' perceptions of the military government are more complicated than the conventional studies have acknowledged. These attitudes are based on Burmese farmers' past and present experiences with different authorities and agricultural policies. Burmese cultivators' ambivalent feelings toward the authorities in power also explain their reluctance to demands for complete transformation of the military regime, which in their view incorporates both positive and negative features. Farmers seem complacent as long as there are piece-meal and partial reforms made to improve negative aspects of the government, whether these are local governing authorities, village chairmen, or a particular agricultural policy.

Chapter 6

The Burmese Experience in Comparative Perspective

Everyday Life Experiences under the Military Regime in Burma
Burma's military regime (1962-current) has been one of the most repressive and authoritarian governments in the world. It cracked down on the unarmed, student-led, nationwide, pro-democracy movement in the period between 1988 and 1989, and it is estimated that about 10,000 people were killed. The killing was indiscriminate; students as young as thirteen were shot, bayoneted, and run over by tanks. Women were robbed, raped, and killed. The army also fired at nurses in the Rangoon General hospital simply because they carried a banner saying "doctors, nurses and hospital workers who are treating the wounded urge the soldiers to stop shooting."[1] Some of those who were injured by the army were carried away in truckloads, taken to the cemetery and burnt alive. Those who were arrested were tortured.[2]

In the meantime, Ne Win, the General who led the military coup in 1962 and who was responsible for mass killings in 1974 and 1988, escaped mass enrage unscathed. He has amassed a fortune by squandering public money and property, and his personal wealth has been estimated as similar to that of Ferdinand Marcos in the Philippines. Bertil Lintner, for instance, writes that Ne Win "owns property in London, West Germany and in Tokyo's most expensive business district, Ginza."[3] He gave his

---

[1] Bertil Lintner, *Outrage: Burma's Struggle for Democracy* (Bangkok: White Lotus, 1990), 103-104.
[2] Some were forced to kneel on sharp pebbles while being bitten by dogs and beaten by interrogators. Others were ordered to perform "motorcycle" or "the helicopter." The "motorcycle" method was used when students were asked to get on the imaginary motorcycle. They had to stand a half-crouch and pretend that they were riding a motorcycle, making engine noises. The interrogators would strike at them for not stopping at a red light or for not obeying the law. This went on for a long period of time. The "helicopter" approach was employed when students were forced to spin around with outspread arms, which made them dizzy. They were beaten and ordered to continue spinning after they lost balance. Other forms of torture included electric shocks and forcing the prisoners to drink their own urine. Bertil Lintner, *Outrage*, 53.
[3] Bertil Lintner, *Outrage*, 61. In March 2002, the junta arrested Ne Win's infamous son-in-law, Aye Zaw Win and three grandsons, Kyaw Ne Win, Aye Ne Win and Zwe Ne Win. They were accused of plotting a coup to form a new regime loyal to Ne Win. On 26 September, 2002, they were all sentenced to death by hanging. The government announced that Ne Win's relatives had

son-in-law, his favorite daughter's husband, one of the most lucrative and coveted positions by appointing him as the head of the government agency that dealt with the pearl trade. He married seven times, twice to the same woman, and his last marriage to a 25-year old Arakanese beauty in 1988 was a superstitious and symbolic act, aiming at preventing the country from falling apart.[4]

The army staged a coup d'état on 18 September, 1988, a propitious day according to the army astrologer. Most of Ne Win's activities, in fact, revolved around number nine, his favorite number. For instance, the coup d'état took place in September, which is the ninth month, and on the 18th (1+8=9). It was hardly surprising then, given his fixation with the number nine that in 1987 the government demonetized 25, 35, and 75 kyat currency notes and introduced new bank notes in the denomination of 45 (4+5=9) and 90 (9+0=9). The army then announced that it would hold a multi-party election and allowed the formation of political parties. Not unexpectedly, the elections were held on May 27 (2+7=9), 1990. Aung San Suu Kyi, the charismatic leader of the main opposition party and the daughter of the late General Aung San, who was a leading nationalist leader in Burma's independence movement, was put under house arrest and banned from running in the election. To the utter dismay of the army, Suu Kyi's party won in a landslide victory in 1990.

The military refused to honor the election results, and went after the opposition leaders, harassing and incarcerating them. Although the military has gradually released political prisoners, there are still 1,000-1,300 of them in prison, and some have died due to torture and the poor prison conditions.[5] Those who were arrested and appeared in court did not get a fair trail. For instance, "four people were arrested, charged, tried and sentenced to death in the space of two days in January 1994 for the alleged murder of a student."[6] Arbitrary arrest and detention are common features of military ruled Burma, and political activists who carry out

planned the coup because they were upset at losing some of their economic and political privileges as Ne Win's influence gradually waned. Ne Win and his daughter Sandar Win were put under house arrest immediately after the rest of the family were arrested. Ne Win died in disgrace in December 2002. British Broadcasting Corporation (26 September, 2002). See Maung Aung Myoe, "Will the failed coup attempt derail the ongoing national reconciliation and political transition in Myanmar?" (Singapore: Institute of Defense and Strategic Studies Commentaries, 3/2002).

[4] Bertil Lintner, 61-62, 107.
[5] Christopher Smith, "More sanctions for Burma", *Asian Wall Street Journal*, September 18, 2002, p.8.
[6] The Human Rights Sub-Committee of the Parliament of the Common Wealth of Australia, Human Rights and Progress towards Democracy in Burma, 22.

peaceful political activity are charged with sentences of seven to twenty years. Prison conditions are harsh. Some ill prisoners have not been given proper medical assistance. As a consequence, Amnesty International reported that about 15 deaths have occurred in custody between 1988 and 1993. Prisoners are subject to beatings, shacking, suffocating, burning, stabbing, torture including death threats, and rubbing open wounds with salt and chemicals.[7]

Outside the prison's thick wall, the situation looks equally bleak. The military strictly controls its citizens through surveillance and intelligence networks and prohibits criticism of the government. Burma is an "informal society in which there is expansive and complete coverage of the country by the intelligence," and there will always be military intelligence around where there are four or five people gathered together.[8] University and high school teachers are held directly responsible for their students' actions. They must help contain students' anti-regime activities, and they are forced to take a variety of political training courses. The government's fear of student protests also leads to the denial of their access to education. According to Christina Fink, "(b)etween 1962 and 1999, universities have been shut down thirteen times, from periods of a month up to more than three years. Between 1988 and 2000, the universities were closed more than they were open. Classes were cancelled from June 1998 to May 1991, from December 1991 to May 1992, and from December 1996 to July 2000."[9]

Along with education, the government has deliberately neglected citizens' social and economic welfare. After the State Law and Order Restoration committee (SLORC) assumed power in 1988, Burma became the largest opium producer in the world. The production of opium increased, especially after the government signed a series of ceasefires with ethnic insurgencies in 1989. The ceasefires gave the former Shan and Wa ethnic insurgent groups a free hand in administering their areas, including the right to carry arms, in return for their agreement to stop fighting. This arrangement created collusion between the ex-insurgent groups, who produce opium, and the military authorities, who engage in opium trading or extort money from opium traders and producers. The Burmese economy has depended mainly on drug-related activities. This causes international outrage because the government, while benefiting from opium production and trade, has not done anything significant to

---

[7] The Human Rights Sub-Committee, 24-25.
[8] The Human Rights Sub-Committee, 16.
[9] Christina Fink, *Living Silence: Burma Under Military Rule* (Bangkok: White Lotus and Zed Books, 2001), 182.

solve drug-related problems such as the increasing numbers of drug addicts, HIV positives, and drug-related deaths. Christopher Smith, the vice chairman of the International Relations Committee in the US House of Representatives, points out that the regime "has pleaded with the international community for increased international aid to help combat their nation's high HIV-AIDs rate and widespread poverty, and yet it found the money to spend US $130 million to purchase 10 MIG fighter jets, and is actively pursuing the development of nuclear power."[10] A 1995 World Bank report estimated that the SLORC spent about 46 per cent of its total spending on defense between 1989 and 1994 while social expenditure (including health and education) declined from 32 per cent to 23 per cent in real terms.

To promote tourism and improve the image of the cities, the government relocated many people without compensation and at short notice. Forced relocation occurred in major cities like Rangoon, Mandalay and reaches as far as the border towns in Northern Rakhine state. The National Coalition of Government of the Union of Burma (the exile government) estimated that the numbers of internally displaced are between 500,000 and 1,000,000 (1995).[11]

The military's treatment of ethnic civilians (the Shan, Chin, Mon, Karen, Karenni), who live in the border areas and have contact with ethnic insurgences, is even more brutal and inhumane. These ethnic civilians often undergo forced relocation and are used as porters, human shields against mines and are subject to arbitrary and summary execution and forced relocation. A porter who escaped from the army's custody, for instance, recalled that a man "could no longer carry anything so a soldier hit him on the chest and head. Then he started hitting him on the shoulder with a 75mm shell. The porter said to the soldier, 'Kill me. I cannot go on anymore.' Then the soldiers just kicked him down the hill so we do not know for sure if he died, but I think so."[12] The army also demanded labor, farm animals, and food supplies from villagers. They raped women, and killed the old, the sick, or the uncooperative. According to a 19 June 2000 report by the Shan Human Rights Foundation, the Burmese military has allegedly raped hundreds of innocent women, including girls as young as five years old. About 135,000 people have fled in fear to Thailand as refugees, and another one million Burmese are internally displaced and living in malaria-infested and harsh jungles.[13]

[10] Christopher Smith, "More sanctions for Burma."
[11] The Human Rights Sub-Committee, 19.
[12] Ibid., 26.
[13] Ibid., 24-25

In fact, Burma, a country that held great promises after it gained independence from Britain, is currently in economic disaster. It experiences forty to fifty per cent annual inflation, and lacks appropriate infrastructure for development (such as road, bridges, electricity, gasoline), a market-determined exchange rate, autonomous financial institutions, control over money supply, and a transparent and uncorrupt legal system. Corruption and rent-seeking activities are rampant, and the government has not been able to create a stable political environment and enforce laws governing economic transaction. Not surprisingly, over forty per cent of the population is said to live below the poverty line, and about 40 percent of the rural populations is landless. The average annual per capita income of Burmese citizen remains as low as between US $ 225 and $ 440. According to the United Nations Development Program, Burma has become one of the very poorest countries in the world, ranking 131st out of 175 countries in 1997.[14]

This book has looked at the Burmese government authorities' relationships with the strategically and economically important populations (Burmese peasants) in the context of a brutal military's negligence of its own citizens. Rice farmers, the focus of this study, are not necessarily exempted from these harsh practices. After all, the state has, most of the time, enforced mechanisms to drain off much of the agricultural surplus from the countryside on terms deleterious to the interests of Burmese rice farmers. Nonetheless, the military's position towards rice producers is qualitatively different from that of other citizens, given Burmese cultivators' strategic role in the economy and their limited political goals.

This project has shed light on a quite extraordinary aspect of the authoritarian patterns of Burmese politics, and demonstrates why it is possible for one of the most repressive and ruthless regimes to enjoy pockets of support in the countryside. To understand this, we must analyze the historical foundations of rice farmers' interactions with various types of authority, their cultural and political orientations, the specific agricultural policies and practices that have bearing on their lives and the constrained political and economic atmospheres within which these farmers have struggled to make ends meet. The analysis demonstrated how, in these circumstances, islands of favorable attitude towards the regime can exist within the sea of palpable tension and mistrust.

---

[14] Peter Carey, *From Burma to Myanmar: Military Rule and Struggle for Democracy* (London: Research Institute for the Study of Conflict and Terrorism: November/December 1997), 18.

The first section of this chapter will provide a brief summary of this book and reassert my main arguments. The second section of this chapter will put Burma into comparative perspective by looking at a number of authoritarian regimes which enjoy comparable bases of rural support. I will discuss the broader implications of my findings on Burma, and demonstrate how the analysis of political legitimacy through the disaggregated state has given us a more grounded and comprehensive understanding of Third World authoritarian regimes.

Paddy Farmers and the State Authorities
Since pre-colonial times, the Burmese cultivators have had to interact directly with two different types of local authorities; centrally appointed officials and local leaders. The relationships between rice farmers and local authorities have varied depending on changes in central government's practices, and the residence and socioeconomic backgrounds of local authorities. Generally speaking, rural residents have held low regard for centrally appointed authorities, who lack interest in local affairs and in establishing social contact with rural populations. Coming from higher educational and socioeconomic backgrounds and being subject to frequent transfer, the centrally appointed authorities usually patronize the uneducated rural poor. They deliberately carry out their social and cultural activities in the major towns and eschew interaction with rural residents. The only circumstance in which these local officials get in touch with residents is when they implement national policies; that is to collect tax, buy crops, demand labor, survey land, provide water, enforce sanitary, educational, and agricultural policies, and monitor cultivation practices. The rural populations therefore see the centrally appointed officials as a mere extension of the coercive arm of the central administration, and usually avoid them as much as they can.

On the other hand, overall, the villagers tend to have positive views towards local leaders, the *myothugyi* or the village chairmen. Most of these leaders were either born in or are permanent resident of the villages they represent. They tend to be protective of their village affairs, responsive to villagers' needs, and shield their residents against the arbitrary demands of central authorities. They may be better off than the majority of the villagers, but their formal education does not usually extend beyond high school. They derive their wisdom and authority from the information handed down by their ancestors and through their accumulated experiences. Most of them are respected and revered by the villagers.

This simplified version of rice farmers' relationships with two different types of local authorities does not accurately capture the variations that exist across the country and at different points of time. As said in chapter two, not all the village leaders in the pre-colonial societies were sensitive to the needs of their residents. Furthermore, many scholars show that the friendly relationships that once characterized native leaders/villagers interaction took a turn for the worse under the British colonial government. Village chairmen became agents of the state and had less capacity to protect their residents because of the more centralized and efficiently organized administrative practices of the colonial government. At the same time, rural residents became mesmerized by appeals from urban nationalist leaders and looked to them for solutions to their grievances. Once these expectations were not fulfilled, Burmese cultivators withdrew their support for the nationalist leaders and took matters into their own hands by taking arms against the British authorities. Urban nationalist leaders' failure to establish alliances with rural residents reinforced age-old mutual suspicion and increased the gap between urban elite and rural poor.

The military government, which came to power in 1962, initially attempted to target Burmese cultivators for their support. Through a series of peasants' seminars, the military encouraged peasants to express their views and exchange information with the highest ranking authorities. It extolled the role of the peasantry in the mass media and in national speeches. It used a more relaxed approach to encourage higher agricultural production by relying on incentives (higher amount of loans and agricultural inputs) and on exhortation rather than on coercion. This approach did not last long. The Burmese peasantry were not only faced with more broken promises of the national leaders but also had to suffer the rigid control and arbitrary demands of the military government. They had very few mechanisms to evade constant supervision and strict orders from above. The centrally appointed local authorities became more demanding and inflexible because of the nature of the strict hierarchical structure of the administration, which placed pressure upon the subordinates to implement irrational national policies. Under the military regime, Burmese farmers encountered heightened hostility and aggression from all sides of authority, whose goals were to maximize the exaction of grain and control over rural populations. Tensions, antagonism, and acrimony were the primary features of state-societal interactions in military-ruled Burma. This does not mean, however, that there was no room for protective and responsive local authorities who shared complementary interests with rice farmers.

Chapter three examined a number of institutional and organizational factors that influenced local authorities' practices and affected their relationships with rice farmers. Most farmers came into contact with these agencies and personnel through their implementation of various agricultural policies. Different local government agencies implemented the same agricultural policies in slightly different manners, and thus the ways in which these officials behaved had a wide range of consequences on rural perception of local and central authorities.

Almost all local officials were corrupt, given their extremely low salaries and little opportunity for upward mobility. However, some of them had had mutually beneficial relationships with the rice farmers. But what types of authorities were more likely to share interests with rice farmers and to be responsive to their needs?

Generally speaking, local officials who come from similar socioeconomic backgrounds as the rice farmers tended to be more sympathetic to farmers' problems. Because of their relatively lower educational level (which is usually the three-year diploma in agriculture), these officials (most of them agricultural officials) were allowed to permanently reside in their place of birth. After all, they had very few opportunities to move up the ladder within the agricultural ministry, and therefore had little reason to be transferred to other places. Promotion within the hierarchical structure of the agricultural administration was, in fact, basically reserved for those who graduated from the five-year college. Thus agricultural officials who held a diploma in agriculture tended to have friendly relationships with the farmers partly because they were local people, and partly because they or their parents relied on farming as their main or partial source of income. Having cultivated the lands themselves and experienced all sorts of problems at first hand, they tended to be protective of their farming residents.

Burmese farmers and agricultural officials held different opinions on Myanma Agriculture Service's (MAS) tendency to inflate the data on crop output, yield, and cultivated acres. Since the primary responsibility of MAS was to promote higher crop yield, production, and cultivated acres, agricultural officials were under pressure to exaggerate their performance to impress their superiors. Rice farmers were indifferent to this practice as long as it did not have a detrimental impact on their lives. They would simply express their annoyance at MAS by making fun of agricultural officials openly or behind their backs. Once these inflated figures affected farmers in terms of a higher procurement quota, farmers became more vocal and confrontational, causing hostility between the two parties.

Farmers, however, tended to have a more favorable view of the land record office, which had no institutional or organizational need to exaggerate crop output or cultivated acres. The land record officials' job was simply to keep track of land titles, location, and types of soil in each farm and village. They tended to report deflated data partly because it has very little effect on their organization's integrity, and partly because it was in their and farmers' interest.

Farmers' overall relationships with agricultural officials, however, were not as intense as their interactions with officials from other agencies and departments that wielded greater control over their lives. Examples were the township PDCs, the irrigation department, and the forestry department. The township PDC officials were the most feared authorities in rural areas because of their access to the use of force. Like most centrally appointed officials, they were insensitive and unconcerned about local difficulties. Using their organizational status as law and order restoration agency, they placed rigid demands upon the local populations, including the exaction of a portion of grain, the drafting of free labor for the construction of roads, bridges and irrigation networks, and the imposition of irrational agricultural policies.

The relationships between rice farmers on the one hand, and local irrigation officials and forestry officials on the other hand varied depending on a variety of conditions specific to the local areas. For instance, there was little reason for the rice farmers to come into conflict with the irrigation office in the areas where water was available for every paddy cultivator. Tensions arose in the water-scarce areas, especially in Upper Burma, where every farmer scrambled to have enough water to grow summer rice. When water supply could not keep up with demand, farmers began to offer money and gifts to irrigation officials, who then took bribes from more people than the irrigation tank could actually accommodate. This caused crop failures and bad harvests, creating tension between irrigation officials and rice farmers.

Those who clashed with the forestry department were the ones who lost all or part of their lands to the forestry department, which was endowed with the authority to reclaim fallow and virgin lands. Since the forestry department took arbitrary measures in some places and not in others, farmers who were not subject to forced relocation did not have any reason to develop hostility towards forestry officials. The land record office also wielded significant control over farmers to the extent that they could refuse to transfer the land ownership title and could require considerable cash to facilitate this illicit transaction. When they did this, they antagonized farmers.

Farmers normally held higher positive regard for the distributive branches of the agricultural agency than the extractive and regulative branches of the agricultural agency. They appreciated cheap loans, subsidized agricultural inputs, and free water especially if the processes for obtaining them did not require cumbersome bureaucratic procedures. However, since the cheap loans and subsidized agricultural inputs were usually insufficient to cover production costs, the rural development bank or the Myanma Agriculture Service, which provided these services, made only a small positive impression on farmers. Rice farmers, however, consistently despised the MAPT (Myanma Agriculture Produce Trading) which bought rice from them at below market prices. Rarely did the MAPT officials interact with rice farmers except at harvesting time when farmers were required to sell a certain amount of rice to the government. Farmers constantly complained about the abuse and exploitation at the buying centers. These complaints will continue as long as MAPT procures a high proportion of farmers' output at low fixed prices, and as long as the MAPT officials use dirty tricks to exact additional grain from the farmers for their personal gain.

Rice farmers' relationships with native authorities also varied according to a number of circumstances. Not all native leaders were protective of their residents. I have shown different characters of village chairmen who were popular and unpopular among their residents. Generally speaking, village chairmen who were farmers while in office were more sensitive to the needs of their villagers. Moreover, a better-off chairman tends to be less exploitative of his residents than his economically worse-off counterpart. He usually has more surplus grain vis-à-vis his villagers, and generally shuns actions that would jeopardize the already precarious situation of his poorer residents. Lacking surplus grain and other income-generating business, an economically worse-off village chairman tends to exact as much as he can from fellow residents who enjoy better or comparable economic situations.

To sum up, rice farmers' relationships with centrally appointed officials and native leaders are conditioned by the socioeconomic backgrounds of local authorities, the goals and organizational resources of the local agencies and departments, the geography and demography of villages and townships, and the nature of the occupation of the village headman. Analyzing the roots of a wide range of local officials' practices is important because it is through these officials that agricultural policies are implemented. This analysis also sheds light on Burmese farmers' predominant concern with good local governance and leadership and their perceptions or expectations of a good government. Burmese rice farmers particularly value village chairmen and local authorities who are impartial, honest, responsive to their needs, sympathetic to their plight, protective of their interests, and who are not too corrupt and abusive of their power and authority. Rice farmers are complacent as long as these qualities are present in local leaders, be they military or civilian officials. Most officials are expected to engage in illicit deals among themselves and with farmers, and they do not necessarily create negative repercussion unless these activities take place at farmers' expenses. Farmers prefer local state officials who share similar interests with them, who dispense resources with a minimum level of corruption, who do not rigidly enforce central policies that are inimical to the interests of farmers, and to whom farmers can openly and frankly express their problems.

A good government, on the other hand, is perceived by Burmese farmers as the one that not only safeguards the material well-being of its citizens but also oversees the appointment of honest, reliable, and sensitive local authorities. While some farmers perceived democracy to be secondary to their concerns, others who wanted democracy associated it with a situation where there is "no corruption," where "we can have autonomy over our economic decision making and we can talk freely," where "we can live in peace and harmony," and where "everything is good, and the government is effective in planning and managing."[15]

Since local authorities implement national policies with small but significant variation, the impacts of particular agricultural policies are not uniformly felt. Thus a combination of particular agricultural policies, the ways in which they are implemented and the extent to which these policies impinge upon their living standards affect farmers' varying regard for authorities. Consequently, Burmese farmers welcome agricultural policies that improve their economic status, require little supervision and monitoring, and exact a smaller proportion of grain.

Generally speaking there was very limited support for the High Yielding Varieties Promotion (HYV), even though it promoted agricultural growth and productivity, because its higher procurement quota and strict supervision of the cultivation processes were not popular with rice farmers. Support for the partial liberalization program was widespread due to the relaxation of the government's grip on rural populations. It also improved farmers' living standards because of the reduction in procurement quotas, better farmgate and procurement prices, and the freedom to grow one's choice of crops. The partial liberalization

---

[15] Conversation with farmers from Rangoon, *Pegu*, and *Irrawaddy* divisions, December 2002.

package did not provide enough input and capital loans, but it enjoyed a higher level of support in the countryside.

There was enthusiastic acceptance of the summer paddy program in the regions with successful experiments in double cropping. The popularity of the summer paddy program had to do with its provision of additional earnings to rice farmers who used to cultivate a single monsoon paddy. Farmers also kept a higher proportion of grain because the central government did not officially procure summer paddy. Furthermore, the fact that summer paddy techniques could be implemented with relative ease (except for the regions with failed experimentation in summer paddy) reduced the likelihood of farmers' opposition. Central authorities however imposed a single set of guidelines in all rural regions, oblivious of the specific circumstances and needs of villages. The summer paddy program therefore was unpopular in regions that lacked access to water or appropriate soil type for it.

The policy on land reclamation was the least popular, since it took away rice farmers' lands, their primary source of survival. The policy itself was designed to benefit private companies and businesses at the expense of poor peasants who were barely scraping by.

The varying levels of support for these agricultural policies, however, did not directly translate into similar degrees of support for central and local authorities. Support for these two different levels of government was mediated by how the local officials implemented these different agricultural programs. For instance, despite the HYV programs' widespread unpopularity, the central government enjoyed legitimacy among a very small number of elite farmers. These farmers were subject to heavy quota demand and strict supervision too, but these pressures were overshadowed by the special attention they were given through the media, government press, and a special state dinner attended by General Ne Win. The central government also received some support from partial liberalization and the summer paddy programs, because of their positive reception in various localities. Central authorities also enjoyed legitimacy due to its "perceived" role as the savior to those who suffered at the hands of local authorities. When convinced that central authorities were unaware of local practices of graft, farmers looked to the central government to solve their problems and sought channels to make their grievances known to the highest authority in Rangoon.

Rural attitudes towards local authorities are based on their execution of agricultural programs. Reasons for the absence of rural support for local government vary from one development program to another. Whereas the popularity of local government under the HYV program was limited by its tendency to over-report performances, the summer paddy program and partial liberalization opened up new opportunities for locally based corruption. Farmers who were left with more grain and cash were now easy prey for local authorities. In the same way, the land expansion program gave local authorities a certain flexibility to make decisions about implementation which led to abuses and exploitation at the village level.

As I have shown in chapter three, local authorities' styles of administration in a particular village or township were by no means uniform. However, the practices of agencies that wielded too much control over farmers' lives provided a basis upon which farmers developed their attitudes towards central authorities. For instance, the MAS and the local governing body (the local Socialist party and People's Council) were the two most influential organizations that monitored and controlled farmers' economic activities during the HYV periods. Both organizations had the tendency to over- report crop performance under their jurisdiction, and both were in charge of introducing, monitoring, and supervising farmers' cultivation practices. These two bodies became a source of resentment in Burma's countryside. Their excessive zeal inadvertently undermined their popularity and on some occasions even created a positive image of central authorities. Some farmers were convinced that central authorities were misled by the exaggerated reports, which led to rice farmers having to give a greater proportion to the government.

The central government's decision to partially liberalize the agricultural sector eliminated local authorities' daily supervision and curtailed their power over Burmese cultivators. Farmers were free to grow crops of their own choice and to sell their surplus grain in the market. The new policy required very little governmental oversight and lessened the local bureaucratic stranglehold on production. The economic conditions of most farmers improved considerably, but they were exposed to new forms of abuse by local ruling authorities. Using a variety of excuses, some local ruling authorities claimed a certain amount of grain or money from farmers who now had extra cash from selling paddy and other crops in the market. This inevitably weakened the foundations of rural support for the local ruling authorities, but sometimes had a very small negative impact on the image of the central authorities, who were assumed to be unaware of local practices. Thus the ways in which different local township and village Law and Order Restoration Committee (LORC) authorities handled the partial liberalization policy had varying implications for farmers' perceptions of the central authorities.

Under the summer paddy program, the irrigation department, along with the local PDCs, exercised considerable authority over paddy farmers. Water is the main ingredient for cultivating rice in the dry season. Thus the local and village PDC's administration of water had a significant influence on how farmers perceived central government. Farmers who had lost their land under land reclamation, on the other hand, basically blamed the Forestry Department and the local PDCs, the two main organizations which implemented the policy. Thus farmers' perceptions of central governing authorities were shaped by local forestry and township PDCs authorities' practices and the extent to which the central government was deemed responsible.

The detailed analysis of the implementation of four different agricultural policies shows that peasants' positive or negative attitudes toward the central government change depending on fluctuations in agricultural policies and local governing structures. It is therefore hardly surprising that farmers developed mixed attitudes toward central authorities. They had an overall negative impression of the military regime, but were friendly with the pro-regime local representative. They showed tacit admiration for Daw Aung San Suu Kyi, but they could not stomach the domineering and patronizing attitudes of the NLD representative in their area. They were very much aware of Lt. General Myint Aung's brutal repression of Karens in the *Irrawaddy* delta and his authoritarian dealing with agricultural staff, but they praised his responsiveness to their demands and his devotion to agricultural development.

Overall, a great majority of farmers held higher regard for *atek lu* than *auk lu*, and attributed *atek lu* as "more lenient," "better," "less corrupt," and having "formulated good policies which have been distorted by *auk lu*."[16] One Karen farmer from Rangoon division, however, commented that both *atek lu* and *auk lu* were "corrupt and bad" and that "they are not very different from each other." He nonetheless remarked on the behavior of Burmese farmers from his neighboring village by saying "their perceptions of *atek lu* and *auk lu* change depending on the situations they are in. When they encountered abuses at the local buying center, they said *auk lu* are bad. When they received low prices for their rice from the government, they said *atek lu* are bad."[17]

Burmese cultivators' ambivalent attitudes toward authorities and their fear of brutal state-based retaliation cautioned them in any notions of

[16] Conversation with farmers from Rangoon, *Pegu,* and *Irrawaddy* divisions, December, 2002.
[17] Conversation with a farmer from Rangoon division, December, 2002.

rebellion that may have endangered their already precarious existence. Rice farmers also relied on a variety of mechanisms (compliance, exit, passive resistance, voice) to deal with the state's claims on their produce and labor, mitigating the chance of open revolt against the regime.

Their initial response was to grudgingly comply with the state's demands or migrate to other areas. If these options were not feasible, they were likely to use passive resistance, which was aimed not only at diluting state demands but also eschewing direct confrontation with authority. Burmese peasants will resort to "voice" or open protest if their call for collective grievance is not heeded by local authorities. Unless they are mobilized by urban leaders, (as happened in the 1988 public demonstration which demanded a complete removal of the government), Burmese cultivators use various forms of protest to remove unwanted policies, and to replace particular local officials who they hold accountable for policy limitations.

Some actions, such as protesting against local/central authorities or threatening to take their complaints to central authorities, were more likely to indicate where farmers' resentment lay. Other strategies, however, were less obvious. We cannot tell for sure whether activities such as under-reporting or over-reporting of their holdings, stealing water from the state-owned irrigation tanks or their neighbors' and selling soaked and impure seeds to the government were symbolic of rice farmers' denial of the legitimacy of authority. In other words, we cannot make judgment about rural perceptions of government based on their passive resistance activities. Regardless, the availability of other options, along with farmers' ambivalent attitudes toward authority and their fear of state reprisal have deterred them from openly challenging government's authority.

My observations of farmers' conduct are confined to the main rice-growing areas that are within the perimeter of central government's control. Thus my analysis is not applicable to peripheral areas and minority ethnic regions which are subject to torture, killings, rape, forced labor, forced relocation, and lootings by government troops. Relatively speaking, local authorities who work in the areas within the reach of central administration operate with greater constraint. Farmers in these areas feel the repressive nature of the state, but they are less subject to abuses, such as torture, killing, and rape. The proximity of the capital also gives farmers certain advantages in their negotiations with local authorities. The awareness that farmers could easily travel to the capital or approach the central authorities constrains local delegates who, after being confronted by farmers, oftentimes revoke unofficial practices.

Central Government as Savior?

A close examination of the relationships between rice farmers and state authorities in Burma gives us a grass-roots understanding of how one of the most repressive regimes in the world can sometimes enjoy pockets of legitimacy. It also shows that neither the nature nor the level of rural support for the regime remains static; they ebb and flow according to different agricultural policies and the extent to which the central government authorities are held responsible for rural problems. This analysis implies that *Burmese cultivators do not always perceive central government in a positive light.* Singularly, Burmese farmers demonstrate certain attitudes that are quite different from their counterparts in Mao's China and tsar's Russia. According to Daniel Field, "Russian peasants were, by and large, destitute and oppressed; their oppressors were the tsar's agents or others acting under the tsar's patent. Yet, whatever their level of misery and discontent, peasants appear to have believed that the tsar was their patron and benefactor."[18] In other words, they believed, up until the beginning of the eighteenth century, that the tsar would take their side "if he knew of their plight."[19] These beliefs were reinforced by peasants' experiences with corrupt local authorities. They became the oppressors, while the "distant tsar," who rarely visited the remote villages, was perceived to be more benevolent than his officials. Similar attitudes can be found among Chinese peasants regarding "chairman Mao." The Great Leap Forward and Cultural Revolution caused millions to die and suffer in the countryside, but most peasants did not blame Mao for these misfortunes. Rather, Chinese peasants accused ideologically-lax local officials who did not live up to Mao's teachings. In the words of Jon Unger, a leading scholar on China's rural politics, Mao was like a "god" to most Chinese peasants.[20]

Historical and contemporary accounts of Burmese rice farmers' interactions with state authorities rarely demonstrate their *complete faith* in a king or the central authority. There are two explanations for this. First, unlike the widespread accepted myth of the tsar as the deliverer of freedom in Russia's countryside, there is no comparable folklore in the history of Burma. To the contrary, the popular myth in Burma associated the government with one of five enemies (along with fire, famine, flood, drought) to mankind.[21] According to Maung Maung Gyi, Burmese citizens

---

[18] Daniel Field, *Rebels in the Name of the Tsar* (Boston: Unwin Hyman, 1989), 3.
[19] Ibid., 1.
[20] Conversation with Jon Unger, the Australian National University, Canberra, 15 September 2002.
[21] Daw Mya Sein, *The Administration of Burma*, 67.

tended to disassociate themselves from politics, and this practice has its roots in their dealings with *repressive kings*, the impersonal administration of the British colonial government, and the authoritarian conduct of the military regime.[22] In addition, although General Ne Win was a long-term autocratic leader in Burma, he never had a cult-like personality as did Chairman Mao. Unlike Mao, not one of the Burmese leaders has been able to command complete subservience and unquestioning loyalty to the state.

Second, Burmese peasants of the current military regime are not completely isolated from the rest of the world. Some of them listen to the radio, watch television and read newspapers. A few of them have graduated from college. For instance, in *Atek* village, which has population of 3,133 (1473 males and 1660 females [1999 statistics]), there were about seven rice farmers who had graduated from college: *U Kaung*, who holds a diploma in agriculture, and has taught at the Agricultural High School before turning himself into a full-time farmer; *U Kaung's* son also graduated from college, and but continues to work in the rice farm; *Ma Pyu*, another college graduate of Burmese literature, also assists her father with preparation of land, transplanting and harvesting. Being the oldest in the family, she felt responsible for her parents and younger siblings, a belief which has prevented her from moving to town in search of better opportunities; *U Hla* holds a bachelor's degree in History, but sees farming as a more profitable venture compared to prestigious but low-paid government employment. He stayed in the village to help his aging father and is likely to inherit the land to continue the family business. *U Kyaw Kyaw* has a law degree, but is now a farmer. *Bo Kyi's* two unmarried daughters who are in their forties are holders of Bachelor's degrees, and work as government employees, but they stay in the village to manage and carry out heavy farm work which can no longer be handled by their eighty-seven year old father.

Educated farmers aside, most farmers are not ignorant of the outside world. According to the 1998 census, only a small percentage of the population (84 out of 3,133 residents or 2.7 percent) in *Atek* village tract was illiterate. Furthermore, most rice villages in Burma are in the same way integrated into the national economy, and connected to major cities. Rice farmers are very much up-to-date in their knowledge of urban culture. Television is a window on the outside world, and an increasing number of rural residents own televisions. In *Atek* village alone about seven out of 169 households have one. Because of growing access to the

---

[22] Maung Maung Kyi, *Burmese Political Values: The Socio-Political Roots of Authoritarianism* (New York: Praeger Special Studies, 1983).

visual media in rural areas, many private pesticide, seed and fertilizer companies increasingly use television as a major source of advertising.

Every evening, villagers flock to the homes of the television owners to watch movies or news. Through commercials, they learn about brand-name consumer products that are not available in their surrounding regions, and through the news hours, they learn about domestic and international affairs. They see high rise buildings and department stores in Rangoon, and they mimic supermodels. They began to speak basic Chinese they have learned from watching Chinese movies, broadcast regularly on the only two government-owned television stations, the *Myawadee* and *Myanmar* Television. Adult males in the villages watch world soccer tournaments through satellite dishes in town, some gamble on the result, behaving no differently from their cosmopolitan counterparts. They know David Beckham, Michael Owen, and Ronaldo. Thanks to television, most villagers are now able to compare their situations with the outside world. They know that their standard of living is considerably lower than those living in the cities, and yet they are grateful that theirs is not as bad as those from "Africa or Ethiopia" who are starving.

Some elderly male villagers possess formidable knowledge well beyond the realm of agriculture. An eighty-seven year old farmer from *Atek* village in Upper Burma, upon finding out that I was a Christian, for instance, asked me whether I belonged to "Protestant, Puritan, or Roman Catholic." He and I discussed a number of issues ranging from NATO's bombing of Yugoslavia to the politics of the United Nations. He knew approximate numbers of UN members, which he recalled were from about one hundred and eighty-five countries. Another forty year old male farmer from the same village, *U Khant*, wanted to know my position on "the US role in Iran-Iraq disputes as well as President Clinton's affair with Monica." Another farmer, *U Panyarr*, from *Taw Latt* village in Upper Burma commented on the Asian currency crisis by ridiculing the "four tigers," which have done well in the past, but have now been relegated to mere "four kitties." Likewise, *Auk* farmers from Lower Burma were curious to know my position on Clinton's affair with Monica and NATO's role in Kosovo. They tuned into world events, and were very much aware of the International Labor Organization's (ILO) accusations of Burma as a forced-labor employer. Being elite farmers, they were unconvinced by

ILO accusations, which according to them paid no attention to Burmese cultural, economic and political contexts.[23]

Thus, although most rural residents were less likely to have passed high school and continued their higher education, their general knowledge did not lag far behind their counterparts. This is true for most rice villagers, except in the very remote and destitute regions. This is not a recent phenomenon, however. Manning Nash, who studied two Burmese villages in the late 1950s, remarked that "in a community like Nondwin, with its high rate of literacy, national issues are part of daily life. Newspapers come into the village although there are only three regular purchases. Many men and women read the papers, and some of the news is discussed. Hand bills, pamphlets, and propaganda tear sheets from political parties in Sagaing and Mandalay also find their way into Nondwin."[24]

Given their awareness of general news and having heard and experienced atrocities committed by the military regime, Burmese farmers do not have blind faith in the central authorities. They develop a degree of acquiescence with central authorities only after experiencing policies which have improved their lives or after concluding that central authorities' policies have been inappropriately implemented, or after the central government has taken action against local abusive practices. A Karen farmer from Rangoon division, for instance, told me that "I heard that Burmese farmers from *Paung Gyi* township, Pegu division approached General Khin Nyunt when he visited their village. They asked for the installation of electricity and the building of primary education. Khin Nyunt accommodated their requests and also told them that 'I would not know your problem if you had not told me.'"[25] The Karen farmer continued saying "*atek lu* are good, but as a Karen, I dare not approach General Khin Nyunt because I am not fluent in Burmese nor am I educated."

On a number of occasions, local authorities warned farmers who were to meet visiting central government officials against making negative comments. This reinforces farmers' suspicions of local

---

[23] Having seen and heard about the world's events does not, however, necessarily give rural residents a clear sense of world geography. A village monk in *Atek* village, for instance, told me that he would like to "stop by" America to visit me on his way to India during his pilgrimage. He was surprised when I told him that America was not on the way to India, and that it would take him another fifteen hours plane ride to get to America from India. My host father and his wife repeatedly confused America with Japan by telling other people that I was from Japan.

[24] Manning Nash, *The Golden Road to Modernity*, 86.

[25] Conversation with a farmer from Rangoon division, December 2002.

exploitation and maladministration. When the farmers heard on the national news that the MAPT would be collecting twelve baskets of paddy per acre from them, and when the township PDC authorities instead asked for fifteen baskets of rice per acre, they had little difficulty identifying the culprits. In the same way, local authorities were the ones to blame for illicit procurement especially after the national government officially announced that it would not procure summer paddy. Farmers were also aware that local authorities were carrying out unapproved activities when they charged about 2,000 kyat per acre for the use of water while the official fee for using irrigation was 10 kyat/acre.

It is debatable whether their perceptions match the reality. Some farmers who had to sell their grain to local military authorities blamed both levels of authority, believing that local actions were carried out with the approval of the military regime. Others interpreted the same practice as local authorities' acting independently. Thus, whether Burmese farmers blamed local authorities or both local and central authorities depended on their previous experiences with various types of authority, and their access to news about national affairs. In other words, farmers' attitudes towards particular authorities may be based on reality or false perceptions, but they are "real" to the extent that they are beliefs and are based on rice farmers' everyday experiences.

In sum, the lack of a historical Burmese legend which extols the role of a benevolent king combined with Burmese cultivators' modern-day awareness of the outside world explain why Burmese farmers, unlike their brethrens from Mao's China and tsar's Russia, usually pause before making positive remarks about central authorities. If they do, they do so with good reason, drawn from their everyday farming experiences and their general knowledge of the national policy.

Burma in a Comparative Framework
The Burmese military is not a unique authoritarian government, which has enjoyed pockets of support in rural areas due to the mediating role of local authorities and its provision of certain benefits accrued to particular agricultural policies. Richar Turits, for instance, found similar rural support for Rafael Leonidas Trujillo Molina, a despotic and repressive leader of the Dominican Republic, who ruled the country from 1930 until 1961. Trujillo was undoubtedly one of the most arbitrary and capricious dictators in the world. He plundered national resources, murdered and violated human rights, abused and exploited Dominican women, exercised absolute control over the appointments of state officials, glorified himself

as the rightful ruler of the country, and blatantly practiced nepotism. To get a clear picture of Trujillo, Turits writes,

> (Trujillo) accumulated a perhaps unparalleled portion of the country's wealth, showing little respect for human and civil rights, including, or especially those of the traditional upper classes. He appropriated and distributed vast properties belonging to certain members of the preexisting rural elites. And he owned a mammoth portion of urban industry. ......Trujillo's son Ramfis was publicly afforded full military honors as a colonel from the young age of four (and as a brigadier general when he turned nine). The dictator was notorious for his sexual exploitation of Dominican women, as he traveled around the country soliciting lovers and then supposedly compensating those he left with houses, jobs, and even husbands...Cities, streets, bridges, parks, national calendars, monuments, and mountain peaks were all named or renamed after Trujillo, his family, and his era. Congressional leaders were obliged upon assumption of office to sign their own resignations, a document that could be handed to them at any moment signifying the immediate end of their term. In some cases, such resignations were reportedly delivered to deputies and senators in the midst of their own speeches before congress. And among many other megalomaniacal acts of violence, Trujillo ordered the abduction from a New York subway station and subsequent murder in the Dominican Republic of a Columbia University Student, Jes'us de Galindez, who was completing a dissertation on Trujillo's dictatorship that was far from laudatory.

However, this dictator, who, in Turit's own words, fits perfectly the "social-scientific models for socially-baseless tyranny and despotic or autonomous rule," had, on closer examination "a substantial social basis and spheres of acceptance." [26] The support for Trujillo mainly came from the countryside, and there were a number of reasons for that. The most fundamental was his land distribution and agricultural assistance program which aimed to benefit the poorest of the poor. Peasants were the main beneficiaries of Trujillo's policies at the expense of "various elite and middle classes for whom state intervention and control had a more destructive impact on their professional and everyday lives."[27] Turits notes that,

> Trujillo's efforts to achieve a type of rural populism and foster paternalistic policies were far more substantial than previously assumed. They were backed by concrete government actions and material benefits for those willing to offer both productivity and outward loyalty in return.

[26] Turits, 7.
[27] Turits, 703.

> Specifically, the regime distributed and maintained peasant access to large amounts of the nation's lands, and thereby helped secure political loyalty or acquiescence among the peasantry.[28]

This type of support is not unlike the support for the central Burmese government, generated by agricultural policies that benefited rice farmers. Furthermore, like the Burmese case, Trujillo's popularity was facilitated by the mediating role of local authorities. Basically, he enjoyed peasants' support because of his appointment of uncorrupt local officials who faithfully carried out his orders.

> Most importantly from the perspective of the peasantry, this system depended on the delegation of substantial power to the alcaldes pedaneos, the lowest-level, submunicipal government authorities....The pedaneos seem to have been a source of legitimacy for the regime (as well as coercion), both because of who was selected to hold these offices and because of the manner in which they generally carried out their obligations.[29]

Trujillo's popularity was also based on his role as local problem solver. Trujillo established channels for peasants to address local corruption, and provided mechanisms to alleviate peasant grievances. This enhanced his credibility and authority in the countryside. Turits writes that,

> The government's control over local corruption , graft, and abuses of power was especially critical for the peasantry given the state's massive role in distributing land, resolving property disputes (whether through local officials or the Land Court), providing irrigation, and trying to eliminate petty theft and crime. Corruption and favoritism in those areas represented serious threats to the peasantry. Yet, most peasants I spoke with asserted that the Trujillo state was responsive to peasant protests when corruption did transpire and that these situations were remedied. When it heard accusations of local officials' improper conduct, the government often sent commissions to investigate these charges...After investigating the matter, the commissioner reportedly held a town meeting, publicly castigated the officials in charge of distributing water, and declared that such corruption would not be tolerated in the future. Letters written by peasants to Trujillo also suggested a certain confidence in the state and their role in denouncing abuse. [30]

---

[28] Turits, 8.
[29] Turits, 617.
[30] Turits, 624-625.

Thus, Trujillo's popular legitimacy was predicated upon the behavior of local authorities to the extent that they carried out central directives to the benefit of the peasantry. It also depended on Trujillo's ability to alleviate local abuse, injustice, and inadequacies. Turits thus writes that "the Trujillo government has been remembered as being responsive to complaints by the rural poor and supportive of its concerns. The state's purported intervention on behalf of these popular classes evidently led some to feel relatively empowered in relation to employers and other superiors."[31]

Trujillo's popularity has also to do with the improvement in peasants' situations after he came to power. According to Turits, there was a break down in law and order in pre-Trujillo period and "liberal rights had never been consolidated, radical critiques never widely circulated, and peasants rarely valorized in national discourse and as members of the nation as they were under Trujillo."[32] Such was the situation in post-Trujillo also. Turits observed that

> Trujillo would not be remembered so positively by many if after his regime the peasantry had fared better economically, if liberal political rights had advanced more, if bureaucratic discipline and government probity had improved rather than diminished, and if national pride had not been piqued by various forces, including dramatic increases in the country's economic dependence.[33]

Thus peasants were generally more satisfied with Trujillo's regime than were the various elite and middle class groups. Like their counterparts in Burma, however, the Dominican peasants did not hold an undifferentiated view of Trujillo. Being the beneficiaries of Trujillo's policies did not eliminate the issue of state repression, creating ambivalence for many peasants. Turits acknowledges that,

> Peasants' recollections of the regime were generally far from simple or one-sided, embracing contradiction and balance and eschewing the type of black-or-white discourse of many written histories.......(P)easants remember various oppressive aspects of everyday life under the dictatorship from earlier years as well, namely seemingly ubiquitous surveillance and harsh repression of even civil offenses...Yet, overall the state was recalled positively.[34]

[31] Turits, 626.
[32] Turits, 663-664.
[33] Turits, 704.
[34] Turits, 677, 702-703.

Marcos' martial law regime in the Philippines also enjoyed support stemming from particular agricultural policies. Ben Kerkvliet, for instance, writes that people from various socioeconomic classes tend to believe that government in postwar periods in general and Marcos government in particular have "become slightly more beneficial and responsive to poorer members of society."[35] The poor peasants benefited not only from land reform (one middle aged tenant for instance stated that "without martial law there would have been no land reform") but also from the policies on non-requirement of collateral loans, expansion of irrigation, and recognition of *Hukbalahap (Huk)*. The *Huk* were guerrillas, who had fought against the Japanese during the war but had been branded communists until Ferdinand Marcos came to power. Marcos officially recognized the *Huk* and promised veterans of the *Huk* medical and education benefits.

Two other authoritarian regimes that have enjoyed some support in agricultural regions are contemporary China and Vietnam. In both countries, the popularity of the central government was determined by local officials' administration of government policies. In China, policies of decollectivization and decentralization of fiscal and administrative authority increased tensions between local authorities and residents. Xiaobo Lu, for instance, observes that the move towards more market-oriented practices in China transferred some fiscal responsibilities from the central state to local states and led to the proliferation of functional and regulatory agencies at the township level. This change increased local cadres' responsibilities and also created opportunities for corruption. Local officials thus became targets of complaints. Xiaobu thus notes that, "conflicts between cadres and peasants have been on the rise, partly as a result of the extractive and corrupt activities, and partly due to the weakening power of rural officials."[36]

These emerging local tensions have led rural residents to turn their attention towards central authorities, where they seek a solution. LianJiang Li and Kevin O'Brien also observe that post-Mao China has been characterized by considerable growth and commercialization and worsening elite-mass relations manifest in a growing number of individual protests, mass demonstrations, and formal collective complaints. These protests, led by "policy-based resisters," usually called for the dismissal of corrupt *local* emperors, the repeal of *local* policies, and the lifting of

---

[35] Ben Kerkvliet, "Martial Law in a Nueva Ecija", *Bulletin of Concerned Asian Scholars* 14 (Oct/Dec 1982): 6-7.
[36] Xiobo Lu, "The politics of peasant burden in reform China", *The Journal of Peasant Studies*, 25 (1) (October 1997): 131.

illegal *local* impositions.[37] According to Li and O'Brien, "policy-based resisters" attempt to challenge the authority of local officials within the framework of law by identifying *local cadres' policy violation*. To become more knowledgeable, they read newspapers, magazines, cadre work style manuals, listened to radio broadcasts, watched television news, or gathered stories of successful resistance from villagers returning from other places.[38] In these ways, their behavior is similar to their counterparts in Burma who want beneficial policies to be implemented scrupulously. Thus "when new local fees are announced, they (policy-based resisters) may first question whether a levy is authorized by higher levels. Then they may calculate whether the total assessment exceeds the legal limit of 5% of a village's income. If the fee is unauthorized or excessive, they may then refuse to pay, claiming the fee contravenes this or that regulation or contradicts a pledge made in a recent speech by a national leader."[39]

Interestingly, however, complaints against authorities have been strictly confined to the local level. Previous popular sayings from China suggest a benevolent role for the central authorities. In the nineties, for instance, peasants said "the center is our benefactor (*enren*), the province is our relative, the county is a good person, the township is an evil person, and the village is our enemy."[40] The recent saying differs slightly in terms of the changing popular impression on the province and county; "there are clear skies at the center, clouds are forming in the province, it's raining in the county, it's pouring in the township, and we're being drowned in the village."[41] Li and O'Brien note that "we have seen little evidence that they (policy-based resisters) question the legitimacy of central laws and policies, not to mention the right of unaccountable leaders at higher levels to promulgate laws and policies."[42] Li and O'Brien also comment that "this is one reason why in up to 60% of collective complaints, complainants bypass one or more levels of government when proceeding

---

[37] LianJiang Li and Kevin O'Brien, "Villagers and popular resistance in contemporary China", *Modern China* 22 (1)(January 1996): 29. According to Li and O'Brien, "policy-based resisters" or diaomin (literally, "shrewd and unyielding people") do not "revere or fear rural cadres, nor do they reject them out of hand as grasping agents of the state." Instead they use "laws, policies, and other official communications to defy local leaders. They accept their duty to observe laws and policies but also insist it is their right to observe only laws and policies." 40.

[38] Ibid., 40. See also Lianjiang Li and Kevin O'Biran, "The politics of lodging complaints in rural China", *The China Quarterly* 143 (September 1995): 756-783.

[39] LianJiang Li and Kevin O'Brien, "Villagers and popular resistance", 40.

[40] Kevin O'Brien, Personal correspondence with author, 22 August 2002.

[41] Kevin O'Brien, Personal correspondence with author, 22 August 2002.

[42] Kevin O'Biran and Lianjiang Li, "The politics of lodging complaints in rural China", 54.

up the state hierarchy; the higher one goes, it is widely believed, the more successful one is likely to be."[43]

Whether the resisters have complete faith in national authorities is hard to say; it is possible that they do for strategic reasons. Kevin O'Brien comments that,

> Rightful resisters know they will lose their high-level supporters and media allies if they challenge the regime, so they have to avoid making claims (or acting illegally, e.g. burning the township police station) that show their challenge to be more than something directed at malfeasant local officials. What they actually believe is an open question, and not a few clearly know that the ultimate source of their problem is higher.[44]

LianJiang Li's recent work on the Chinese peasants' view of the state however suggests that peasants' faith in central authorities may have been a myth, especially if it did not confirm to their experiences with higher authorities. Li's findings challenge the notion that Chinese peasants never question the legitimacy of the national authorities. Rather, Li identifies ambivalent attitudes in rural areas towards toward authorities at all levels, and summarizes three different perspectives on the Party-State.[45] The first view sees all levels of party committees as "trustworthy," (party state is united and benevolent), and the second view holds that all levels of authorities are "untrustworthy" (party-state is united and predatory). The third view holds a high regard for central authorities but a low regard for local authorities (central policies are very good, but they are all distorted when they reached lower levels)."[46] Li finds that the better-educated and wealthier villagers are more likely to distrust all levels of party committees because most of them are migrant workers, peddlers, construction workers, or transportation operators. They are likely to work outside their villages and be the subjects of harassment and exploitation by various levels of governments. Another group of peasants who have lost trust in both local and central authorities are those who have had frustrating experiences lodging complaints about local corruption to higher levels. They were able to take their complaints to the capital, but encountered "beastly rude" high-ranking authorities, bureaucratic red tape, and long waiting periods. These hurdles were enough to undermine central authority's credibility and legitimacy.[47]

[43] Ibid., 43.
[44] Kevin O'Brien, Personal correspondence with author, 22 August 2002.
[45] LianJiang Li, "Political trust in rural China", unpublished paper.
[46] Ibid., 2.
[47] Ibid., 6.

According to Li, Chinese peasants' attitudes towards state authorities still show that most respondents had more trust in higher-level officials than they had in lower-level officials.[48] His survey, nevertheless, demonstrates that "many villagers do not consider the Party-State to be monolithic Leviathan with a single face. They disaggregate it."[49]

Another authoritarian government rural residents look to for solutions is Vietnam's Communist Party, which has been the only legitimate political party. It is hostile toward the idea of a multi-party system, and has very little tolerance for potential rival political activities.[50] Vietnam's state is even more rigid and centralized than the Chinese Communist party, which allows for at least a few small opposition parties, and the Burmese military government, which, at least, makes promises to hold multi-party elections.

Like its counterpart in China, the Vietnam's Communist Party has witnessed unprecedented rates of local corruption after decollectivization. Ben Kerkvliet notes that corruption has been a problem under the Communist party since the early 1960s but confined to officials taking "small amounts of rice or money that belonged to the state or taking for their own use cement or other construction materials that were supposed to be used for public buildings."[51] These amounts were tiny compared to those of the 1990s when the level of corruption increased dramatically. Kerkvliet notes that "figures from police reports show, that, on average, each known case of corruption in 1999 amounted to about US$ 86,000 going into official pockets."[52]

To strengthen central government's hold over the conduct of local cadres, Vietnamese peasants have used official and unofficial channels to complain about local corruption, and these "allegations of wrongdoing reported through official channels have helped to prompt authorities to investigate and enforce anti-corruption law."[53] Like the Chinese and Burmese farmers, Vietnamese farmers mainly target local authorities and "mandarins" "who abused their authority and used their positions to benefit themselves," who "engaged in corruption, violating the ownership rights of the people," who "pocketed proceeds from selling land that did not belong to them", who used "local tax revenues for their own

---

[48] Ibid., 2.
[49] Ibid., 4.
[50] Benedict Tria Kerkvliet, "An approach for analyzing state-society relations in Vietnam", *Sojourn* 16(2) (2001): 245.
[51] Benedict Tria Kerkvliet, "An approach for analyzing state-society relations in Vietnam", 264.
[52] Ibid.,
[53] Ibid., 265.

purposes," and imposed excessive fees on the local populations. [54] For instance, in late 1996 in Thai Binh province, peasants took to the street to demand higher authorities investigate and punish corrupt local authorities, but by early 1997 their petitions had not been heeded by the provincial authorities. This led to violence clashes between police and demonstrators. National authorities finally intervened. They relied on limited force and on dialogue with demonstrators. They investigated complaints and concluded that villagers' allegations of local officials' siphoning of government funds were well founded, and that provincial and other local authorities were negligent for not responding promptly when villagers' first began to complain. Consequently, the central government "disciplined" 2,000 officials, including the provincial secretary of the Communist Party and the chairperson of the provincial council. Some officials were removed and others were imprisoned. Some protesters were also charged with destroying property and provoking unrest. [55]

Vietnamese peasants' bold action against local corruption and the central authorities' occasional intervention in their favor enhanced government's role as fixer of local grievances. There have been only a few studies on Vietnamese peasants' attitudes to the party state but, we can conclude that the Vietnamese peasants, like their Burmese, Dominican and Chinese counterparts, do not see the state as monolithic. They too hold significantly different opinions of central and local authorities.

When central authorities intervene on behalf of the rural peasants, a tacit alliance between the highest ranking authorities and the grass-root population is formed. Jonathan Fox calls this tactics a "sandwich strategy," which seeks coordinated pressure from above and below to achieve a particular goal of the rural poor. [56] Satumino Borras refers to the same strategy as a "*bibingka* strategy" to describe the alliance between the pro-land reform movement below and pro-land reform initiatives from above. *Bibingka* is a native Filipino rice cake baked in a homemade two-layer oven, where in each panel on top of and underneath the cake are smouldering charcoals. [57] Peasants and central authorities in Burma,

---

[54]Ibid., 265.

[55] Ben Kerkvliet, 266-267.

[56] Jonathan Fox, *The Politics of Food in Mexico* (Ithaca: Cornell University Press, 1992), 164.

[57] Satumino Borras, "The *bibingka* strategy to land reform and implementation: Autonomous peasant mobilizations and state reformists in the Philippines", (The Hague: Working Paper Series No. 274, Institute of Social Studies, March 1998).

Dominican Republic, Communist China and Vietnam have used the strategy. Jon Unger, for instance, writes that

> Beijing, for its own part, is increasingly willing today to promote the viewpoint among disgruntled peasants that errant local cadres are to blame for their plight, painting itself as a good, caring government. National leaders see sense in posing as allies and protectors of the farmers, just as the farmers see the sense of appealing to the central authorities in hopes of playing them off against the local officialdom.[58]

Mexican and Indian peasants who are the subjects of local elite abuses use the sandwich or *bibingka* strategy, also. India is a democratic country with a free press and freedom of expression, but peasants who live in the countryside are no less vulnerable to entrenched authoritarian practices by the local elite than their counterparts in non-democratic countries. Robert Wade has observed ongoing tension between Indian farmers and irrigation officials, and farmers' subsequent attempts to complain against corrupt officials. Wade noted that farmers are often willing partners to bribery because some of them will rush to pay if their crops are at risk, and are willing enough to pay for water for unauthorized irrigation. However

> (I)f an engineer comes into a post and starts demanding significantly more from farmers and contractors than was usual previously, then they may try to take action to check or avoid his demand. They may in some locations break the channel banks for sluice gates to by-pass his control....*The letters, probably anonymous....will go to the CE (Chief Engineer), to the Minister, to the MLA, to the ACB (Anti Corruption Bureau), to anyone the authors think might be able to harm the man--perhaps with a copy to the man himself........*But his mechanism is limited to the extent that farmers fear that the engineer and local staff will strike back at them, perhaps by cutting off their water supply if they complain. It is also limited by differential willingness of MLAs to act. A village which has some wealthy, influential farmers can expect to have its complaints receive more attention than a village of poor, low caste farmers. [59]

The preceding examples illustrate a common pattern in authoritarian countries; that is, farmers look to higher authorities to arrest local abuse and corruption. Like Burma, China, Vietnam, and the Dominican Republic, Mexico is one of the most powerful and interventionist states in Latin America. On the one hand, the state needs to occasionally fulfill

---

[58]Jonathan Unger, *The Transformation of Rural China*, 215.
[59] Robert Wade, "The system of administrative and political corruption: Canal irrigation in South India", *The Journal of Development Studies* 18 (3) (April 1982): 311.

some promises to reestablish political legitimacy among peasants. On the other hand, almost all measures to redistribute land and wealth in the countryside have failed because of opposition from entrenched rural elites. Successive governments in Mexico therefore have relied on distribution of goods and services rather than on land reform to address problems of rural poverty. These efforts, however, have met with limited success. According to Fox, the only program that has survived its creator, President Lopez Portillo (1980), and continued to function well in some regions was the rural consumer food subsidy program, the CONASUPO-COPLAMAR. This program, which delivered a nutritional subsidy to thousands of Mexico's most impoverished villages, has survived for two reasons. The first was the effort of the reformist-oriented policy makers from "above" who created a legitimate channel for expressing dissatisfaction. They formed a democratic community organization to increase accountability of government food agencies. The second factor was the ability of targeted beneficiaries to take advantage of the program's resources and participatory procedures to build their own representative organizations.[60] The "sandwich" or "*bibingka*" strategy which mutually reinforces pressure from above and below, has been utilized on regular basis by the poor farmers from Third World authoritarian countries. Whether they sincerely believe in the central authorities' benevolence and "good intention," however, remains a subject of scholarly debate.

What Does Burma Teach Us Now?
A brief examination of the policies and practices of the extremely interventionist, centralized, and authoritarian governments in Burma, Trujillo's Dominican Republic, Communist China and Vietnam, and Portillo's Mexico shows that some authoritarian governments do not rely solely on "coercion" and "force" to strengthen their standing. They also rely on the provision of "incentives" to legitimize their governments. Burmese military promoted partial liberalization and summer paddy to improve farmers' lot, from which they receive considerable positive feedback. After realizing that collectivization was a failure, the governments in Communist China and Vietnam introduced household-based farming, relaxed control over rural populations, and encouraged private owned-small enterprises. Trujillo undertook agrarian reform in the Dominican Republic to redistribute land to marginalized and disenfranchised farmers. Portillo introduced food sufficiency in Mexico

---

[60] Robert Wade, 311.

by subsidizing agricultural inputs, loans and offering higher prices for peasants' produce. These definite policies, when implemented with minimal corruption and when successfully encountered entrenched opposition at local levels, gave certain benefits to most poor peasants. They also support legitimacy claims of authoritarian regimes.

Another way in which authoritarian governments enjoy popular legitimacy is their "perceived" role as the defenders of rural interests. The strength of this perception depends on farmers' knowledge of national affairs and their experiences in dealing with different levels of government. Peasants may hold a superficial belief in the "benevolent role" of the central authorities for strategic reasons; i.e. to play one level of authorities against the other. Regardless, complete faith in central authorities' benevolence is rare. Consequently, even those who benefit from particular government policies hold ambivalent attitudes toward the central authorities. Farmers also develop conflicting views about local authorities, depending on how responsive are these officials towards their needs.

In sum, some authoritarian regimes do have substantial support in the countryside, but the approval rating of the regime changes depending on political and economic environments and on the conduct of local authorities. Furthermore, rice farmers' tendency to improve their lot, and their periods of favorable inclination towards authority do not deter them from challenging authorities if there were a more open political system, and if there were favorable conditions for undertaking such action. Farmers' support for these authorities must be analyzed in the context of long-term coercive, repressive and often brutal authoritarian government. Thus a degree of satisfaction with state authorities merely neutralizes the rural opposition. Authoritarian governments will enjoy political legitimacy in the rural areas as long as there is the potential for upward mobility; as long as there is periodic partial reform; and as long as there are sympathetic officials who guard local interests against the arbitrary decisions and demands from the capital, and central authorities who protect the rural residents from local exploitations.

Bibliography

Adas, Michael. *Prophets of Rebellion: Millenarian Protest Movements Against the European Colonial Order*. Chapel Hill: University of North Carolina Press, 1979.

Adas, Michael. "From avoidance to confrontation: Peasant protest in pre-colonial and colonial Southeast Asia." *Comparative Studies in Society and History* 23 (1981): 217-247.

Adas, Michael. "The village and state in Vietnam and Burma: An Open and shut case?" First publication of the paper delivered at a Workshop on "The Village Revisited: Community and Locality in Southeast Asia," Asian Studies Center, University of Amsterdam, April 1988.

Adas, Michael. "Bandits, monks, and pretender kings: Patterns of peasant resistance and protest in Colonial Burma, 1826-1941." In *Power and Protest in the Countryside: Studies of Rural Unrest in Asia, Europe, and Latin American*, edited by Robert Waller and Scott Guggenheim. NC: Ruham, 1982.

Agricultural Corporation. "Farmers with Production over 150 baskets per acre in 1978/79." (in Burmese). Yangon: 1980.

Alagappa, Muthiah, ed. *Political Legitimacy in Southeast Asia: The Quest for Moral Authority*. California: Stanford University Press, 1995.

Appadurai, Arjun. "Small-scale techniques and large-scale objectives." In *Conversations between Economists and Anthropologists: Methodological Issues in Measuring Economic Change in Rural India*, edited by Pranab Bardhan. Oxford: Oxford University Press, 1989.

Asian Watch. *A modern Form of Slavery: Trafficking of Burmese women and Girls into Brothels in Thailand*. New York: Human Rights Watch, 1993.

Aung-Thwin, Michael. "1948 and Burma's myth of independence." In *Independent Burma at Forty Years: Six Assessments*, edited by Josef Silverstein. Ithaca: Southeast Asian Program, 1989.

Aye, Dephane Khin Shwe Shwe. "The Rice Situation in Burma." unpublished paper, 1998.

Badgley, John. "Burma: The nexus of socialism and two political traditions." *Asian Survey* 3 (2) (February, 1963): 89-95.

Badgley, John. "Intellectuals and the national vision: The Burmese case." *Asian Survey* 9 (8) (August, 1969): 598-613.

Badgley, John. "Burma's zealot wungyis: Maoists or St. Simonists." *Asian Survey* 5 (1) (January, 1965): 55-61.

Bandyopadhyay, Sekhar. *Burma To-Day: Economic Development and Political Control Since 1962.* Calcutta: Papyrus, 1987.

Barker, Rodney. *Political Legitimacy and the State.* Oxford: Claredon Press, 1990.

Beetham, David. *The Legitimation of Power.* New Jersey: Humanities Press International, Inc., 1991.

Borras, Satumino. "The bibingka strategy to land reform implementation: Autonomous peasant mobilizations and state reformists in the Philippines." The Hague, the Netherlands: Working Paper Series No. 274, Institute of Social Studies, March 1998.

British Broadcasting Corporation, September 26, 2002.

Brown, Ian. "Tax Remission and tax burden in rural lower Burma during the economic crisis of the early 1930s." *Modern Asian Studies* 33 (2) (1999): 383-403.

Bryant, Raymond. "The politics of forestry in Burma." In *The Politics of Environment in Southeast Asia: Resources and Resistance,* edited by Philip Hirsch and Carol Warren. London and New York: Routledge, 1998.

Burma Issue: News, Analysis and Peoples' Stories 9 (7) (Bangkok, Thailand: July 1999): 2-3.

Burma Issue: News, Analysis and Peoples' Stories 9 (10) (Bangkok, Thailand: October 1999): 3-7.

Cady, John. *A History of Modern Burma.* Ithaca: Cornell University Press, 1958.

Callahan, Mary. *The Origins of Military Rule in Burma.* A Ph.D. dissertation submitted to the faculty of the Graduate school of Cornell University, May 1996.

Carey, Peter. *From Burma to Myanmar: Military Rule and Struggle for Democracy.* London: Research Institute for the Study of Conflict and Terrorism, November/December 1997.

Deh, Hsaw Wah (Independent Human Rights Monitoring Group). Report on farmers' reaction against procurement policy in *Irrawaddy* division. Washington DC: Human Rights-Trade Union Rights Section, Federation of Trade Unions-Burma, 2 May, 1998.

The Economist Intelligence Unit. *Country Report: Myanmar (Burma).* Washington D.C: 4th quarter, 1998.

Fairclough, G. "That's an Order." in *Far Eastern Economic Review* (August 31, 1995): 27.

Field, Daniel. *Rebels in the Name of the Tsar*. Boston: Unwin Hyman, 1989.

Fink, Christina. *Living Silence: Burma Under Military Rule*. Bangkok: White Lotus and Zed Books, 2001.

Forestry Department. *Country Profile for Forestry Sector Outlook in Myanmar*. Yangon: Ministry of Forestry, 1997.

Forward, 22 March 1966, 8-9.

Forward 22 May 1963, 12-13.

Forward. November 1979. 3-7.

Fox, Jonathan. *The politics of Food in Mexico: State Power and Social Mobilization*. Ithaca: Cornell University Press, 1993.

Fox, Jonathan (ed.). *The Challenge of rural democratization: Perspectives from Latin America and the Philippines*. Portland: Frank Cass, 1990.

Furnivall, J.S. *Colonial Policy and Practice: A Comparative Study of Burma and Netherlands India*. Cambridge: Cambridge University Press, 1948.

Gillis, Malcolm, et al., *Economics of Development*, 4th edition. New York: W.W. Norton & Company, 1983.

Guyot, James. "Bureaucratic transformation in Burma." In *Asian Bureaucratic Systems*, edited by Ralph Braibanti. NC: Duke University Press, 1966.

Guyot, James. "Burma in 1988: Perestroika with a military face." *Southeast Asian Affairs* (1989): 107-136.

Gyi, Maung Maung. *Burmese Political Values: The Socio-Political Roots of Authoritarianism*. New York: Praeger Special Studies, 1983.

Han, Dr Ba. "Aspects of Burmese rural live of old." *Journal of Burma Research Studies* (June 1968): 9-10.

Herbert, Patricia. *The Hsaya San Rebellion (1930-1932) Reappraised*. Australia: Monash University, 1982.

Hirschman, Albert. *Exit, Voice, and Loyalty: Responses to Decline in Firms, Organizations, and States*. Cambridge: Harvard University Press, 1970.

Hill, Hal, and Sisira Jayasuriya. *An Inward-Looking Economy in Transition: Economic Development in Burma since the 1960s*. Singapore: Institute of Southeast Asian Studies, 1986.

Houtman, Gustaaf. *Mental Culture in Burmese Crisis Politics*. Tokyo: The Institute for the Study of Languages and Cultures of Asia and Africa, 1999.

241

Human Rights Solidarity. Report on *Food Security in Burma*, 10 (4) (Hong Kong: Asian Human Rights Commission, April 2000).

Huntington, Samuel and Joan Nelson. *No Easy Choice: Political Participation in Developing Countries*. Massachusetts: Harvard University Press, 1976.

Huntington, Samuel. *The Third Wave: Democratization in the late Twentieth Century*. Norman: University of Oklahoma Press, 1991.

Hyden, Goran. *Beyond Ujamaa in Tanzania: Underdevelopment and an Uncaptured peasantry*. London: Heinemann, 1980.

The IMF. *Myanmar: Recent Economic Development*. Washington D.C: 1995.

Kerkvliet, Benedict Tria. "An approach for analyzing state-society relations in Vietnam." *Sojourn* 16(2) (2001): 238-278.

Kerkvliet, Benedict. "Martial law in Nueva Ecija village, the Philippines." *Bulletin of Concerned Asian Scholars* 14 (October/December 1982): 2-19.

Kerkvliet, Benedict. "Land regimes and state strengths and weaknesses in the Philippines and Vietnam." In *Weak and Strong States in Asia-Pacific Societies*, edited by Peter Dauvergne. Sydney: Allen & Unwin, 1998.

Kyi, Khin Maung. Pattern of accommodation and bureaucratic authority in a transitional culture." A Ph.D. thesis presented to the Faculty of the Graduate school of Cornell University (June 1966).

Kyi, Khin Maung. "Modernization of Burmese Agriculture." *Southeast Asian Affairs* (1982): 113-131.

Kyi, Khin Maung and associates. "Process of communication in modernization of rural society: A survey report on two Burmese villages." *The Malayan Economic Review* 18 (1) (April, 1973): 55-73.

Kyi, Maung, Myo Nyunt, and Mya Than. "Economics of production and farm size in Burmese agriculture with reference to paddy farming." Yangon: Department of Research Institute of Economics, 1975.

Lane, Robert. "The legitimacy in bias." In *Legitimation of Regimes*: *International Framework for Analysis*, edited by Bogdan Denitch. Beverly Hills, California: Sage Publication: 1979.

Liddle, William R. "Indonesia's democratic past and future." *Comparative Politics* 24 (July, 1992): 443-462.

Lintner, Bertil., and Paul Handley. "Rancor over Rice." *Far Eastern Economic Review* (10 August, 1989): 58.

Linter, Bertil. *Outrage: Burma's Struggle for Democracy*. Bangkok: White Lotus, 1990.

Lissak, Moshe. *Military Roles in Modernization: Civil-Military Relations in Thailand and Burma.* London: Sage Publications, 1976.

Li, Lianjiang and O'Brien, Kevin. "Villagers and popular resistance in contemporary China." *Modern China* 22 (1) (January, 1996): 28-61.

Li, LianJiang. "Political trust in rural China." Unpublished paper, 2002.

Loathamatas, Anek. "A tale of two democracies: Conflicting perceptions of elections and democracy in Thailand." In *The Politics of Elections In Southeast Asia,* edited by Robert Taylor. Cambridge: Cambridge University Press, 1996.

Lu, Xiabo. "The politics of peasant burden in reform China." *The Journal of Peasant Studies,* 25 (1) (October, 1997): 113-138.

Matthews, Bruce. "The present fortune of tradition-bound authoritarianism in Myanmar." *Pacific Affairs* 71 (1) (Spring 1998): 7-23.

Maung, Mya. *The Burma Road to Poverty.* New York: Praeger, 1991.
Maung, Mya. "The Burmese approach to development: Economic growth without democratization." *Journal of Asian Economics* 7 (1) (1995): 97-129.

Maung, Mya. *The Burma Road to Capitalism.* New York: Praeger, 1998.

Mills, J.A. "Burmese peasant response to British Provincial Rule 1852-1885." In *Peasants and Politics: Grass Roots Reaction to Change in Asia,* edited by D.B Miller. New York: St. Martin's Press, 1978.

May, Ron, Lawson, and Viberto Selochan. "Introduction: Democracy and the military in comparative perspective." In *The Military and Democracy in Asia and the Pacific,* edited by R.J. May and Viberto Selochan. Bathurst, NSW: Crawford House Publishing; London: C. Hurst & CO. LTD, 1998.

Migdal, Joel. *Peasants, Politics, and Revolution: Pressure toward Political and Social Change in the Third World.* New Jersey: Princeton University Press: 1974.

Migdal, Joel. *Strong Societies and Weak States.* New Jersey: Princeton University Press, 1988.

Migdal, Joel, Kohli, and Shue. *State Power and Social Forces: Domination and Transformation in the Third World.* Cambridge: Cambridge University Press, 1994.

Migdal, Joel, *State in Society: Studying How States and Societies Transform and Constitute One Another.* Cambridge: Cambridge University Press, 2000.

Ministry of Agriculture and Irrigation. *Information of Myanmar Agriculture: 1996.* Yangon: 1996.

Moore, Sally. "Legitimation as a process." In *State Formation and Political Legitimacy*, edited by Ronald Cohen and Judith Toland. New Brunswick: Transaction Books, 1988.

Myint-U, Thant. *The Making of Modern Burma*. Cambridge: Cambridge University Press: 2001.

Myint, Kyaw. *Study on the Changes of Rice Production in Myanmar*. Yangon: MAI, 1999.

Myoe, Maung Aung. "Will the failed coup attempt derail the ongoing national reconciliation and political transition in Myanmar?" Singapore: Institute of Defense and Strategic Studies Commentaries, 3/2002.

Nash, Manning. *The Golden Road to Modernity: Village Life in Contemporary Burma*. Chicago: University of Chicago Press, 1965.

Nash, Manning. "Party building in Upper Burma." *Asian Survey* 3 (4) (April, 1963): 197-201.

The NLD. Official letters to the SPDC authorities. 2 May 1998, 21 December 1999, and 23 December 1999.

Nelson, Joan and Samuel Huntington. *No Easy Choice: Political Participation in Developing Countries*. Massachusetts: Harvard University Press, 1976.

O'Brien, Kevin and Lianjiang Li. "The politics of lodging complaints in rural China." *The China Quarterly* 143 (September, 1995): 756-783.

Oo,Tin Htut. "Myanmar agriculture under the economic transition: Present situation and emerging trends." Tokyo: The Institute of Developing Economies, March 1996.

Pare, Luisa. "The challenges of rural democratization in Mexico." In *The Challenge of Rural Democratization: Perspectives from Latin America and the Philippines*, edited by Jonathan Fox. Portland: Frank Cass, 1990.

Pakulski, Jan. "Legitimacy and mass compliance: Reflections on Max Weber and Soviet type societies." *British Journal of Political Science* 16 (1986): 35-56.

The Parliament of the Common Wealth of Australia. *Human rights, and Progress toward Democracy in Burma*. Canberra: The Australian Government Publishing Service, 1995.

Popkins, Samuel. *The Rational Peasant: The Political Economy of Rural Society in Vietnam*. Berkeley: University of California, 1979.

Pye, Lucian. *Politics, Personality, and Nation Building: Burma's Search for Identity*. New Haven: Yale University Press, 1962.

244

Raup, Philip M. "Some interrelationships between public administration and agricultural development." In *Political Economy of Development,* edited by Charles Wilber. New York: Random House, 1988.

The Shan Herald Agency. Reports on 22 Feb 2000, and 24 Feb 2001.

Saito, Teruko. "Farm household economy under paddy delivery system in contemporary Burma." *The Developing Economies* 19 (4) (1981): 367-397.

Sann, Naw Tin Thet. "Life conditions of the rural population in the Ayeyarwady-Delta/Myanmar: Disadvantages and Remedies." English version of the thesis submitted to the Institute fur Regional Wissenschaft, Universitat Karlsruhe for Postgraduate Degree of Licentiata in Regional Science, 1999.

Schatzberg, Michael. *Political Legitimacy in Middle Africa: Father, Family, Food.* Bloomington and Indiana: Indiana University Press, 2001.

Schwarz, Adam. *A Nation in Waiting: Indonesia in the 1990s.* St. Leonards, N.S.W: Allen & Unwin, 1994.

Schendel, W. *Three Deltas: Accumulation and Poverty in Rural Burma, Bengal and South India.* New Delhi: Sage Publications, 1991.

Scott, James. *The Moral Economy of the Peasant: Rebellion and Subsistence in Southeast Asia.* New Haven: Yale University Press, 1976.

Sein, Daw Mya. "The historical background of the new constitution." In *The Future of Burma in Perspective: A Symposium,* edited by Josef Silverstein. Ohio: Center for International Studies, Southeast Asia Series No. 35, Ohio University, 1974.

Sein, Daw Mya. *Administration in Burma.* London: Oxford University Press, 1973.

Shue, Vivienne. *The Reach of the State: Sketches of the Chinese Body Politics.* Stanford: Stanford University Press, 1988.

Silverstein, Josef. *Burma: Military Rule and the Politics of Stagnation.* Ithaca: Cornell University Press, 1977.

Silverstein, Josef. "Burma: Ne Win's revolution considered." *Asian Survey* 6 (2) (February, 1966): 95-102.

Solomon, Robert. "Saya San and the Burmese Rebellion," *Modern Asian Studies,* 3 (3) (1969): 209-223.

Spiro, Melford. *Anthropological Other or Burmese Brother.* New Brunswick: Transaction Publishers, 1992.

Steinberg, David. "Military rule in Burma since 1962." In *Military Rule in Burma: A Kaleidoscope of Views,* edited by. F. Lehman. Singapore: Institute of Southeast Asian Studies, 1981.

Steinberg, David. *The Future of Burma: Crisis and Choice in Burma.* New York: University Press of America, 1990.

Steingberg, David. *Crisis in Burma: Stasis and Change in a Political Economy in Turmoil.* Bangkok, Thailand: Institute of Security and International Studies, 1989.

Steinberg, David. *Burma: A Socialist Nation of Southeast Asia.* Boulder: Westview Press, 1982.

Taylor, Robert. *The State in Burma.* Hurst: London, 1987.

Taylor, Robert. "Elections in Burma/Myanmar: For whom and why?" In *The Politics of Elections in Southeast Asia*, edited by Robert Taylor. Cambridge: Cambridge University Press, 1996.

Text of US Department of Agriculture on Burma Rice Procurement Policy, *Dow Jones*, December 1, 1997.

Than, Mya. "Burma's agricultural development since 1962." In *Unreal Growth: Critical Studies on Asian Development,* edited by Nyo Manh-Lah. Delhi: Hindustan Publishing Corporation, 1984.

Than, Mya. "Little change in rural Burma: A case study of a Burmese village (1960-80)." *Sojourn* 2 (1) (1982): 55-87.

Than, Mya. "A Burmese village revisited." *The South East Asian Review* 2 (2) (February, 1978): 1-15.

Than, Mya and Nobuyoshi Nishizawa. "Agricultural policy reforms and agricultural development." In *Myanmar Dilemmas and Option,* edited by Mya Than and Joseph Tan. Singapore: Institute of Southeast Asian Studies, 1990.

Than, Tin Maung Maung. "Neither inheritance nor legacy: Leading the Myanmar state since Independence." *Contemporary Southeast Asi*a 15 (1) (June, 1993): 24-63.

Than, Tin Maung Maung. "Burma in 1983: From Recovery to Growth?" in *Southeast Asian Affairs* (1984): 89-122.

Than, Tin Maung Maung. "The Political Economy of Myanmar's Development Failure: 1948-88." Paper presented at Burma Studies Conference, Center for Burma Studies, Northern Illinois University, Dekalb, Illinoise, October 2-4, 1998.

Thawnghmung, Ardeth Maung. "Paddy farmers and the state: agricultural policies and political legitimacy in rural Myanmar." A Ph.D. dissertation submitted to the Political Science Department, University of Wisconsin, Madison, 2001.

Thein , Myat and Maung Maung Soe. "Economic reform and agricultural development in Myanmar." *ASEAN Economic Bulletin* 15 (1) (April, 1998): 13-29.

Ting-tus, Ch'u. *Local Government in China under the Ch'ing*. Stanford, California: Stanford University Press, 1962.

Turits, Richard. "The Foundation of Despotism: Peasants: Property, and the Trujillo Regime (1930-1961)." A Ph.D. Dissertation submitted to History Department, University of Chicago, August 1997.

The UNDP, *Agricultural Sector Development in Burma: A Trend Analysis of Published Statistics*, 1987/88-1996/97. Yangon: UNDP, 1998.

The US embassy, *Country Commercial Guide*. Rangoon, 1998.

The US embassy, *Country Commercial Guide*. Rangoon: 1996.

The US embassy. *Foreign Economic Trend Report: Burma*. Rangoon: 1996.

Unger, Jonathan. *The Transformation of Rural China*. New York: M.E. Sharpe: 2002.

Vu, Tuong H. "Of rice and moral rule: The politics of Beras and State formation in Indonesia, 945-1949." Paper presented at the American Political Science Association Annual meeting, Boston, August 29-September 1, 2002.

Wade, Robert "The system of administrative and political corruption: Canal irrigation in South India." *The Journal of Development Studies* 18 (3) (April, 1982): 287-328.

Wiant, Jon and David Steinberg. "Burma: the military and national development." In *Soldiers and Stability in Southeast Asia*, edited by J Soedijati Dijiwandono and Yong Mun Cheong. Singapore: Institute of Southeast Asian Studies, 1988.

Wiant, Jon. "The political symbolism of Taw-Hlan-Ye-Khit." In *Military Rule in Burma Since 1962*, edited by F.K. Lehman. Singapore: Institute of Southeast Asian Studies, 1981.

Win, Khin. *A Century of Rice Improvement in Burma*. Manila, Philippines: International Rice Research Institute, 1991.

Win, Khin and Kyi Win. *Burma's Experience in Rice Improvement: 1830-1985*. Manila: IRRI Research Paper Series, the International Rice Research Institute, 1990.

Wolf, Eric. *Peasants Wars of the Twentieth Century*. New York: Harper and Row, 1969.

The World Bank. *The World Bank Report on Myanmar*. Washington D.C: 1999.

Working People's Daily. Rangoon: 27 February 1968.

Working People's Daily. Rangoon: 28 February 1975.

Young, Cramer and Wailes. *An Economic Assessment of the Myanmar Rice Sector: Current Developments and Prospects*. Arkansas:

Arkansas Agricultural Experiment Station: University of Arkansas, 1998.

Interviews and Correspondence
Myint, Ye. Personal correspondence with author, April 11, 1997.
Charlie. Interview by author, Washington D.C, May 30, 1998.
Sindeler, Scott. Agricultural Attache, United States Department of Agriculture, Bangkok, Thailand. Interview by author, January 19, 1999.
O'Brien, Kevin. Personal correspondence with author, 22 August 2002.

Index

215; third world, 201, 219, 221, 224-225

B
Bachelor's degree: by agricultural officials, 97-100, 115; by farmers, 212
Bad harvest: of Burmese peasants, 75, 102, 111, 117; summer paddy, 149, 205
Badgley, John, 9, 60, 65-66, 69-70
Bassein, 46, 124
Beans: official policy on, 127, 136-138, 140, 152, 154; production of, 140, 150; procurement of, 141
Beetham, David, 5, 14-15, 37
Better-off farmers, 23, 96-97, 103
Bibingka strategy, 39, 223-224
Billboards, 99
Bogalay township, 113
Borras, Satumino, 39, 223
Bribery: for water, 1, 106, 108, 117, 119, 148, 205, 223; for land revenue and tax reduction, 31, 151; in elections under civilian government, 61; of government officials under British administration, 50-51, 175; of village chairmen, 92, 94-95, 97; of agricultural officials, 98, 106, 158, 184
British colonial government: annexation and occupation of Burma, 48; peasants' revolt, 19, 24, 57, 161, 175; administration of Burma, 30, 49, 51-52, 54, 202, 212; nationalist movement, 53-55, 79, 202;
Broadcasting method, 148
Bu athin, 55
Buddhism, 19, 21-22, 64, 79
Buddhist kingdom, 52
Buddhist monks: under British colonial rule, 19, 55; under civilian government, 60; under military government, 21, 167, 169, 177-178, 186, 190

Bukiran peasants: perceptions of government, 17, 24, 28
Bureaucracy: expansion under British Occupation, 50, 57, 175; under military regime, 120
Bureaucratic procedures, 119, 142, 205
Bureaucrats: in military regime, 109, 116, 133, 150
Burma Independence Army (BIA), 57, 58
Burma Socialist Program Party (BSPP), 125, 128, 163, 181, 183, 187
Buying depots: operation of, 87; abuses and exploitation at, 130, 135, 141
Byei, U Lum, 28

C
Cady, John, 42, 44-46, 49, 50, 52
Capitation tax, 53-54
Caretaker government, 63, 65
Cee, U Pyet, 94-95, 97
Central/national authorities: popularity and unpopularity, 79, 132-135, 140-143, 148-151, 155-157, 207-209, 216, 219; farmers' perceptions of, 1-2, 5-7, 120, 170, 172, 189-190, 208, 211, 214-215, 219-220, 223-224; relations with farmers, 11, 28, 41, 78, 186, 193-194, 201-202, 210, 221, 225; policies and practices, 29, 31, 33, 168, 170, 172, 174, 187, 189, 193, 207-208; relations with local authorities, 81, 84, 107, 186, 211, 222
Central Committee for the Management of Culturable Land, Fallow Land, and Wasteland, 152
Central Party and Council organizations, 134. See also BSPP
Chei, 168-170
Chemical fertilizer: HYV promotion 89, 91; use of, 141, 149, 150-151; distribution, of 103, 113, 116, 126-127, 144, 169, 171; costs of, 166, 202; using fertilizer bag for other purpose, 201

197; interpretations of, 123, 131, 161, 176, 206

The Department of Agricultural Planning (DAP), 85, 93

Deputy Head of Branch: land record officials, 98; official ranking in agricultural ministry, 89. See also Village Extension Manager

Deputy Minister of Agriculture, 92, 172

Din, U Aung, 69

Din, U Tha, 68

Director General: of land record, irrigation,
and agriculture offices, 86, 89, 93

Disaggregated state, 6, 36, 201

Distributional resources: of local agencies,
118, 121

District Peace and Development Council (PDC), 89, 91, 93, 95, 106-108, 187

Divide and rule strategy, 115. See also Bogyoke Myint Aung

Divisional Peace and Development Council
(PDC), 84, 89, 92, 99, 107, 110, 113, 142

Do Bama Asi-ayon, 57

Dominican Republic, 2, 12, 173, 215-216, 223-225

Double cropping, 95, 207

Dream township, 114

Dry zone, 42, 87, 103, 145

Duya seminar, 68

Dyarchy rule, 54-55

E

Economic census: under British government, 58; village level, 99; *Alei* township in Upper Burma, 101-102, 212

Economic performance, 3-5, 9, 37, 148

Economy: moral economy of peasant, 38, 159; agrarian economy, 33, 142; national economy in pre-colonial periods, 47; national economy under post-colonial civilian government, 59; national economy under military regime,
66, 89, 144, 183, 199, 201, 212 ; local economy under military regime, 94-96;

market-oriented, 125; socialist, 141

Education: of Burmese elite under colonial
administration, 52; constraints and opportunities under military government, 66-67, 79, 199-200; of village chairman, 97; of local officials, 114, 121, 202-203, 214; of farmers, 97, 164

Election: national, 14; 1990 national election, 3, 22, 80, 162, 198, 221; under
post- colonial civilian government, 25, 27, 60-61, 64; in Africa, 25, 35; in the Philippines, 28; in Thailand, 34; in Mexico, 173; under British colonial government, 54-55; for Burmese village
chairmen, 91

Elite farmers, 93, 132, 134, 207, 213

The Emerald Operation, 129

England, 53

Enren, 220

Environmental damage, 77, 153

Equity: concerns of lower class members, 37; promotion of, 38

Ethnic insurgencies, 124, 199-200

Exit, 11, 174, 177, 180-181, 192-193, 210

Export licenses for agricultural products, 154

Extensification, 125

Extension managers/workers, 85-86, 97-103, 111, 119, 124, 126, 130-131, 155-156, 159

F

Fairclough, Gordon, 147

Fallow land: policies under colonial government, 55; policies under SPDC, 77, 87, 152-153; local authorities' administration of, 107, 110, 154, 205

Farmers' Income Generating Group (FIGG), 180

Field, Daniel, 211

Fink, Christina, 199

Forced labor, 145, 210, 213

Forced relocation, 175, 200, 205, 210

Foreign exchange, 8-9, 74, 76, 143-144, 153

Foreign investment, 136

252

132, 136, 138

Politicians: citizens' support for, 26; under
civilian government, 60-61, 63, 79; in India, Philippines, and Latin America, 33; in Thailand, 35; in colonial periods,
56; motivation and behavior, 27, 33, 56,
60, 64; rural perceptions of, 35, 65; socioeconomic background, 65-66
Pon, 62
Pongyi, 19. See also Buddhist monks
Popa, 68
Popularity: definition, 16; of military, 162;
of central government authorities, 1, 36,
135, 140, 142, 159-160; bases of government's, 5-6; of local authorities, 134-135, 140, 142, 155, 159, 208; relationship with economic development, 38; of village chairman, 90, 96 of agricultural policies, 5, 9; of HYV, 130-131; of partial liberalization,
136, 138; of summer paddy program, 148, 207; of Trujillo, 216-217; of Chinese Communist Party and Vietnamese Communist Party, 219
Porter, 200
Post-colonial: elite-peasants relations, 41, 78, 80; appeal to Buddhist based legitimacy, 79; voting, 61
Praise township, 146
Prefectoralism, 84
Pre-colonial: Burmese cultivators' perceptions of legitimacy, 18-19, 21, 23,
51, 80; elite-peasants relations, 29-31, 33, 41, 46, 50, 52-53, 78, 81, 174-175, 201-202; economy, 42; administration, 43-44; Burmese kings, 66
Private companies: in land reclamation, 152, 154, 207; employment opportunities by, 157, 180; means of advertising in rural areas, 213
Private enterprises: 152, 154, 225
Private entrepreneur: under land reclamation, 77, 152, 154
Private money lender: as powerful rural

elite, 90; source of help for farmers, 139,
177-178; under colonial government, 49,
55
Private trader: in partial liberalization, 76; as powerful rural elite, 90; illicit deals by, 108, 142, 184, 199; a source of help to farmers, 139
Process-oriented approach: aspects of, 13, 34, 36-38. See also political legitimacy
Pro-democracy movement: declining support for the military regime, 22; rural
situations during, 92; involvement of farmers, 80, 162, 191; farmers' reaction
toward, 123, 131; suppression of, 197
Prome, 187-188
Protest: against central and local authorities, 210; in rural China, 34; as sign of illegitimacy, 14; of African peasants under British colony, 24; of Burmese students, 199; 1988 pro-democracy movement, 36; against British occupation of Burma, 46, 48; peasant protest under military regime, 161, 189-191, 194, 210; lack of,
161-163, 192; types of rural protest, 174, 177, 219, 222
Pu, U, 167
Public projects, 147
Pulses: procurement, 138, 141; export of, 136; policy on cultivation of, 76, 127, 136-137, 152; production of, 136, 140
Pye, Lucian, 111
Pyinmana, 58, 60, 107, 124
Pyone, Maung, 181-182
Pyu, 42
Pyu, Ma, 212
Pyswar Directorate, 64

Q
Quadrant one, 156
Quadrant two, 156
Quadrant three, 133-134, 152, 155, 158
Quadrant four, 133, 140, 152, 158

Taylor, Robert, 29-30, 34, 53-54, 57, 61-62,
  64, 79
Tax: collection during pre-colonial periods,
  29, 42, 44-45; collection under colonial government, 30-31, 47-51, 53-54, 194, 202; opportunities for tax evasion under colonial government, 55, 57, 175; collection under civilian government, 62; opportunities for tax evasion under military government, 182; tax evasion by multinational corporation, 194; the role of local authorities in collecting, 174; local corruption, 108; SLORC's policy on, 76; exemption for private companies in land reclamation, 153
Teak Curtain, 1, 8
Technical and human support: perceptions of farmers toward, 131; during HYV promotion periods, 131; under land reclamation, 153; responsibilities of agricultural officials in providing, 99-100
Teik-Kyi township, 87, 124
Television: access to, 23, 97, 103, 171; coverage of, 22
Tenancy: situations under colonial government, 48-49
Tenant: under martial law in the Philippines, 218; numbers of tenants under land reclamation, 77, 153; situations under colonial government, 48; percentage of tenants in post-colonial Burma, 59, 67, 77
Tenasserim, 46, 84
Thailand, 10, 34, 36, 61, 168, 181, 200
Thakin, 57-58, 60, 62
Thamu-Hnamu, 28
Than, Mya, 9, 59, 67, 72, 125, 183
Than, Tun, 93
Thathameda tax, 47
Thein, Myat, 9, 136
Thibaw, king, 47
Third World: popularity of central government, 2; foundations of legitimacy, 4, 11, 13, 15, 201; concerns

of farmers, 28; agricultural implementation, 104; covert activities, 182; strategies of farmers, 224
Thugyi: relations with local populations, 29-31
Tin, U Ba, 68
Tin, Thakin, 60
Toungoo, 42, 71
Township Peace and Development Council
  (PDC): relations with farmers, 1, 95, 107, 120-121, 141-142, 188-189, 204, 209, 214; behavior and practices, 108, 155; organizational structure, roles and responsibilities, 89-91; relations with subordinate and other agencies, 92-93, 99, 105-106, 110, 112
Tractor: possession of farmers, 23, 97, 102;
  distribution of, 66; imports of private companies, 153
Traditional values: defining: 20-21; dynamic of , 36; of Revolutionary Council, 65
Transplanters, 126, 131, 178
Trujillo, Rafael Leonidas: policies and practices, 215-216; popularity, 216-218
Tsar: Russian peasants' perceptions of, 211,
   215
Tun, Thakin, 62
Turits, Richard, 2, 173, 215-218

U
U, Ba, 57
Under-reporting: by village chairman, 94; by farmers, 102, 106, 139, 182, 210; by
  land record officials, 105, 119; by local
  officials, 134; as passive resistance, 177, 210
Union of Burma Agricultural Product Marketing Board (UBAM), 67
The Union of Solidarity and Development Association (USDA): census in Upper Burma, 101-102; activities in rural areas, 188; local representatives, 165-166

rise to power, 41, 63; transfer of power
to U Nu in 1960, 64; policy on
agriculture, 74, 162; political situations
under Ne Win, 187; protest
against, 190, 192; after 1988 pro-
democracy demonstration, 197;
activities and personality, 198, 212
Women's Income Generating Group, 180
World Bank, 153, 200
Wunthanu athin, 54-55
Wunza, 75, 181

Y
Yamethin district, 62
Yezin, 98, 114
Yield: high-yielding rice, 74, 92-93, 125,
134; under-reporting, 94, 103, 172,
177,
193; string-row transplanting method,
96, 145; pressure to produce high-
yielding crops, 99, 103, 105, 119, 130,
132, 135, 149, 178, 204; rice yield,
101-
102, 127, 129, 145, 185; knowledge of
crop yield, 107
Youn, U, 28
Ywa Ngwe village, 166
Ywathugyi, 46

For Product Safety Concerns and Information please contact our EU
representative GPSR@taylorandfrancis.com
Taylor & Francis Verlag GmbH, Kaufingerstraße 24, 80331 München, Germany